Computer Animation and Simulation '95

Proceedings of the Eurographics Workshop
in Maastricht, The Netherlands,
September 2–3, 1995

D. Terzopoulos and
D. Thalmann (eds.)

Eurographics

SpringerWienNewYork

Prof. Dr. Demetri Terzopoulos
Department of Computer Science, University of Toronto,
Toronto, Canada

Prof. Dr. Daniel Thalmann
Computer Graphics Lab, Swiss Federal Institute of Technology,
Lausanne, Switzerland

© 1995 Springer-Verlag/Wien
Printed in Austria

Typesetting: Camera ready by editors and authors
Printing: Druckerei Novographic, A-1238 Wien
Binding: Fa. Papyrus, A-1100 Wien

Graphic design: Ecke Bonk

Printed on acid-free and chlorine-free bleached paper

With 156 partly coloured Figures

ISSN 0946-2767
ISBN 3-211-82738-2 Springer-Verlag Wien New York

Preface

This volume contains research papers that were presented at the *Sixth Eurographics Workshop on Animation and Simulation* which took place at Maastricht, The Netherlands, September 2–3, 1995. A core area within computer graphics, animation is concerned with the computer synthesis of dynamic scenes. The creation of realistic animation based on the simulation of physical and biological phenomena is a unifying and rapidly evolving research theme. This series of workshops, an activity of the Eurographics Working Group on Animation and Simulation, is an international forum where researchers representing the animation and simulation communities convene to exchange knowledge and experience related to this theme and to physics-based modelling, human modelling, motion control, visualization, etc. Of keen interest at this sixth workshop were novel animation techniques and animation systems that simulate the dynamics and interactions of physical objects—solid, fluid, and gaseous—as well as the behaviors of living systems such as plants, lower animals, and humans. The workshop continued to promote the confluence of animation and simulation as a leading edge of computer graphics research that is providing animators with sophisticated new algorithms for synthesizing dynamic scenes.

The call for extended abstracts for the workshop, issued in February 1995, elicited an enthusiastic response. Each submitted abstract was reviewed by two members of the international program committee comprising the following experts:

Bruno Arnaldi	(IRISA Beaulieu Campus, France)
Norman Badler	(University of Pennsylvania, USA)
David Baraff	(Carnegie–Mellon University, USA)
Ronan Boulic	(Swiss Federal Institute of Technology, Switzerland)
Sabine Coquillart	(INRIA, France)
David Forsey	(University of British Columbia, Canada)
Marie-Paule Gascuel	(iMAGIS/IMAG, France)
Gerard Hegron	(Ecole des Mines of Nantes, France)
Pedro Lopes	(INESC Multimedia Centre, Portugal)
Annie Luciani	(ACROE-LIFIA, France)
Nadia Magnenat–Thalmann	(University of Geneva, Switzerland)
Dimitri Metaxas	(University of Pennsylvania, USA)
Kees van Overveld	(Eindhoven University of Technology, The Netherlands)
Michiel van de Panne	(University of Toronto, Canada)
David Zeltzer	(Massachusetts Institute of Technology, USA)

Based on the reviews, we selected 16 abstracts for presentation at the workshop and invited the authors to prepare full papers for inclusion in this volume. The members of the program committee deserve special acknowledgment for reviewing the extended abstracts promptly in accordance with a tight schedule aimed at publishing this volume in time for the workshop. We are pleased with the scope and quality of the papers and express our appreciation to the authors for their contributions to the workshop and to this book.

The local arrangements coordinator, Tanja van Rij, of the Centre for Mathematics and Computer Science in The Netherlands contributed substantially to making the event a reality. Our appreciation goes to the Eurographics Society and to Werner Purgathofer of the Technical University of Vienna for his support in publishing the workshop proceedings as a volume of the Springer–Verlag Eurographics Series. We thank Xaviar Pueyo of the University of Girona for publicizing the workshop. Maria Cuda of the University of Toronto provided valuable administrative assistance during the review process. Finally, our special thanks goes to Gerard Hegron, Co-Chair of the Eurographics Working Group on Animation and Simulation, for encouraging us to organize this sixth workshop and for his generous assistance.

We acknowledge financial support from the following funding agencies: Terzopoulos was supported by the Canadian Institute for Advanced Research, the Natural Sciences and Engineering Research Council of Canada, and the Information Technologies Research Center of Ontario. Thalmann was supported by the Swiss Federal Institute of Technology and the National Swiss Foundation for Research.

Demetri Terzopoulos (Co-Chair)   Daniel Thalmann (Co-Chair)
University of Toronto   Swiss Federal Institute of Technology
Toronto, Canada   Lausanne, Switzerland

Contents

VIII

Part I:
Animating Physical Objects

Two-dimensional simulation of gaseous phenomena using vortex particles

Manuel Noronha Gamito
Pedro Faria Lopes
Mário Rui Gomes
INESC, Rua Alves Redol, 9, 2°, 1000 LISBOA
E-Mail: {maglpfllmrg}@inesc.pt

Abstract. This article presents a simple, fast and stable method for the animation and visualisation of turbulent gaseous fluids in two dimensions. We draw on well known methods from computational fluid dynamics to model the fluid using vorticity and velocity fields. While the vorticity is transported by a particle system, we use a uniform grid to compute velocities and displacements for each particle. This mixed approach where free particles move on a fixed grid requires little computational power, making it suitable for computer animation. The method simulates the behaviour of fluids in situations where the contact between fluid masses with different velocities generates an intermediate mixing layer which can give rise to turbulence phenomena. Unlike previous algorithms, it is possible to generate quasi-turbulent patterns, where large scale coherent vortex structures are still discernible in the flow.

1 Introduction

The modelling and animation of fluids are among the greatest challenges anyone working in computer graphics can face. Fluids are a constant presence in our lives, from the water that covers two thirds of our planet to the air that surrounds us. There is an understandable desire to portray such objects side by side with other more tractable geometric objects.

In this article a method is presented for the animation and visualisation of gaseous fluids based on a vorticity model [12]. The vorticity is a measure of the amount of circulation of the fluid at each point in space. If the vorticity field is known at some instant it is possible to obtain its evolution for all subsequent instants. The vorticity field is represented with a particle system [14]. A vortex particle (also know as a *vorton* in the computational physics literature) carries around a given amount of vorticity and can be thought of as an infinitely small whirlpool. When all these small whirlpools are added together the final flow pattern arises. Vortex particles continually form and evolve over time, giving rise to highly complex and appealing motions. Common examples can be a column of smoke rising through the air or the foam pattern a ship's propeller leaves behind it on the water.

We use a regular grid to store an equivalent sampled version of the vorticity field. A velocity field is calculated over the grid as the solution to a Poisson equation with suitable boundary conditions. The particles are then advected according to this velocity field. This method is particularly useful for the simulation of fluid flows with low viscosity and in the presence of large velocity gradients. This type of flows is characterised by small regions of concentrated vorticity, which can eventually become turbulent.

At present, the method is only applicable for two dimensional flow fields. It has, however, very low computational costs and can handle systems with large numbers of particles, which makes it an attractive method for the generation of complex animated textures. Such textures can then be mapped onto the surface of three-dimensional objects, much like Gardner's textures [8].

2 Previous Work

Several models for fluid flow including turbulent effects, have already been presented in the literature. In early works, turbulence was functionally defined as the superposition of band-limited noises over consecutively smaller scales [13]. This *ad-hoc* definition of turbulence was used for the synthesis and animation of clouds [7,16]. The results, although quite good for static images, were forcefully unrealistic when it came to simulating the dynamics of the clouds.

Yaeger was the first to use a vorticity model in computer graphics to animate the atmosphere of the planet Jupiter [23]. The vorticity field, corresponding to an initial cloud pattern, was sampled on a grid and the evolution of vorticity was solved over that grid using pseudo-spectral techniques. Methods such as this, that sample and solve field equations over grids, are known as Eulerian methods. For a grid with a resolution of $N \times N$ the method must solve a system of N^2 differential equations, one for each node where a vorticity value is stored. Clearly, Eulerian methods are not particularly efficient when highly detailed animations are desired.

Haumann was able to build arbitrarily complex flow patterns by the addition of basic flow primitives [10]. These primitives were simple solutions to the fluid mechanics equations for incompressible fluids and included uniform flows, sinks and sources of fluid and vortex effects. A static flow field could be built and particles would be advected through it.

Sakas considered the turbulence of a fluid to be a stochastic noise superposed on a constant flow [15]. The noise was synthesised from a power spectrum given by the Kolmogorov distribution. The patterns obtained by such spectral synthesis methods correspond to the description of fully developed turbulence. Turbulence can be described as a superposition of an infinite number of vortices, or eddies, with sizes varying over all scales [21]. From the large scale eddies, energy is transmitted down to smaller ones without loss. The energy of the fluid is finally dissipated to the environment when it reaches the smallest eddies. The large scale eddies are the first ones to appear in the temporal evolution of a turbulent flow. These eddies then break up into smaller ones until the whole range of scales is present and a fully developed turbulence regime is established. Spectral synthesis with the Kolmogorov power spectrum does not take into account the dynamics of the large scale eddies and so cannot model quasi-turbulent flows where fully developed turbulence has not yet been reached. A cigarette smoke is a typical example of this type of flow. The smoke near the cigarette tip is mostly non turbulent and the turbulence gradually increases as the smoke rises in the air.

Stam also used spectral synthesis to define a turbulent velocity field at the microscopic scale [19]. To this, a deterministic flow field was added to describe the large scale motion of the fluid. A particle system is advected over the resulting field. The particles are treated as opaque blobs and rendered with a ray-tracing paradigm to give the fluid a gaseous look. The animations obtained with this method are fairly convincing but it is still not possible to model the large scale vortical motion since the macroscopic flow field is deterministic. Also, energy and momentum transfers between this and the small scale velocity field are not considered, making it impossible to model the onset of turbulence arising from the macroscopic motion of the fluid.

Recently Chiba used a vorticity model to build animated two-dimensional velocity fields [4]. These fields were used to advect particle systems and to create flame and smoke simulations. Vortices are randomly dropped in a three-dimensional field (two spatial coordinates plus one temporal coordinate) according to a given probability distribution. The vortices are considered as spheres of constant vorticity and induce a rotational velocity field around them. This model is perhaps closest in spirit to the functional noise model [13] and suffers from the same limitations.

3 Vorticity Dynamics

The fluid behaviour is governed by two equations: a continuity and a dynamics equation. For incompressible fluids (and ignoring external forces like gravity) these two equations take the form:

$$\nabla \cdot \mathbf{v} = 0 \tag{1}$$

$$\frac{\partial \mathbf{v}}{\partial t} + (\mathbf{v} \cdot \nabla)\mathbf{v} + \frac{1}{\rho}\nabla p = \upsilon \Delta \mathbf{v} \tag{2}$$

At every instant the flow is described by the velocity field $\mathbf{v}(\mathbf{x},t)$, $p(\mathbf{x},t)$ is the pressure distribution, ρ is the density (a constant) and υ is the kinematic viscosity. Equation (1) represents the law of mass conservation. The amount of fluid entering any given volume must equal the amount of fluid going out. Equation (2) is the fluid mechanics equivalent to Newton's second law $F = ma$. The existence of a pressure gradient inside the fluid gives rise to a flow $\mathbf{v}(\mathbf{x},t)$ which seeks to eliminate it.

We will consider the flow to be purely rotational, i.e. there will always be a vector field $\psi(\mathbf{x},t)$ which allows the flow to be written as:

$$\mathbf{v}(\mathbf{x},t) = \nabla \times \psi \tag{3}$$

Since the flow $\mathbf{v}(\mathbf{x},t)$ is planar (let us suppose it lies on the x-y coordinate plane) the field $\psi(\mathbf{x},t)$ is bound to be everywhere coincident with the z axis. It can be considered as a scalar field $\psi(\mathbf{x},t)$ since its direction is already know. The equation (3) becomes:

$$\mathbf{v}(\mathbf{x},t) = \nabla \times \psi \mathbf{e}_z \qquad (4)$$

where $\mathbf{e}_z$ is the direction of the z axis. Using the rotational flow greatly simplifies the dynamics by replacing the general vector field $\mathbf{v}(\mathbf{x},t)$ with the scalar field $\psi(\mathbf{x},t)$, known as the *stream function*. It can be seen by plugging (3) or (4) in (1) that a rotational flow automatically verifies the continuity equation.

The vorticity represents the amount of fluid circulation in every point in space and through time, being given by:

$$\omega(\mathbf{x},t) = \nabla \times \mathbf{v} \qquad (5)$$

Again we have that the vorticity is a vector always normal to the plane of the fluid. It therefore suffices to consider only its magnitude $\omega(\mathbf{x},t)$. By taking the curl on both sides of (2) and using (1) one gets:

$$\frac{\partial \omega}{\partial t} + (\mathbf{v} \cdot \nabla)\omega = \upsilon \Delta \omega \qquad (6)$$

Notice that the curl applied on the left side of (2) managed to take the pressure gradient out of the way. The dynamics are now further simplified since only a stream function $\psi(\mathbf{x},t)$ and a vorticity field are needed to fully describe the flow. Yaeger used this equation in his model to simulate the Jovian atmosphere. To try and find a more efficient method the variable ω is instead considered to be the vorticity carried by an infinitesimal fluid particle along its trajectory and through time. Equation (6) becomes:

$$\frac{d\omega}{dt} = \upsilon \Delta \omega \qquad (7)$$

The partial derivative of the vorticity relative to time is replaced with a total derivative because ω has no longer an explicit dependence on the spatial coordinates. This equation means that the vorticity of a particle is gradually diffused around it due to viscous effects. The vorticity is initially concentrated in the centre of the particle and will spread to a disk of increasing radius. In the particular case of an inviscid fluid ($\upsilon = 0$), the vorticity is a conserved quantity of every particle. The equation of motion for a given particle i is now:

$$\frac{d\mathbf{x}_i}{dt} = \mathbf{v}(\mathbf{x}_i, t) \qquad (8)$$

Each particle takes the velocity of the flow at its current position. Comparing (7) and (8) with (6) it can be seen that a particle system is a natural representation of the dynamics of a turbulent flow. Particles tend to concentrate on high vorticity areas and with more accentuated dynamics. This means the computational effort is concentrated in areas where it is most needed, while other areas, with little or no activity, are ignored.

To complete the vorticity model, we relate the flow (in terms of its stream function $\psi(\mathbf{x},t)$) to the vorticity field by plugging (3) into (5) to yield the Poisson equation:

$$\Delta\psi = -\omega \tag{9}$$

From the vorticity field at any given time it is now possible to get $\psi(\mathbf{x},t)$ as a solution of (9) and then obtain the flow $\mathbf{v}(\mathbf{x},t)$ from the curl (4), which in two dimensions takes the simplified form:

$$v_x = \frac{\partial\psi}{\partial y}, \qquad v_y = -\frac{\partial\psi}{\partial x} \tag{10}$$

4 A Particle-Grid Model

Our hybrid model combines a particle system with a fixed uniform grid [6,11]. The particles transport vorticity while the grid is used to solve the field equation. Each iteration of the algorithm can be briefly summarised in the following steps:

- Interpolate particle vorticities to the grid, according to equation (11).
- Numerically solve the field equation (9) on the grid to obtain the stream function.
- Calculate velocity field on the grid from the stream function, according to eq. (4).
- Calculate particle velocities using interpolation from the grid (equation (13)).
- Advect particles (equation (15)).

The first step builds a representation of the vorticity field over the grid, based on the vorticity information carried by the particles. Fig. 1 shows the vorticity interpolation scheme.

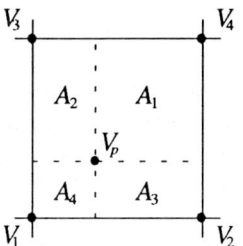

Fig. 1. Vorticity interpolation.

The particle vorticities are accumulated on the grid in such a way that each particle contributes to the four grid points that surround it. The particle vorticity V_p is bilinearly interpolated to the grid points V_1 to V_4. For V_i $(1 < i < 4)$ we have:

$$V_i = \frac{A_i}{h^2} V_p \tag{11}$$

where A_1 to A_4 are the areas subtended by the particle and the grid points and h is the grid spacing. This scheme conserves the total vorticity of the system.

With the vorticity grid at hand, the Poisson equation (9) is now solved relative to the stream function $\psi(x,y)$ on a rectangular domain $a \leq x \leq b$, $c \leq y \leq d$. On the edges of this domain, boundary conditions must be imposed in order to have a complete formulation of the problem. A simple condition specifies that $\psi(x,y)$ be equal to zero for $x = a$, $x = b$, $y = c$ and $y = d$. This condition, coupled with the definition of the flow (10), implies that $v(x,t)$ can only have a tangential component along the boundaries. No inflow or outflow is possible and the fluid remains constrained inside the computational domain. The Laplacian operator in (9) is approximated with finite differences in order to solve the equation. The *FISHPACK*[*] library was used, containing a set of FORTRAN routines to solve both Poisson and Helmholtz type equations over a variety of coordinate frames [20].

At this point we have a discrete representation $\psi_{i,j}$ of the stream function over the grid. From this representation, the fluid's velocity field $v_{i,j}$ can be obtained. For a given grid point (i,j) the curl (10) is approximated by the following differences:

$$v^x_{i,j} = \frac{\psi_{i,j+1} - \psi_{i,j-1}}{2h}, \quad v^y_{i,j} = \frac{\psi_{i-1,j} - \psi_{i+1,j}}{2h} \tag{12}$$

A particle's velocity is now calculated with an interpolation scheme similar to the one previously used to interpolate vorticities. Considering again Fig. 1, where the grid points now store the velocities v_1 to v_4, the velocity v_p of the particle is calculated through a bilinear interpolation:

$$v_p = (A_1 v_1 + A_2 v_2 + A_3 v_3 + A_4 v_4)/h^2 \tag{13}$$

During the advection stage, each particle is displaced according to:

$$x_p(t + \Delta t) = x_p(t) + v_p(t)\Delta t \tag{14}$$

where Δt represents the time increment. Equation (14) can be easily identified with the Euler method for the solution of ordinary differential equations. More robust methods, like the Runge-Kutta, could have been used, with increased computational costs.

Up to now the viscous effects, represented by the right hand side of the vorticity transport equation (7), have been neglected. Equation (14) updates the position of the particles but their vorticity remains constant, resulting in the simulation of an inviscid fluid. To simulate viscous diffusion of vorticity into the environment a simple random walk procedure can be used after the advection stage of each particle [5]. The advection of a particle p is now:

$$x_p(t + \Delta t) = x_p(t) + v_p(t)\Delta t + \delta x \tag{15}$$

---

[*] This library is part of the NetLib archive, available world-wide through anonymous FTP.

where δx is a vector whose components $(\delta x_1, \delta x_2)$ are independent gaussian variables with zero mean and variance $2v\Delta t$. The random walk simulates the diffusion of vorticity in a statistical sense. Although the vorticity of each particle remains concentrated around the particle's centre, the particles themselves suffer a diffusion process which effectively spreads the vorticity field according to equation (7).

5 A Turbulent Jet Stream

The vorticity model, described in the previous section, will be applied to the animation of gaseous phenomena. In particular, we wish to animate a column of smoke rising through the air. This type of animation can be used to simulate cigarette smoke. The combustion process occurring at the tip of the cigarette heats the air around it. Hot air, having lower density than ambient air, will rise until its thermal energy is dissipated through convection. At the same time, small ash particles are released from the cigarette tip and transported along with the rising jet. These particles are opaque and give a visual representation of the flow, which otherwise would have been invisible to the naked eye.

To avoid performing a full-scale physical simulation of the phenomenon, the model of a mechanical jet will be used as an approximation to the behaviour of the much more complex thermal jet. In the mechanical jet, the heating and convection considerations are ignored. This amounts to dropping the variables of heat and density and retaining only the fundamental variables of the vorticity model, namely the vorticity and the stream function. The upward motion of the smoke will be imposed with a uniform vector field. Vortices are automatically created at the cigarette tip and will follow this uniform flow while interacting with each other. This situation is depicted in Fig. 2 and corresponds to a jet of fluid ensuing from an orifice of width W with a constant speed U_0.

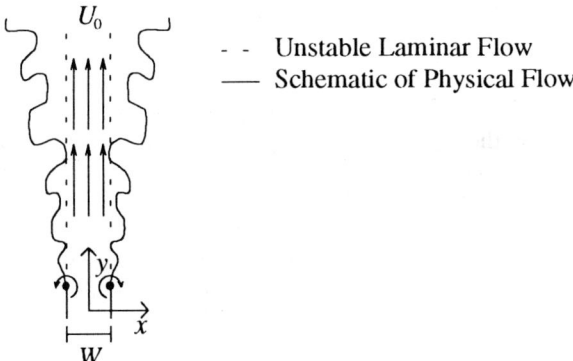

Fig. 2. A turbulent jet with upward velocity U_0 and width W. The two dots represent two fluid particles and their respective circulations at the separation of the flow.

If we ignore for a moment any bulk rotational motion of the fluid we will have a uniform flow inside the region $-W/2 < x < W/2$ with upward speed U_0 and outside of this region the fluid will remain at rest. There are two interfaces at $x = -W/2$ and $x = W/2$ where the two masses of fluid slide through each other. The vorticity is zero everywhere except at the interfaces where it is uniformly distributed along the height. For the interface at $x = -W/2$ the vorticity is positive, corresponding to a counter-clockwise sense of rotation of the fluid. Reversibly, any fluid point lying along the line $x = W/2$ will have negative vorticity and will tend to spin in a clockwise manner. What we have then are two parallel vortex sheets with opposite vorticity.

This scenario is mathematically possible but it is also completely unstable from a physical point of view. Abernathy has shown that tiny disturbances in the two sheets will quickly develop into a stable pattern, consisting of a succession of pairs of large counter-rotating eddies [1]. This type of pattern arises in a wide variety of flow situations and is known as the *Karman vortex street*. The intrinsic instability of the two vortex sheets is quite pronounced. In our algorithm, errors due to finite approximations are sufficient to trigger the formation of the Karman street.

Vorticity is continually created at the two points $x = \pm W/2$, $y = 0$ at a constant rate given by:

$$\frac{d\Gamma}{dt} = \pm \frac{1}{2} U_0^2 \qquad (16)$$

where the positive value refers to the left point. The variable Γ is called *circulation* and is related to the vorticity by the relation:

$$\Gamma = \iint \omega \, dx \, dy \qquad (17)$$

According to (16), as more fluid is ejected the total circulation and the total vorticity of the system increase steadily. The quadratic rate of increase relative to the ejection speed U_0 makes the system very sensitive to this parameter. The vorticity created at the two exit points of the jet then travels upward with speed $U_0/2$. This value comes from the fact that the vorticity lies in the interface between two masses of fluid travelling at speeds of 0 and U_0 so that it will tend to have an average speed of $U_0/2$. This uniform vertical flow is superposed over the rotational flow given by (10).

To discretize the model of the turbulent jet, the continuous vorticity filaments which are shed at the exit points must be replaced by a sequence of vortex particles. The algorithm consists of iterating over the consecutive time instants $t_i = i.\Delta t$ for $i \in N_0$. At the start of each iteration every particle is displaced vertically by an amount $U_0 \Delta t/2$ and a new pair of vortex particles is placed at the exit points, with circulations given by:

$$\Gamma_i = \pm \frac{\gamma \Delta t}{2} U_0^2 \qquad (18)$$

where the additional parameter γ gives an animator control over the vorticity creation mechanism.

It can be shown that the finite difference approximations, present in the Eulerian part of the algorithm, are responsible for the introduction of an artificial viscosity term, which has the effect of spreading the vorticity of a particle around its position [11]. The exact expression for this spreading effect is rather complicated and for simplicity reasons we will assume that the vorticity is uniformly distributed inside a circle whose radius we know to be proportional to the grid cell size h. With the above said and using (17) one gets:

$$\Gamma_i \propto h^2 \omega_i \qquad (19)$$

This equation is then plugged into (18) to arrive at a formula giving the vorticities ω_i of newly created particles. Notice that the constant of proportionality implicit in (19) can be hidden inside the γ parameter.

6 Rendering

Having the means to generate the time evolution of the jet stream, we must now turn to the question of how to visualise it. As previously said, the microscopic ash particles released from the cigarette and transported by the flow are responsible for the visible properties of the smoke. It seems natural to use particle elements again for rendering purposes. Such particles will act as fluid markers, being advected by the flow according to the advection equation (15), and will be passed on to the rendering module.

At the start of every iteration and at the same time as new vortex particles are created, the span $-W/2 \leq x \leq W/2$, $y = 0$ (refer to Fig. 2) is filled with equispaced markers. All previously existing markers have been advected upwards by the flow so that a continuous stream is created at the origin. The creation process is controlled by a concentration parameter, measured in number of particles per grid cell, which determines the spacing and the amount of markers introduced. The random walk component of equation (15), induced by the viscosity of the fluid, has a jittering effect and prevents the occurrence of visual artefacts in the particle stream. Fluid markers are renderend using *spot noise*. For a more detailed explanation of this technique refer to [22].

7 Results

Colour plate 1 (see Appendix) shows frames from an animation of a turbulent smoke jet produced over a grid of 32×128 resolution, spanning an area of 0.25×1.0 spatial units. The jet has an initial width of 0.015625 (equivalent to a span of two grid cells) and initial velocity $U_0 = 0.5$. The dynamics of vorticity is controlled by a factor $\gamma = 0.2$ and the viscosity is $\upsilon = 1.5 \times 10^{-5}$. The jet has a concentration of about eight particles per grid cell for an image of 128×512 pixels. Particles are automatically deleted from the system when they hit the upper limit of the computational domain.

This animation illustrates the transition from laminar to turbulent flow. The jet has an initial uniform upwards flow but the instability of the vortex sheet model soon manifests and the flow evolves into a complex pattern of turbulent eddies. This onset of turbulence is an example of how the macroscopic motion of the fluid can influence its microscopic motion (a uniform flow generates large eddies which decompose into smaller and smaller eddies).

The computation times were measured on a Silicon Graphics Indigo^2 machine. The frame with the highest number of particles took 3.6 seconds to generate (0.43s for the solution of the Poisson equation, 2.29s for particle advection and field interpolations and 0.88s for rendering) for a total of 19676 particles (1905 vortex particles and 17771 fluid markers).

Colour plate 2 (see Appendix) shows another animation of the same jet, this time with a width of 0.078125 (spanning 10 grid cells). The system reached a peak value of 64769 particles with a peak time of 11.89s per image.

The time complexity of the algorithm is $O(k) + O(mn.\log n)$ for a system with k particles and an $m \times n$ grid. The algorithm can be quite efficient, even for large numbers of particles, provided the grid resolution is kept small (typical values are between 32 and 256 cells along each side of the grid). The $O(k)$ complexity on the number of particles is quite remarkable since previous particle dynamics algorithms had $O(k^2)$ or $O(k.\log k)$ [3]. This complexity is independent of the distribution of particles throughout the domain. To the authors knowledge, the only other particle algorithm with $O(k)$ complexity is based on a multipole expansion of the inter-particle interactions [9].

8 Future Developments

Many improvements can be made on the algorithm. The first and most obvious one is the extension to a fully three-dimensional vorticity model. In three dimensions, the concept of a vortex particle as the basic building block of the vorticity field must be replaced by the concept of a *vortex filament*; a thin, closed line, carrying a constant amount of circulation. A term must also be added to the right side of the vorticity transport equation (6) to account for a new phenomenon, known as *vortex stretching* [17]. Because of the orthogonality properties already explained in section 3, the vortex stretching term vanishes in two dimensions.

During the evolution of the flow, vortex filaments tend to stretch and to become highly entangled in each other as a result of the vortex stretching mechanism. An initially smooth filament may end up having sections with high radius of curvature. These effects are a manifestation of the turbulent properties of the flow. In a discrete model of three-dimensional vorticity, a vortex filament must be represented with a collection of points, linked together with straight line segments or other higher order interpolants. As the filaments stretch and distort intermediate points must be inserted in the collection to keep a good accuracy of the representation [2]. Such a three-dimensional vorticity algorithm will be harder to implement and will certainly be much slower. It is questionable whether such an algorithm can be useful for computer animation purposes.

An interaction of the jet with an externally supplied wind field could also be modelled. At present the environment is considered to be at rest, which is not a very realistic assumption. The smoke stream would look more natural if small wind drafts could introduce disturbances in the flow. Along the same lines, the source of fluid should be able to move during the animation. Such an effect would cause a bending of the smoke stream in a direction opposite to the movement of the source.

Another interesting possibility is the interaction of the fluid with rigid bodies. The fluid should be able to detect the presence of other bodies and adapt itself to avoid interpenetrations. In practical terms this would imply the specification of interior boundary conditions to the equation of the flow (9). The presence of viscous effects would vastly complicate this situation because a boundary layer and a vorticity creation mechanism would have to be considered along the surface of the objects [18]. In the opposite direction, the fluid should be able to influence the movement of the rigid bodies through the actuation of drag and lift forces. These two mechanisms would allow fluid dynamics algorithms to be integrated in a transparent manner with already existing rigid body dynamics algorithms.

9 Conclusions

We have presented a method for the simulation of turbulent behaviour in fluids. The method is based on computational techniques, well established in the CFD domain for some decades. We have taken some applications of fluid dynamics out of the realm of large vector supercomputers and have made them usable for medium sized workstations, where they may find application in computer graphics.

All the control variables of the model can be conveniently abstracted so that any animator, with no prior knowledge of fluid mechanics, can rapidly take advantage of it. For the animation of smoke, for instance, one only has to specify simple parameters like the concentration of particles, the thickness and initial velocity of the smoke or the desired degree of turbulence.

The algorithm is stable. The vorticity of a particle is uniformly distributed inside a circle centred at the particle's position. The radius of the circle is a function of the grid spacing and the quantification errors made by the finite difference approximations. This fuzziness of the particle's vorticity makes the interaction force between particle pairs go smoothly to zero for short ranges. The possibility of hard collisions is avoided and the total energy of the system can be efficiently conserved.

The algorithm is fast since its complexity changes linearly with the number of particles. We have produced animation sequences using large numbers of particles, which would have been impracticable or even impossible to produce with previous particle dynamics algorithms.

The algorithm is also easy to implement. Apart from the Poisson equation solver, which can be implemented with public domain software, all other operations consist of trivial bilinear interpolations and particle advections.

The main disadvantage of the method lies in its two-dimensional nature. It produces animated textures which later can be mapped onto three-dimensional objects. Three-dimensional algorithms are possible and several implementations already exist. However, the increased complexity of three-dimensional vorticity models reflects on both the complexity and the computational costs of these algorithms.

In this article the vortex particle method was applied to the animation of a turbulent smoke stream but many other applications of the same basic algorithm can be devised. Several animations are currently under development, namely the animation of turbulent planetary atmospheres (along the lines of [23]), the generation of wakes behind moving bodies and the simulation of foam on the surface of water streams.

Acknowledgements

The authors wish to express their gratitude to Joaquim Jorge for reviewing the text and to Gavin Pringle for helpful criticisms along the way. The first author would also like to thank Mafalda Barbosa for showing an incredible amount of patience at a time when other more urgent work was needing immediate attention.

References

1. Abernathy, F.H., Kronauer, R.E., "The formation of vortex streets", Journal of Fluid Mechanics, vol. 13, pp. 1-20, 1962.

2. Almgren, A.S., Buttke, T., Colella, P., "A Fast Adaptive Vortex Method in Three Dimensions", Journal of Computational Physics, vol. 113, pp. 177-200, 1994.

3. Appel, A.A., "An Efficient Program for Many-Body Simulations", SIAM Journal on Scientific and Statistical Computing, vol. 16, n. 1, pp. 85-103, 1985.

4. Chiba, N., Muraoka, K., Takahashi, H., Miura, M., "Two-dimensional Visual Simulation of Flames, Smoke and the Spread of Fire", The Journal of Visualisation And Computer Animation, vol. 5, pp. 37-53, 1994.

5. Chorin, A.J., "Numerical Study of Slightly Viscous Flow", Journal of Fluid Mechanics, vol. 57, n. 4, pp. 785-796, 1973.

6. Christiansen, J.P., "Numerical Simulation by the Method of Point Vortices", Journal of Computational Physics, vol. 13, pp. 363-379, 1973.

7. Ebert, D.S., Parent, R.E., "Rendering And Animation of Gaseous Phenomena by Combining Fast Volume and Scanline A-buffer Techniques", ACM Computer Graphics, vol. 24, n. 4, pp. 357-366, (Proc. SIGGRAPH '90).

8. Gardner, G.Y., "Visual Simulation of Clouds", ACM Computer Graphics, vol. 19, n. 3, pp. 297-363, (Proc. SIGGRAPH '85).

9. Greengard, L., Rokhlin, V., "A Fast Algorithm for Particle Simulations", Journal of Computational Physics, vol. 73, pp. 325-348, 1987.

10. Haumann, D., Wejchert, J., Arya, K., Bacon, B., Khorasani, A., Norton, A., Sweeney, P., "Aspects of Motion Design for Physically-Based Animation", Scientific Visualisation of Physical Phenomena, (CG International '91 Proceedings), Springer-Verlag, Tokyo, June 1991, pp. 147-158.

11. Hockney, R.W., Eastwood, J.W., "Computer Simulation Using Particles", IOP Publishing, Bristol, 1988.

12. Leonard, A., "Vortex Methods for Flow Simulation", Journal of Computational Physics, vol. 37, pp. 289-335, 1980.

13. Perlin, K., "An Image Synthesiser", ACM Computer Graphics, vol. 19, n. 3, pp. 287-296, (Proc. SIGGRAPH '85).

14. Reeves, W.T., "Particle Systems- A Technique for Modelling a Class of Fuzzy Objects", ACM Computer Graphics, vol. 17, n. 3, pp. 359-376, (Proc. SIGGRAPH '83).

15. Sakas, G., "Modelling and animating turbulent gaseous phenomena using spectral synthesis", The Visual Computer, vol. 9, n. 4, pp. 200-212, 1993.

16. Saupe, D., Peitgen, H.O., "The Science of Fractal Images", Springer-Verlag, Berlin Heidelberg New York, 1988.

17. Sethian, J., "A Brief Overview of Vortex Methods", Vortex Methods and Vortex Motion, Gustafson, K.E., Sethian, J., (Eds.), SIAM, 1990

18. Sethian, J., Brunet, J., Greenberg, A., Mesirov, J.P., "Two-Dimensional, Viscous, Incompressible Flow in Complex Geometries on a Massively Parallel Processor, Journal of Computational Physics, vol. 101, pp. 185-206, 1992

19. Stam, J., Fiume, E., "Turbulent Wind Fields for Gaseous Phenomena", ACM Computer Graphics, vol. 27, n. 4, pp. 369-376, (Proc. SIGGRAPH '93).

20. Swarztrauber, P., Sweet, R., "Efficient Fortran SubPrograms For The Solution Of Elliptic Equations", NCAR TN/IA-109, July, 1975, 138 pp.

21. Tennekes, H., Lumley, J., "A First Course in Turbulence", MIT Press, Cambridge, 1972.

22. van Wijk, J.J., "Flow Visualisation with Surface Particles", IEEE Computer Graphics & Applications, pp. 18-24, July, 1993.

23. Yaeger, L., Upson, C., Meyers, R., "Combining Physical and Visual Simulation: Creation of the Planet Jupiter for the Film 2010", ACM Computer Graphics, vol. 20, n. 4, pp. 85-93, (Proc. SIGGRAPH '86).

Editors' Note: see Appendix, p. 225 for coloured figures of this paper

A Physical Model Of Turbulent Fluids

A. Luciani, A. Habibi, A. Vapillon, Y. Duroc
ACROE - LIFIA
INPG - 46 avenue Félix Viallet
38 031 Grenoble cedex - FRANCE
Tél : (33) 76 57 46 69 - Fax : (33) 76 57 46 02
e-mail : acroe@imag.fr

Abstract

Turbulent phenomena are a subject of great interest for the computer graphics community as well as for the physics community. In computer graphics, current models of turbulent flow are mostly kinematic and stochastic models. The models presented in this paper are all physically-based and totally deterministic. They were achieved using the *Cordis-Anima* physical modeller-simulator, which is based upon point physics connected by physical interactions. In order to obtain physically and visually fine phenomena, while using a rather low number of particles, we resort to multi-scale modelling : the turbulent phenomena are modelled by a medium-scale physical model, whereas the refinement is achieved by a small-scale linear physical model. The final simulation is achieved by coupling these models. The resulting simulations present various phenomena inherent in turbulent fluids (curls, vortices, dissipation, diffusion). We also succeeded in reproducing several specific observed phenomena such as Kelvin-Helmholtz and Von Karman turbulences.

Discrete vs continuous models

There are mainly two types of approaches for the modelling of physical phenomena : the continuous approach and the discrete approach. As shows [Gre 73], in classical modelling (figure 1) :

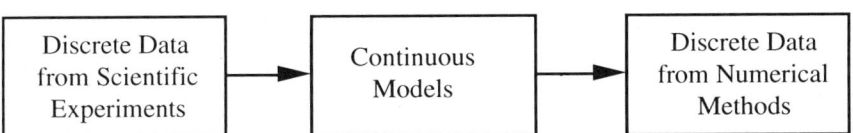

figure 1 the classical scientific procedure - [Gre 73]

continuous models can be directly replaced by discrete models to great advantage enabling the study of unpredictable or highly non-linear phenomena, for which the continuous formal equations are difficult to solve. This is all the more true for modelling the dynamic behaviour of non-stationary turbulent or chaotic systems such as fluids in non-laminar flow, smoke, propagation in complex environments (organic tissues, superconductors, porous substrata). All produce turbulent phenomena in which structured shapes such as vortices spontaneously appear, maintain themselves and possibly disappear; In these systems energetic dynamics play an important role. Vortices, curls, dissipation, diffusion and other turbulences appear as consequences of these very energetic exchanges.

1. Previous works
1.1. Motion modelling
In the field of computer graphics, the turbulent phenomena in smoke and in flames are often modelled by superimposing a velocity field and physical objects. In [MP 89] and [LJCFR91], viscous flow has was modelled, but no turbulences were observed. In [WH 91] and in [CMTM 94] physical particles are carried by a fluid which is often represented by a kinematically defined velocity field. This is why the relation between the fluid and the particles is one-way (fluid → particle). The resulting animations represent deformable leaves moving in turbulent wind field in [WH 91], flames and their spreading in [PP 94] and the visual simulation of fire in [CMTM 94].

In [SF 93] the velocity field has one large-scale field determined as in [WH 91] and one small-scale field which corresponds to a filtered white noise. But the velocity of the particles is directly determined kinematically by the value of the velocity field at that point. This results in the simulation of turbulent phenomena such as smoke and vapour.

1.2. Shape modelling
When one uses particle modelling in the aim to obtain an image, the various particles that compose the object must appear as one continuous stretch of matter. This implies that each particle be replaced by an elementary volume.
[INA 90] considers that each particle is the center of a time-independent spherical density function. The density functions add up and form a global density field that is volume-rendered. Thus the elementary shapes mentioned above do not depend on the motion of the particles. In [SF 93], the density functions are time-dependent. Diffusion and dissipation are modelled by the variation in size and in value of each density function according to a predetermined law. In [PP 94], each particle is associated with a Gouraud shaded regular hexagon. The shape of these polygons changes according to an explicitly time-dependent law. In [CMTM 94] as well as in [PP 94], each particle leaves on the final image, a trace that represents its successive positions in the course of time. This is the "long exposure" method. In this case, the elementary shape associated with each particle depends also on its motion.

1.3. Our aim
Our aim is to obtain a generic physical model of these phenomena that may produce a great variety of different behaviours and, in particular, react to unpredicted external physical events. Therefore, the kinematic or semi-kinematic models are not adequate. The model must be totally dynamic. We use a discrete model based upon point physics. In view of the importance of the energetic interactions in these phenomena we will take into account the physical interactions between the particles but also the actions from the environment on the particles, and the feedback (from the particles on the environment). This is a closed-loop interaction.
As for shape modelling, we extend this to the notion of *refinement*. The shape is also generated by physical modelling in order to obtain a deformable shape around each matter point. This deformation must not be arbitrary. It must be coherent with the physical properties (e.g. diffusion and dissipation) of the global model. In this paper it is modelled by a local physical model already described in [LHM 95] in accordance with the reference phenomena that are to be reproduced and in accordance with the physical behaviour of the particles.

18

2. Cordis - Anima modeller-simulator

Cordis-Anima is a physical modeller-simulator based on point physics [CLF 93]. It is a well-proven system on which all of our previous works were carried out. It is based on the construction of physical models by the assembly of a possibly large number of a very limited set of automata. These automata are divided in two types : mass elements and interaction elements. The input of the former is a force value and the output is a position. The input of the latter is two positions and the output is two opposite forces. The first type is characterized by only one algorithm (Newton's second law). The second type is characterized by linear or piecewise linear, or discontinuous elastic or viscous interaction functions. All of our models are constructed by the assembly of these algorithms in networks in which the nodes are mass automata and arcs are interaction automata.

3. The viscous interaction hypothesis : theoretical aspects
3.1. Viscosity as an emergent phenomenon - the *mixing layer*

Let us consider a set of particles, or a fluid at a microscopic level, in which motion is composed of thermal motion and a global motion called convection. If there is a velocity gradient between two zones of such a fluid , they exchange momentum at the junction of both zones by particle diffusion, by molecular collisions. Thus, the zone with higher velocity loses momentum and the slower fluid gains momentum. At a macroscopic level, these collisions define an emergent shear force proportional to the velocity gradient. The proportionality coefficient is the *dynamic viscosity* . The junction between these zones is an interface called the *mixing layer*. (figure 2) This layer is unstable and may go into oscillation and thus trigger whirlpools [Les 94].

3.2. Viscous particle model

This interaction phenomenon between two zones of molecular particles may be modelled by a set of particles linked to a substratum by a viscous interaction. The involved particles are not at a molecular scale, but at a scale sufficient for the representation of viscous resistance to flow (figure 2).

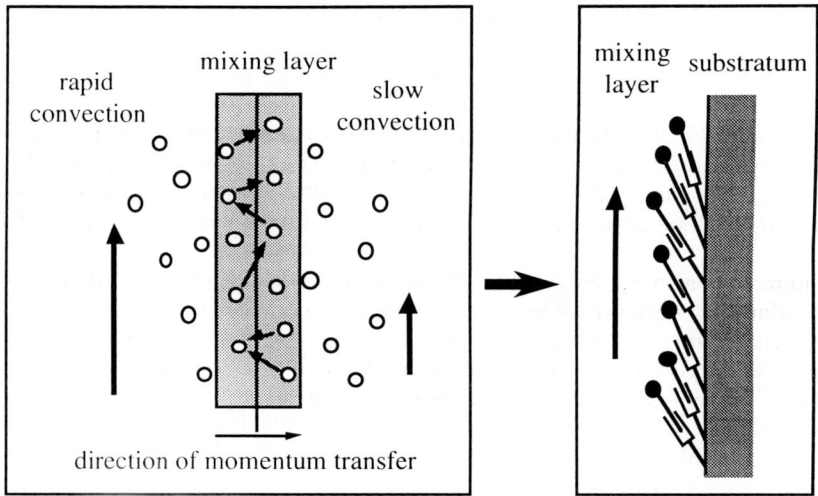

figure 2 Dynamic viscosity accounts for the collisions in the mixing layer

This is a discrete physics particle implementation of the "newtonian fluid" model. It represents the Newton's third law : "The resistance occurring within a fluid is proportional to the velocity at which the different elements of the fluid move apart from each other". The Navier-Stokes equation is the formalization of this very law. More generally, in the mixing layer, viscosity is always higher than in other zones. The simplest particle model able to account for this phenomenon is composed of a set of particles in two-state viscous interaction with each other and with a substratum. The interaction law is described below :

$$F_{pp} = Z_{pp} \cdot Vr_{pp} \qquad F_{ps} = Z_{ps} \cdot Vr_{ps}$$
$$\text{If } D_{pp} < T_{pp} \quad Z_{pp} = Z_1 \quad \text{else } Z_{pp} = Z_2$$
$$\text{If } D_{ps} < T_{ps} \quad Z_{ps} = Z'_1 \quad \text{else } Z_{ps} = Z'_2$$

where F_{pp} (resp F_{ps}) are the inter-particle (resp. particle-substratum), forces
D_{pp} (resp. D_{ps}) are the inter-particle (resp. particle - substratum) distances
Vr_{pp} (resp. Vr_{ps}) : relative velocities of the particles (resp. of particle - substratum)
T_{pp} (resp T_{ps}) is the threshold of the inter-particle (resp particle-substratum) interaction

In what follows, this type of interaction will be called thresholded viscous interaction, and the value of Z_2 and Z'_2 will be zero.

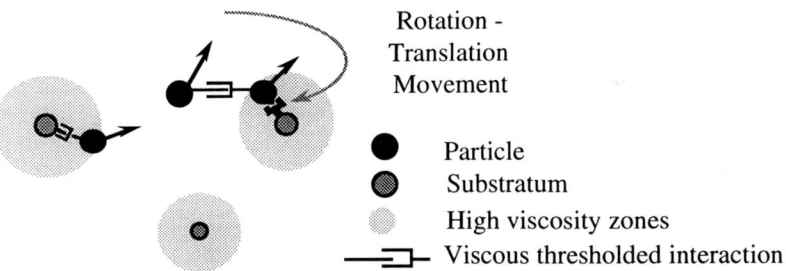

figure 3 : The generation of translation-rotation movements

When two masses (P_1, P_2) are linked ($D_{pp} < T_{pp}$), and one of them (P1) enters the high viscosity zone of a substratum mass ($D_{ps} < T_{ps}$) while P2 remains free, then P1 is slowed down. The velocity difference between P1 and P2 causes translation-rotation movements which are the basis phenomena that prime curls and whirlpools (figure 3).

The substratum may also be deformable. These deformations can be modelled by a mass-spring-damper network. The energy exchange goes in both directions (particles↔ substratum). In this way, the motion of the substratum can influence the motion of the particles, i.e. play the role of perturbation and bring the jet of active particles in oscillation and thus, trigger and intensify whirlpools.

20

3.3. Experiments : curls, whirlpools, and Kelvin-Helmholtz turbulences in the discrete viscous model

A first model is composed of a jet of particles in thresholded viscous interactions with each other and with a deformable substratum. These particles flow out of a particle injector represented by two large circles at the bottom of figure 4. The substratum is composed of a grid of masses linked by visco-elastic interactions. The position of the jet is not symmetrical in comparison with the grid. When the jet is fired on this substratum it produces curls, whirlpools, heaps, fractures, with dissipation.

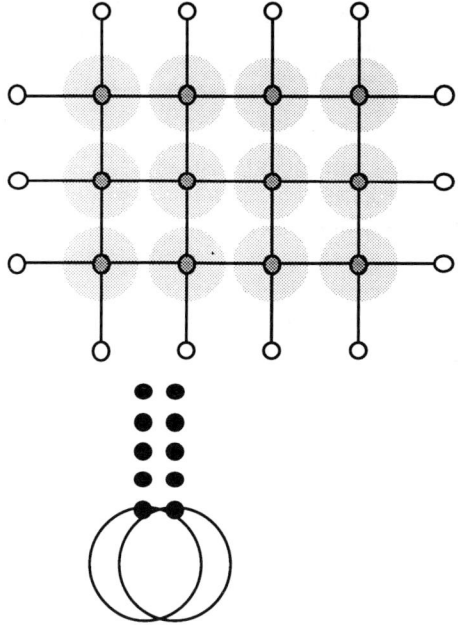

On figure 4 the jet is represented in black and the substratum in grey. We obtain simulations in which we observe : (1) the deformation of the medium (represented by the larger circles), (2) the curls of the flowing particles (represented by points), (3) the dissipation of the flow, (4) its dispersion and (5) the final accumulation on the walls

Different behaviours were observed for different values of the visco-elasticity of the substratum, and the radius of influence of the local viscosities. For the same parameters of the substratum and the flow, the main parameter which determines the nature of the resulting phenomenon is the initial velocity of the flow. For very high velocities, the flow passes through the substratum with very low oscillations. For very small velocities, the flow is dissipated as soon as it enters the substratum.

figure 4 A flow of particles fired in an ambient medium or substratum composed of visco-elastically attached points

Figures 5 to 8 show the variety of behaviours that can be obtained simply by the variation of physical parameters. Each figure corresponds to two instants in the same simulation. The tested parameters are respectively : the ambient tension in the substratum.(figure 5), the initial velocity of the active particles (figure 6), the size of the substratum in terms of number of points (figure 7), and confinement (figure 8).

3.3.2. Double-layer whirlpools

The previous model in which the substratum had a very constrained movement is not general enough to produce other typical profiles of turbulent phenomena such as Kelvin-Helmholtz eddies. A much more general model of the Newton's third law is composed of two sets of particles in thresholded viscous interaction.

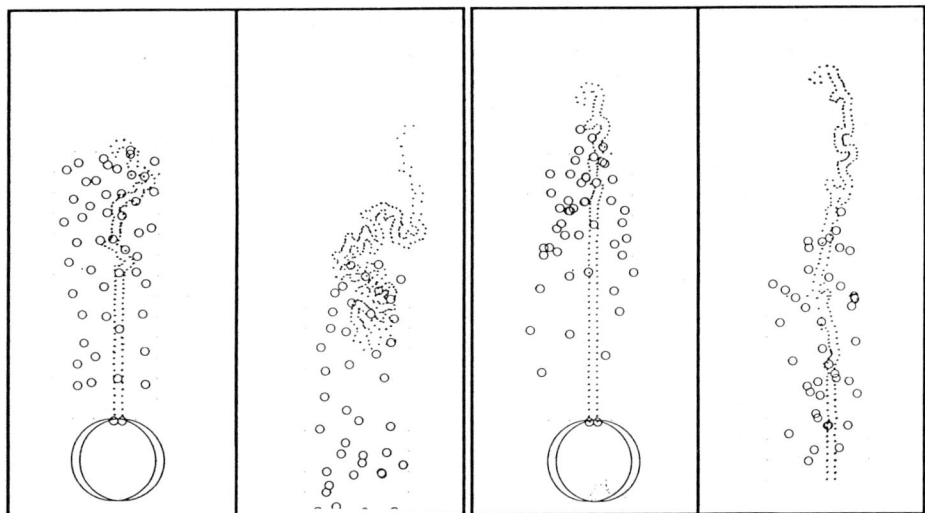

figure 5 Looser substratum   **figure 6** Flow with greater initial velocity

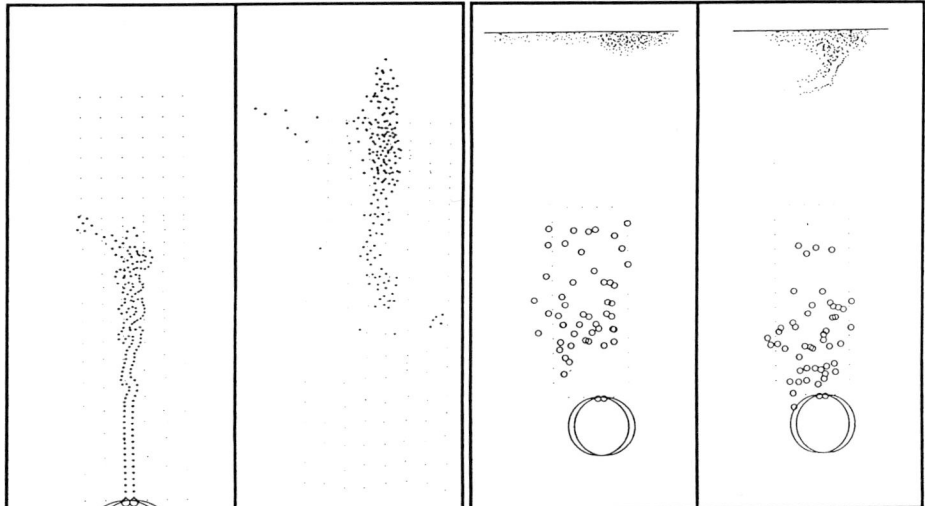

figure 7 Larger substratum   **figure 8** Confinement

Let there be two fluids with different convection velocities V1 and V2 (figure 2.a). We can consider with no loss of generality that the velocities are opposite. We obtain this configuration by placing two sets of particle injectors on each side of the scene, facing each other and vertically shifted, in such a way that the two produced jets move along each other in opposite directions (figures 9, 10 and 13) The gap between the opposite jets is chosen in order that the jets do not collide and thus avoid a front effect which is in contradiction to the mixing layer effect. When the flow of the two jets has reached a steady regime, we disymmetrically introduce a perturbation composed of one punctual mass in elastic buffer interaction with the fluids.

Figure 9 shows the resulting porperly formed Kelvin-Helmholtz whirlpools in the case of thin mixing layers, obtained with two particle jets of two layers each.
On this figure, the perturbation is introduced between image b and c. The particles of both jets cling to each other by viscosity and thus start a Kelvin-Helmholtz eddy. Then both vertically shifted and opposite jets exert a torque on the eddy. This is *vorticity*. The most central particles of the mixing layer coil first. Afterwards, as the eddy grows larger it propagates to outer layers.

3.3.3. Multi-layer whirlpools
Now let us experiment whether the eddy propagates in the fluid. This requires thicker jets. The same whirling phenomenon is observed. In addition, the eddy grows until the whole mixing layer is rolled. It can be noted that all particles do not roll in the eddy. In the previous experiment, all particles were involved, which produced one eddy alone in an empty space. Unlike this previous experiment, it can be observed that the flow is not stopped by the eddy. In view of the thickness of the simulated fluid and the shape of the eddy at the end of the simulations, we can assume that it would grow in the same manner in an infinite simulated environment.

The test parameters were : the inter-particle distance at injection, the gap between each jet, the injection velocity and frequency and the value of the viscous interactions.

The movement may remain global or divide depending on the viscosity. For very small viscosities, there is no eddy at all. For very great viscosities, we observe paste effects. The intermediate values offer the whole range of more or less fluid behaviours. In some of our simulations, made with low viscosities, the fluid divides into two or three smaller eddies within the mixing layer. More or less laminar fluids can be obtained depending on the radius of the viscous interactions in comparison with the inter-particle distances. In these fluids laminar layers can easily be distinguished from coexisting turbulent layers.

4. Introducing pressure by adding elastic components-

4.1. Why and how to introduce elasticity
In fluids, two phenomena coexist. Viscosity for which shear forces are parallel to flow, and shocks for which the irrotational forces are perpendicular to the direction of convection. Moreover, the concurrent effects of collisions cause another emergent phenomenon : pressure, which intensifies agglomeration effects (superpressure) or diffusion (depression) and which causes the formation of a third characteristic profile of turbulent fluid behaviour, that is Von Karman eddies. Now the question is : how to introduce pressure in a punctual mass model.

4.2. Compressed elasiticity model
Local pressure can be modelled by adding a thresholded elastic interaction between the particles of the same jet and between the particles of different jets. In the same way as for viscosity, we can say that pressure is an emergent phenomenon and we must try to model it without necessarily getting down to the scale of molecular thermal motion. Therefore we establish between the particles a thresholded elastic interaction with a low intensity and a large threshold in comparison with the threshold of the above viscous interaction. This is what we call a compressed elasticity model.

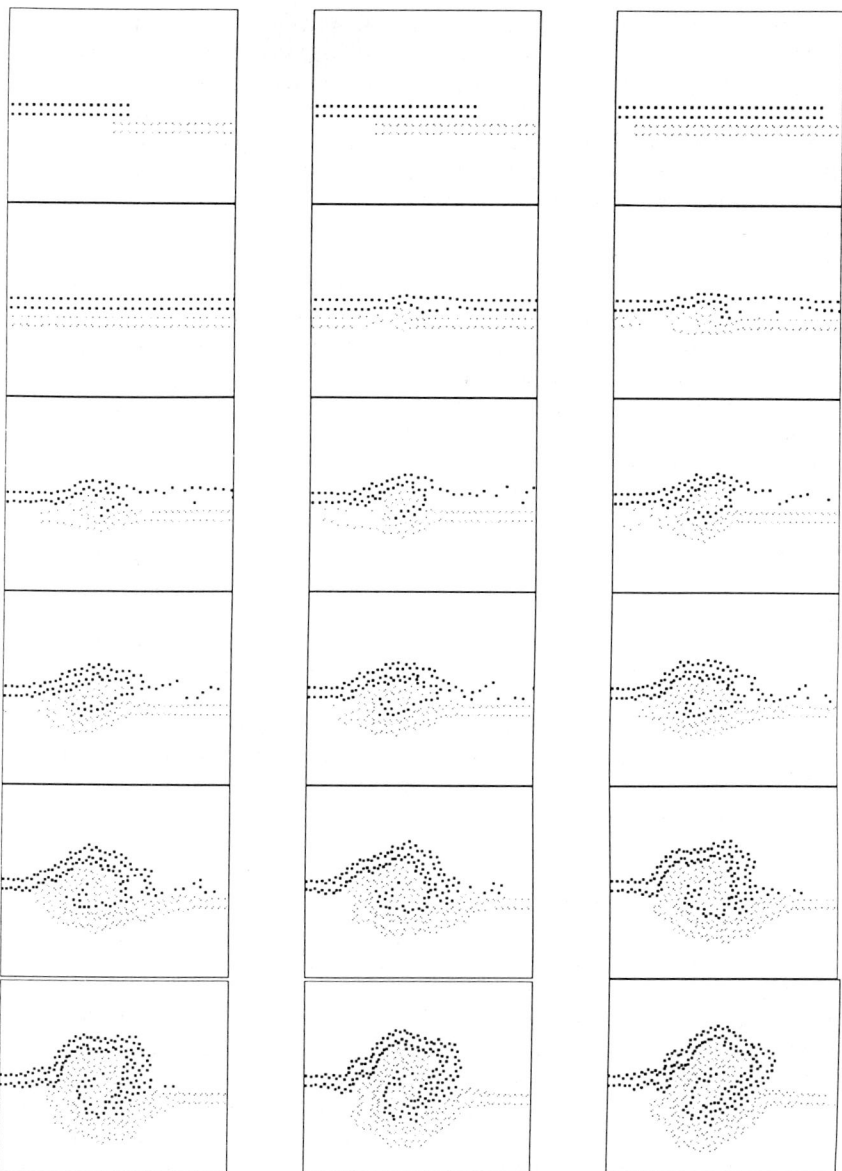

figure 9 Double-layer whirlpool. The time step of this chronogram is 1 sec

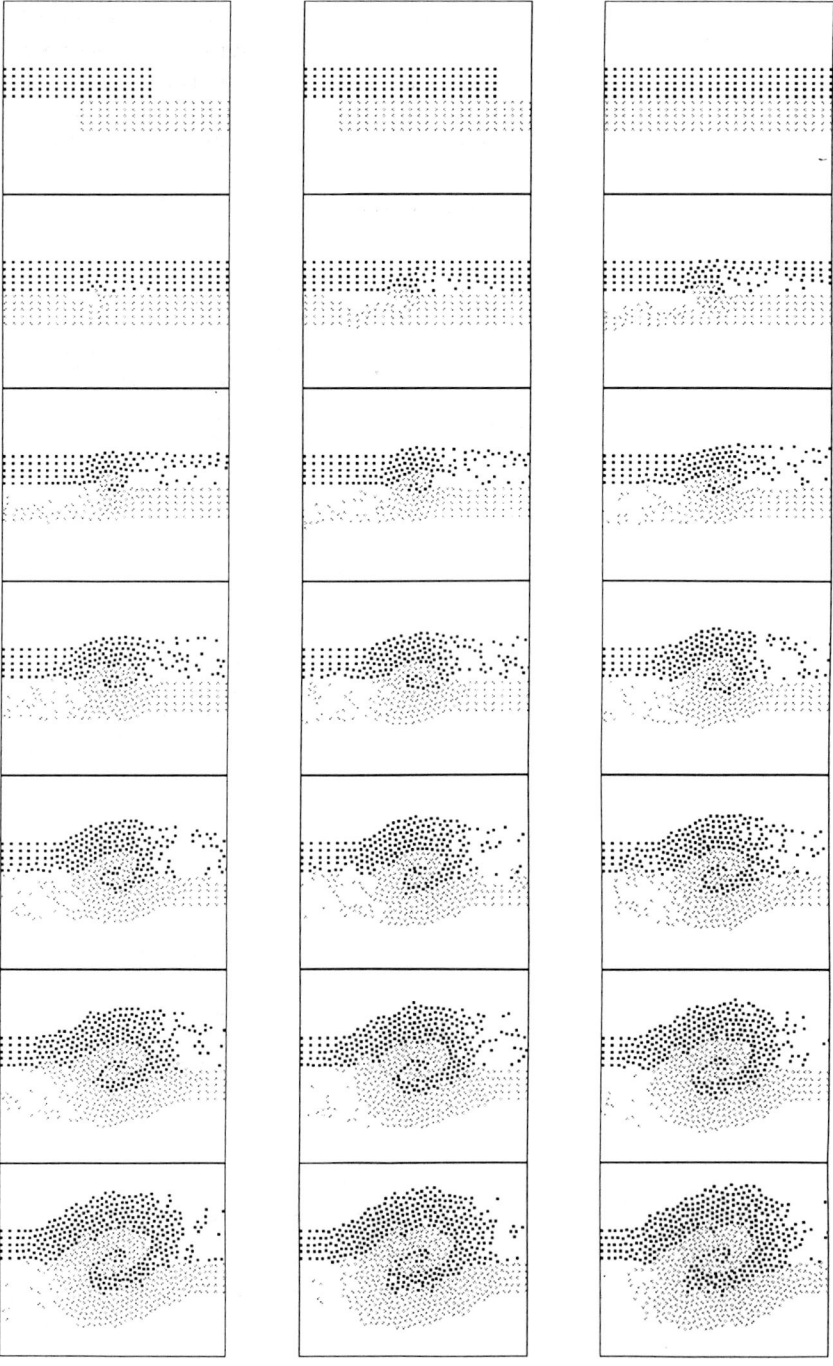

figure 10 Multi-layer whirlpool. The time step of this chronogram is 1 sec

This elastic repulsion force has a very low stiffness, and it only weakly prevents the particles from entering the neighbouring particles' high-viscosity zones. When the particles are linked by viscous interactions, they are in a confined state. Since the threshold is large, the repulsion between the masses is not caused by proper individual collisions. It is integrated on a neighbourhood through the overlapping of the elastic interaction zones. Thus each particle is in repulsive interaction with several neighbouring particles (about 15, in our simulations)(figure 11).

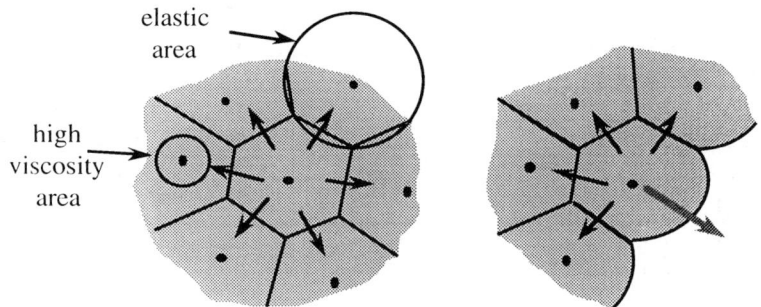

figure 11 Model of pressure

4.3. Global confinement

The introduction of a repulsion force requires a confined system. Such a confinement can be modelled by setting a visco-elastic buffer interaction with external masses acting as walls. This interaction must not be too stiff, in order to avoid the occurrence of shock waves from the walls. Fairly loose elastic buffer interactions enable us to model external pressure instead of rigid walls.

4.4. Results

Figure 12 shows the depression that appears behind an obstacle. The obstacle is represented by a visco-elastic buffer interaction.

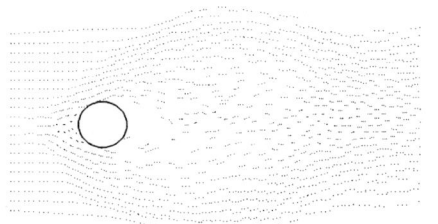

figure 12 Depression behind an obstacle

We also obtained elastic oscillation effects propagating on laminar flows. (figure 13)
If one of the jets is replaced by a set of particles scattered over the simulation space we obtain the major effects that appear in a fluid flowing in a medium. Figure 14 shows the shock wave effects in the medium. Figure 15 shows von Karman profiles with inversed Kelvin-Helmholtz eddies.

Thus smoke behaviour has been modelled, including all the phenomena mentioned above : laminar flow, whirlpools, Von Karman eddies, dissipation (figure 16)

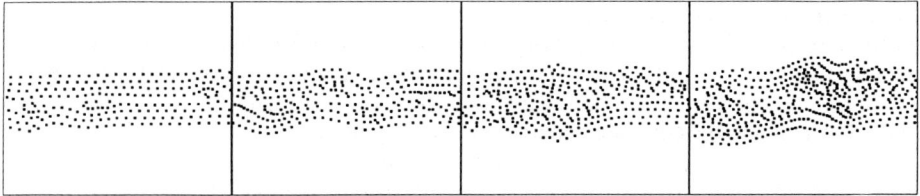

figure 13 Propagation (the time step of this chronogram is 1 sec)

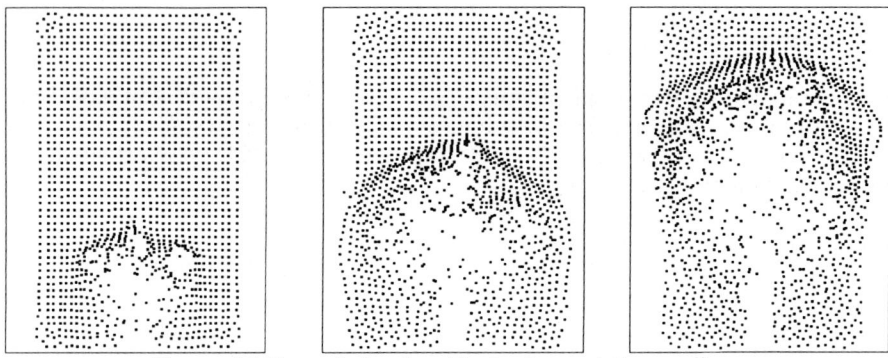

figure 14 Frontal shock with the jet and the medium

5. Refinement
5.1. Principles : physically-based refinement

When the motion of the particles corresponds to a correct motion, each of these particles has to be associated with an elementary volume in order that the combination of all these volumes forms the global volume of a specific turbulent material.

In accordance with the high deformability of this type of material, we know that this volume must also be highly deformable. Furthermore, the deformation of this elementary volume cannot be arbitrarily defined. It must correspond to the physical properties of the modelled phenomenon and it cannot be independent of the movement of the particle.

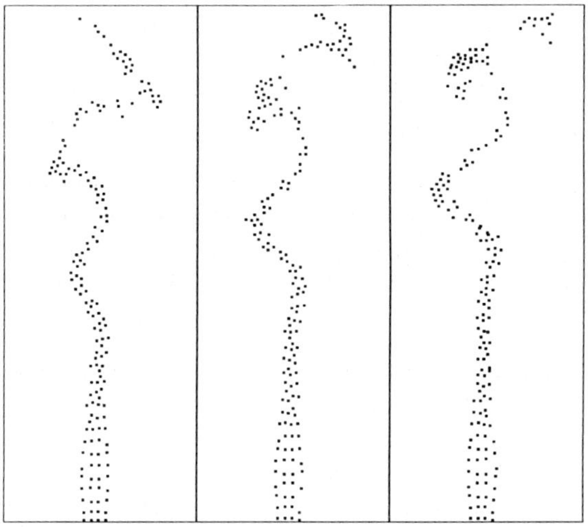

We consider the dynamic phenomena involved in turbulent materials as the combination of a global dynamic behaviour (the behaviour of the particles) and a local dynamic behaviour (the behaviour of the particles' shape) This is the reason why, our refinement model is a physical model.

figure 15 Von Karman eddies in smoke

5.2 Multi-scale modelling

Our hypothesis is that the local dynamic deformations involve low energies. Therefore they are influenced by the global dynamic behaviour but the converse is not true. Thus the final animation is obtained by coupling the particle model with a refinement model that will add the finer deformations to the sequence.

The fact that we work with two separate physical models enables us to simulate each of them at its own simulation rate, with its own resolution and according to its proper specific requirements. A rather small number of particles (300 to 1500) seems to be sufficient for the observation of phenomena such as curls, eddies, Kelvin-Helmholtz and Von Karman turbulences.

In order to obtain smooth wisps of smoke, a far higher resolution is required, but the properties of this model may be much simpler since the turbulences have already been obtained. This is called *multi-scale modelling* [LHM 95] and it makes it possible to produce quality motions at reasonable costs.

5.3.The refinement model

Our refinement model is a linear physical model already described in a previous publication [LHM 95]
Refinement is performed by a deformation field DF. Each point M_{ijk} of the simulated space is characterized by a scalar dynamic variable called the deformation value $a_{ijk}(t)$. The whole scene is characterized by a deformation field DF(t). The particles passing through the scene deform this field. What we represent on the final image is not the particles but their *zone of influence* ZI (t) on the deformation field DF(t), that is, the set of points for which the deformation value is greater than a specific threshold value. In this work, the light intensity of each point is proportional to its deformation value. The zone of influence ZI(P,t) of particle P is the elementary volume V(P,t) that we associate with each particle (Cf § 5.1). This is very comparable with the implicit surface methods.[Blinn 82][BS 91] The novelty consists in the way in which the particles modify the deformation field. We perform physical refinement by endowing this field with physical properties : The deformation value of each point varies as the position of a punctual mass with one degree of freedom *(a phyxel)*. This mass is attached to a fixed substratum by a visco-elastic interaction and to its neighbouring masses by other visco-elastic interactions. Therefore The deformation field DF returns to a specific rest value after each transient deformation.

Thus, the volume S(P) depends on the motion of the particle. For example, the zone of influence of a particle at rest is a sphere with gradations and a blur, but the ZI of a moving particle has also a "comet's tail" whose size, direction and intensity distribution depends on the particle's velocity and trajectory. In addition, a group of close particles is visualized as a blurred continuous stretch of matter (figure 16).

6. Conclusions

Our final particle model (sections 3 and 4) : (1) is at a larger scale than the molecular scale and models emergent effects such as viscosity and pressure with punctual masses in interaction; (2) integrates cohesion forces (viscous forces) that cause eddies, and repulsion forces that cause superpressure and depression, that intensify confinement or the fluid's dispersion and that also cause shock wave propagation, (3) properly reproduces the major characteristic figures of turbulent fluids such as plain curls, Kelvin-Helmholtz eddies and Von Karman wakes. Thus we have modelled various behaviours of turbulent objects : more or less viscous pastes, fluids, gasses, smokes.

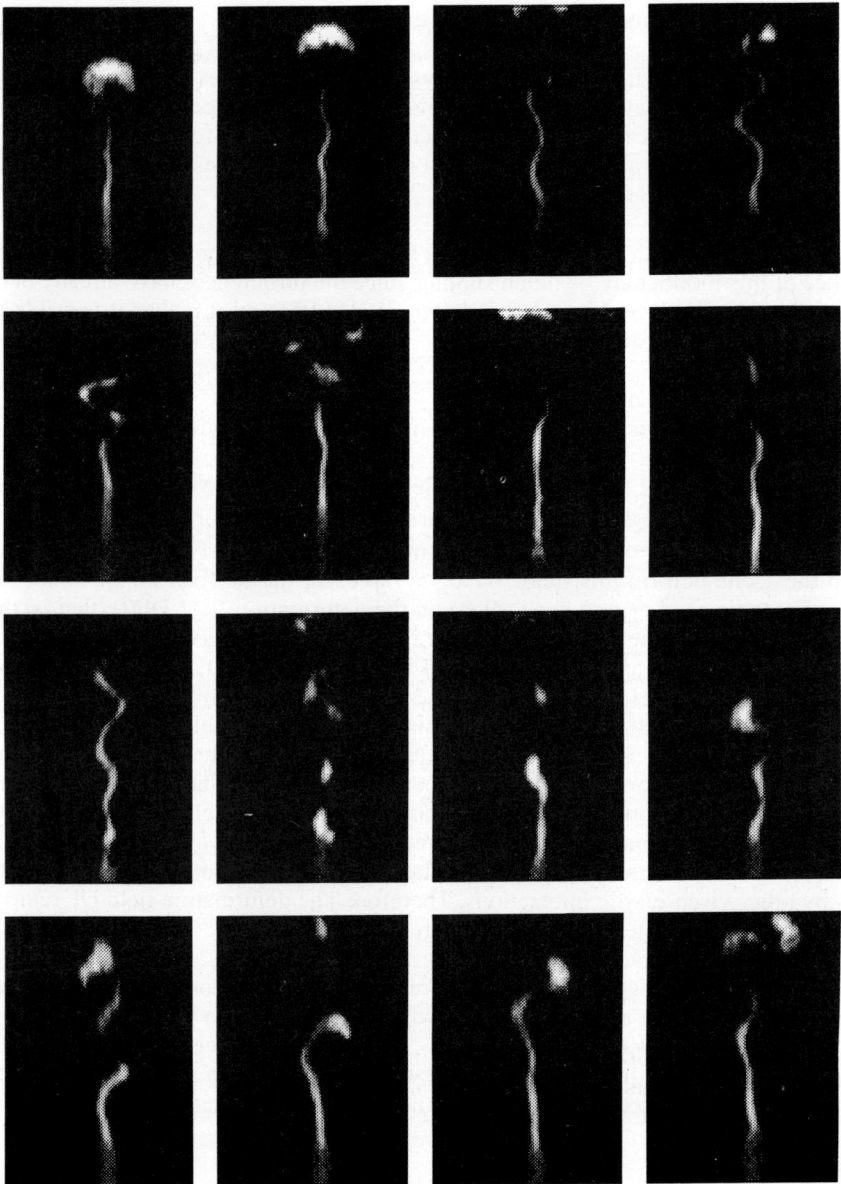

figure 16 A refined model of smoke. The time step of this chronogram is 1 sec

Moreover, the dynamic model constructed by the Cordis-Anima formalism, which is based on point physics and interactions makes it possible, at any instant, to act upon any given mass (respectively interaction automaton) in the system. This action may consist in the application of forces (respectively positions) of the external environment. Thus the operator or an object of the real world can act upon the simulated fluids without affecting the physical consistence of the system.

These simulations were carried out at 1050 Hz. The refinement model is a finely discretized 1D linear O(n) model. The final results are displayed on the chronogram on figure 16. These refinement simulations, with 400 smoke particles and 57 600 phyxels, at the simulation frequency of 300 Hz required 7.06 seconds per frame on a Silicon Graphics Indigo 2 Extreme. However, this refinement model can easily be parallelized and implemented on a massively parallel machine.

References

[Gre 73] D. Greenspan *Discrete Models*, Reading in Applied Mathematics, Addison Wesley, 1973

[MP 89] G. Miller, A. Pearce *Globular Dynamics : A Connected Particle System For Animating Viscous Fluids*, Computer & Graphics Vol 13, No. 3, pp 305-309 1989

[LJCFR91] A. Luciani, S. Jimenez, C. Cadoz, J.L. Florens, O. Raoult *Computational Physics : a Modeler - Simulator for Animated Physical Objects*, Proceedings of Eurographics Conference, 1991, Vienna, Austria

[WH 91] J. Wejchert, D. Haumann *Animation Aerodynamics* In Proceedings of SIGGRAPH' 91 Volume 25, Number 4, July 1991

[CMTM 94] N. Chiba K. Muraoka H. Takahashi and M. Miura *Two-dimensional Visual Simulation of Flames, Smokes and the Spread of Fire*. The Journal of Visualization and computer Animation, vol 5, pp 37-53, 1994.

[PP 94] LC. H. Perry, R.W. Picard *Synthesizing Flames and their Spreading* Proceedings of the Fifth Eurographics Animation and Simulation Workshop (Oslo,

[SF 93] J. Stam and E. Fiume *Turbulent Wind Fields for Gaseous Phenomena* ACM Computer Graphics (SIGGRAPH' 93), p 369-376, August 1993

Norway September 17-18 1994)

[INA 90] M. Inakage *A Simple Model of Flames* Proceedings of CG International'90, pp. 71-81

[LHM 95] A. Luciani, A. Habibi, E. Manzotti *A Multi-Scale Physical Model of Granular Materials* Proceedings of Graphics Interface' 95.

[CLF 93] C. Cadoz, A. Luciani, J.L. Florens *CORDIS-ANIMA A Modelling and Simulation System for Sound and Image Synthesis - The General Formalism*, Computer Music Journal, 1993, 10(1), 19-29, M.I.T. Press

[Les 94] M. Lesieur *La Turbulence* Presses Universitaires de Grenoble 1994

[Gre 73] D. Greenspan *Discrete Models* Addison-Wesley Reading M.A. 1973

[Blinn 82] J.F. Blinn *A Generalization of Algebraic Surface Drawing* ACM Transactions on Graphics Vol. 1, No.3, July 1982, Pages 235 - 256

[BS 91] J Bloomenthal, K. Shoemake Convolution Surfaces Proceedings of SIGGRAPH'91 Computer Graphics Volume 25, Number 4, July 1991

Acknowledgements

Thanks to Jean Loup Florens (ACROE) and Benoît Chanclou (LIFIA) who advanced the primary ideas of this work. Parts of this work have been used for an artistic work called ESQUISSES created for the IJCAI conference on August 31st 1993

The financial assistance of the French "Ministère de la Culture", the "Centre National Cinématographique", and the IMAG Institute is gratefully acknowledged.

Using Simulated Annealing to Obtain Good Nodal Approximations of Deformable Bodies

Oliver Deussen and Leif Kobbelt and Peter Tücke

Institute for Operating and Dialog Systems, University of Karlsruhe
76128 Karlsruhe, Germany
Net: [oliver l kobbelt l tuecke]@informatik.uni-karlsruhe.de
WWW: http:// i31www.informatik.uni-karlsruhe.de/[~oliver l ~kobbelt l ~tuecke]

Abstract. In this paper we present a method to obtain good approximations of deformable bodies with spring/mass systems. An iterative algorithm based on voronoi diagrams is used to get a good mass distribution. The elastic properties of the system are optimized by simulated annealing. Results are shown, and some applications are discussed.

Keywords:

Simulation, Spring/mass lattice, Modeling, Deformable Bodies, Computer Graphics

Real time simulation and interactive control of deformable bodies are of great interest to computer graphics and other fields like pattern matching or medical visualization.

Spring/mass (or nodal) systems are often used to obtain efficient simulations of deformable objects if lower requirements for the simulation precision are given.

Terzopoulos and Waters [15, 13] used them for modeling and simulating facial tissue. Simulation of woven clothes was done by Breen [4]. In an early work, Miller [11] used nodal models to simulate utricular objects.

In medical research similar systems are used to simulate human organs for training tasks in endoscopic surgery [10, 6], and for general surgery simulation and planning [5].

To reproduce a specific mechanic behaviour of a spring/mass system, parameters like spring constants can either be preset, or optimized iteratively. We show that within some general limits, such optimizations yield systems which approximate objects with given elastic properties quite well.

1 Nodal Approximations

In general, a spring/mass system (SMS) is a collection of points (or particles) with a specific mass, that are connected by springs, dampers or plastic elements. The discrete Lagrangian equation of motion for a point p_i at position $\mathbf{u}_i$ and mass m_i has the simple form (cf. [15]):

$$m_i \ddot{\mathbf{u}}_i + \gamma \dot{\mathbf{u}}_i = \mathbf{F}^e - \sum_{j \in N_i} \mathbf{F}_{ij}, \qquad (1)$$

where γ is a general damping coefficient, and $\mathbf{F}^e$ denotes an external force acting on the point. The forces $\mathbf{F}_{ij}$ are exerted by elastic, viscotic and plastic connectors between p_i and neighbour points p_j (N_i: set of neighbours).

1.1   Finite Element Formulation of Nodal Systems

The idea of approximating a deformable body with a system of springs is surprisingly old. In 1868, Kirsch [9] derived the fundamental equations of elasticity from a system of springs approximating a small cube. His work was one of the bases of the finite element method (FEM).

Today pin jointed trusses (assemblages of axially loaded elastic bar elements) are used in structural mechanics as idealizations for many problems. The FEM approach is widely used for such systems.

Those trusses can be seen as spring/mass systems. The only difference is that within trusses bars have a mass and joints are massless whereby in a SMS massless springs are connected by mass points that behave like spherical joints. In both cases, the mass distribution can be expressed by a mass matrix $\mathbf{M}$.

If only elastic and viscotic connectors are used, equation (1) can be written in matrix calculus (cf. [2]) by:

$$\mathbf{M}\ddot{\mathbf{u}} + \mathbf{D}\dot{\mathbf{u}} = \mathbf{F}^e - \mathbf{K}\mathbf{u}. \qquad (2)$$

In this equation, $\mathbf{u} = (u_{1x}, u_{1y}, u_{1z}, ..., u_{nx}, u_{ny}, u_{nz})^T$ is the vector of all point positions[1], $\mathbf{D}$ is the damping matrix and $\mathbf{F}^e$ denotes the external forces acting on the nodes. $\mathbf{K}$ is the systems stiffness matrix. This matrix describes the forces on nodes as a result of deformations and can be seen as a generalized spring constant.

In comparison to other systems of finite elements, nodal systems do have the advantage of $\mathbf{M}$ being diagonal, which is simple and convenient for mathematical handling (cf. [8]). In addition, equation (2) can be solved by local application of equation (1) to each node. This leads to more efficient algorithms (cf. [15]), especially if parallel computers are used.

Table 1 shows some computation rates (calculations per second). The local simulation method based on equation (1) is independent of the bandwidth of $\mathbf{K}$. FEM methods based on equation (2) do have low computation rates if $\mathbf{K}$ is recalculated in every step. This has to be done to make the FEM method comparable with the local algorithm. If $\mathbf{K}$ is updated every eighth step, the computation rates for systems with a small bandwidth are close to that of the local method.

For small deformations (the geometric linear case) $\mathbf{K}$ can be assumed constant. In this case the computation rates are high, but simulation precision decreases.

The calculation of equilibrium states is computational expensive because a linear equation system based on $\mathbf{K}$ has to be solved.

---

[1]More precisely $\mathbf{u}$ describes the displacements of points to an initial position with zero inner energy of the system (indicated by $|\mathbf{K}\mathbf{u}| = 0$).

Table 1: Computation rates (calculations per second, SUN Sparc 20)

Bandwidth of $\mathbf{K}$	49	37	25	21
1) Local integration	37	37	37	37
2) FEM ($\mathbf{K}$ updated every step)	8	9	10	10
3) FEM ($\mathbf{K}$ updated every eighth step)	19	23	31	33
4) FEM ($\mathbf{K}$ constant)	25	32	43	48
5) Equilibrium calculation	2.5	4	7	9

Investigated was a system with 84 nodes, 231 edges and different bandwidth of $\mathbf{K}$. 1) computation with local method; 2) FEM solution with updating of matrix $\mathbf{K}$ in every step; 3) FEM solution, $\mathbf{K}$ is updated every eighth step; 4) FEM solution without updating; 5) computation of equilibrium.

As a consequence, we use a finite element method based on band matrices to obtain equilibrium states within the optimization process (in section 5.3) and local methods for the efficient solution of equation (2) during simulation.

2   Optimal Elastic Systems

Given a deformable body B with mass density $\rho(\mathbf{u})$, surface A and elastic properties represented by a function $\mathbf{G}$ (cf. [7]). This function determines the stress-strain relation

$$\sigma = \mathbf{G}(\epsilon), \tag{3}$$

and thus the forces needed to deform a body in a certain way (see section 5.1).

In the most general case, we have $\mathbf{G} \in I\!R^9 \times I\!R^6$. For linear problems and elastic homogeneous and isotropic materials, $\mathbf{G}$ is a symmetric 6×6 matrix. In this form the relationship is known as *Hooke's law*. For many natural materials in the linear elastic case, $\mathbf{G}$ can be expressed by two independent constants, usually E (*Young's modulus*) and ν (*Poisson's ratio*).

The optimization process will be demonstrated in two-dimensional space with linear elastic loads of homogeneous materials. Extensions to 3-D and to anisotropic and inhomogeneous materials are discussed below.

To get an optimal spring/mass system, we have to approximate the mass distribution by discrete mass points, and elasticity by the topology of the connections together with their spring constants. This is done in two steps. First, we find positions and masses of the points, then we insert and optimize the connections.

3   First Step: Positioning Points

Given an arbitrary body B with surface A, two ways of point positioning were tested. Regular grids (see below) with predefined connection structures were used as well as systems based on randomly given points.

3.1 The Iterated Voronoi Approach

Our observation was, that systems with arbitrary given points do not lead to good results in simulating elastic behaviour of homogeneous bodies. To solve this problem we developed a method of moving the points slightly in order to obtain a more homogeneous point positioning.

For each given point $p_i \in P$, the corresponding Voronoi region $V(p_i, P)$ is defined by

$$V(p_i, P) = \{|q - p_i| < |q - p_j|, q \in \mathbb{R}^3, p_j \in P - \{p_i\}\}.$$

The set of resulting regions for all p_i is a tesselation of the plane, it can be computed in $O(n \log n)$ time for n given points in two-dimensional space (cf. [12]). Since the boundary of each V is polygonal, we can easily intersect it with A.

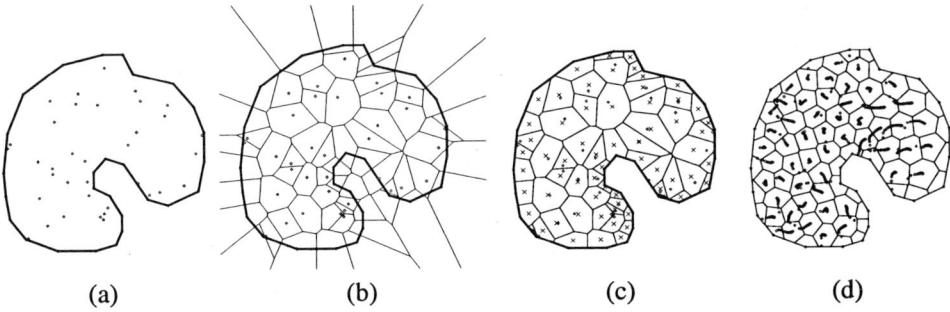

(a)	(b)	(c)	(d)

Figure 1: Point positioning - a) random points; b) Voronoi regions; c) cutted regions with moved points; d) regions after 15 iterations, together with point motion.

Next, the p_i are moved to the center of gravity of the corresponding Voronoi region (Figure 1). This process can be iterated. During iteration, the standard deviation of the point to point distances reduces as well as the standard deviation of the Voronoi-region sizes (Figure 2).

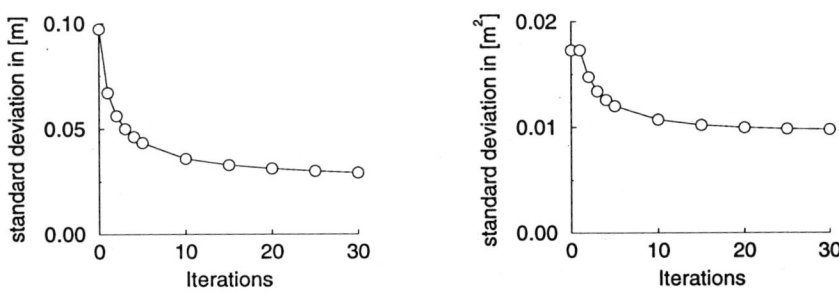

Figure 2: Standard deviation during iteration - a) point to point distances; b) sizes of Voronoi-regions.

Both results indicate a more homogeneous point positioning after some iterations. After the last iteration the weights are computed according to section 4 (see below).

34

3.2 Regular Grids

Besides random positioning of points, we used regular grids together with specific connection topologies. These configurations lead to good approximation results with the investigated loads (see below), but may have an anisotropic behaviour because of their regularity (like crystals do).

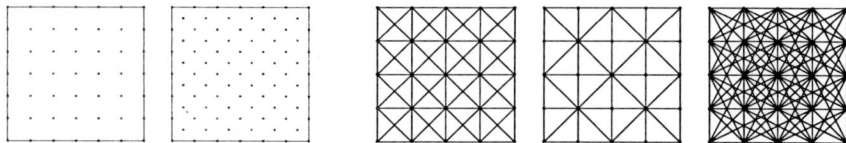

Figure 3: a) regular grids used; b) Suitable topologies to connect the grids.

To combine regular grids with arbitrary surfaces, tesselation is necessary. In the context of our quantitative study in the following paragraphs, we omit such tesselations because their results are hard to interpret.

4 Second Step: Calculation of the Mass Distribution

If the point positions $\mathbf{u}_i$ are known, we have to approximate the mass distribution of B by assigning masses $m(\mathbf{u}_i) := m_i$ to the points. The approximation of B by a set of tupels $(\mathbf{u}_i, m_i)$ is considered to be good, if the mass moments p_{jkl} up to order two coincide. These moments determine the linear and angular accelerations to external forces and torques.

The relevant mass moments p_{jkl} of B are computed by

$$p_{jkl} = \int_B u_x^j u_y^k u_z^l \rho(\mathbf{u}) \, d\mathbf{u} \qquad j + k + l \leq 2. \tag{4}$$

Substituting B by a finite set of points $\mathbf{u}_i$ corresponds to approximating this integral by the sum

$$p_{jkl} = \sum_{i=1}^{n} u_{xi}^j u_{yi}^k u_{zi}^l \, m_i \qquad j + k + l \leq 2. \tag{5}$$

Equation (5) can be considered as the application of a cubature formula for the integrand function $f(\mathbf{u}) = u_x^j u_y^k u_z^l \rho(\mathbf{u})$ over the domain B, where the points $\mathbf{u}_i$ are the sample points and m_i are the weight coefficients for the formula. Hence, the approximation $(\mathbf{u}_i, m_i)$ of B meets all relevant mass moments if and only if this cubature formula has at least *quadratic polynomial precision*, i.e., if and only if

$$\mathbf{A} \, \mathbf{m} = \mathbf{p}, \tag{6}$$

where $\mathbf{m} = (m_1, \ldots, m_{n-1})^T$ is the vector of mass coefficients, $\mathbf{p} = (p_{000}, p_{100}, p_{010}, p_{001}, p_{110}, p_{101}, p_{011}, p_{200}, p_{020}, p_{002})^T$ is the 10-dimensional vector of exact moments of B, and $\mathbf{A}$ is the $(10 \times n)$-matrix with

$$\mathbf{A}^T = \begin{pmatrix} 1 & u_{x1} & u_{y1} & \cdots & u_{y1}u_{z1} & u_{x1}^2 & u_{y1}^2 & u_{z1}^2 \\ 1 & u_{x2} & u_{y2} & \cdots & u_{y2}u_{z2} & u_{x2}^2 & u_{y2}^2 & u_{z2}^2 \\ \vdots & \vdots & \vdots & \ddots & \vdots & \vdots & \vdots & \vdots \\ 1 & u_{xn} & u_{yn} & \cdots & u_{yn}u_{zn} & u_{xn}^2 & u_{yn}^2 & u_{zn}^2 \end{pmatrix}.$$

The solution of the under determined system (6) with least Euclidian norm $\|\mathbf{m}\|_2$ is of the form $\mathbf{A}^T\mathbf{x}$ with $\mathbf{x} \in I\!R^{10}$ [3]. Hence, the mass coefficients $\mathbf{m} = \mathbf{A}^T\mathbf{x}$ can be found by solving

$$\mathbf{A}\,\mathbf{A}^T\mathbf{x} \;=\; \mathbf{p}. \tag{7}$$

Since $\mathbf{A}$ is a Vandermonde matrix, $\mathbf{A}\,\mathbf{A}^T$ is regular if there is a collection of 10 points $\mathbf{u}_i$ which does not lie on a polynomial surface $p(x, y, z) = 0$ of degree less than or equal to two.

Capturing third or higher order moments of B yields no significant improvement of the approximation und thus the degrees of freedom for the choice of the m_i are used in a way that $\|\mathbf{m}\|_2$ is minimal. In this case the masses are distributed as uniform as possible.

5 Third Step: Optimizing Elasticity

Given n points with positions and masses. The connections can be found as follows: If the points are distributed randomly, we use a Delaunay triangulation to obtain pairs of points to be connected by springs. Two points are joined if they have a common edge in the Voronoi diagram. This triangulation method is widely used in finite element mechanics.

For regular grids, we tested several topologies in order to find suitable elastic approximations. Good results are given by structures as those shown in Figure 3(b).

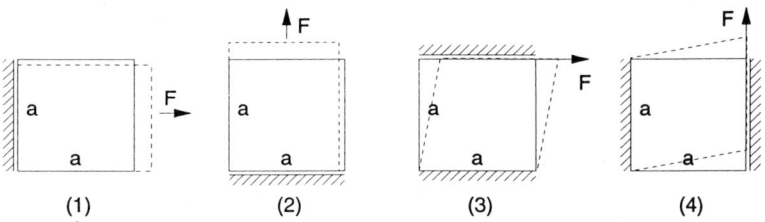

Figure 4: Test configurations with resulting deformations of a surface.

A good approximation of the elastic properties is found if the system's displacement due to some basic loads is similar to that of the given body B. Figure 4 shows the configurations used, B is a square plate. In situations (1) and (2), stretching loads are applied, shearing is done in situations (3) and (4).

5.1 Getting Reference Values

For some simple bodies and special configurations it is possible to get an analytic solution of the resulting displacements due to external forces (cf. [2]). [2]

As a reference, we calculate the deformation of the square plate shown in Figure 4(1). In this situation a uniform distributed force is applied to one side, the opposite one is constrained in x-direction, but not in y-direction.

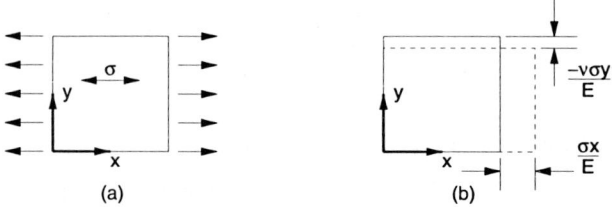

(a)   (b)

Figure 5: a) Plate with uniform distributed load to two opposite sides; b) resulting deformation.

This situation is equivalent to the application of a uniform distributed load σ to two opposite sides, whereby the body is constrained such that rigid body motions are permitted (Figure 5).

We assume a linear elastic deformation and a material that can be expressed by Poisson's ratio ν and Young's modulus E. In section 2 we gave the general formulation of the strain-stress relation (see equation (3)). This relation, now written in matrix calculus, has to be satisfied:

$$
\begin{pmatrix} \epsilon_x \\ \epsilon_y \\ \gamma_{xy} \end{pmatrix} = \frac{1}{E} \begin{pmatrix} 1-\nu & \nu & 0 \\ \nu & 1-\nu & 0 \\ 0 & 0 & 2(1+\nu) \end{pmatrix} \begin{pmatrix} \sigma_x \\ \sigma_y \\ \tau_{xy} \end{pmatrix},
\tag{8}
$$

as well as the equilibrium condition

$$
\begin{pmatrix} \frac{\partial}{\partial x} & 0 & \frac{\partial}{\partial y} \\ 0 & \frac{\partial}{\partial y} & \frac{\partial}{\partial x} \end{pmatrix} \begin{pmatrix} \sigma_x \\ \sigma_y \\ \tau_{xy} \end{pmatrix} = \begin{pmatrix} F_x \\ F_y \end{pmatrix}
\tag{9}
$$

and the strain-displacement relation

$$
\begin{pmatrix} \frac{\partial}{\partial x} & 0 \\ 0 & \frac{\partial}{\partial y} \\ \frac{\partial}{\partial y} & \frac{\partial}{\partial x} \end{pmatrix} \begin{pmatrix} u_x \\ u_y \end{pmatrix} = \begin{pmatrix} \epsilon_x \\ \epsilon_y \\ \gamma_{xy} \end{pmatrix}.
\tag{10}
$$

Since rigid body motions are permitted, we have $F_x = 0$, $F_y = 0$ and assume

$$
\sigma_x = \sigma, \qquad \sigma_y = 0, \qquad \tau_{xy} = 0
$$

[2] For more complicated bodies and situations more precise finite element methods are used to get reference values.

which satisfies equation (9). The stresses can be computed by application of Hooke's law (equation (8)):

$$\epsilon_x = \frac{\sigma}{E}, \qquad \epsilon_y = -\nu\frac{\sigma}{E}, \qquad \gamma_{xy} = 0.$$

Integration according to equation (10) leads to the desired displacements

$$u_x = \frac{\sigma x}{E} + f(y), \qquad u_y = -\nu\frac{\sigma y}{E} + g(x).$$

We set $f(y)$ and $g(x)$ to zero, the proof of correctness for doing this is omitted here.

5.2 Initial SMS Configuration

The initial spring constants of the SMS are set according to Young's modulus (E). For a spring of resting length s_0, the spring constant is set heuristically to $K = E * s_0/4$. The upper part of Figure 8(a) shows the calculated displacements of the initial SMS, approximating the deformations of the given surface. They are drawn using dotted lines.

5.3 Fast Calculation of Displacements

During the optimization process, the displacements $\mathbf{u}$ of the SMS which are due to the applied forces $\mathbf{F}^e$ have to be calculated very often. Within the equilibrium state of the system they are obtained by solving

$$\mathbf{F}^e - \mathbf{Ku} = -\mathbf{F}^b, \qquad (11)$$

which is the solution of equation (2) with vanishing $\ddot{\mathbf{u}}$ and $\dot{\mathbf{u}}$. The additional vector $\mathbf{F}^b$ describes the bearing forces in fixed points. The equation system is solved on the base of band matrices, the necessary node enumeration is done with an optimization method in a preprocessing step. Because $\mathbf{K}$ is changed in every optimization step, it can not be inverted in advance.

5.4 Quality Criteria

For each point position of the SMS and each of the test configurations, the reference displacement $\mathbf{u}^{ref}$ is calculated according to paragraph 5.1. The aforementioned FEM approach is used to compute the actual displacements $\mathbf{u}$ during optimization.

One possibility to describe the quality of an SMS approximation is the standard deviation between actual and reference displacements of all its points:

$$G_s := \sqrt{\sum_{i=1}^{4}\left(\mathbf{u}^{i,ref} - \mathbf{u}^i\right)^2}. \qquad (12)$$

Here, $\mathbf{u}^i$ denotes displacements according to the test configuration i of Figure 4. Other criteria are weighted standard deviations where border and corner points have a stronger influence. We denote the weight factors as $G_{a:b:c}$, where a is the weight of inner points, b that of border points and c of corner points.

5.5 Optimization by Simulated Annealing

Simulated annealing (cf. [1, 14]) is used as optimization method. This algorithm was originally designed for discrete problems but was later adapted to continuum problems. The method seems to be adequate because a pure gradient-descent delivered bad results, and analytic methods were very inefficient because of the high degree of freedom within the system. Another advantage is the simple algorithm (Figure 6).

```
temperature := initial_temperature;
G_min := 10^34;                                    { or some other good initial value :-) }
for i := 0 to no_of_temperatures-1 do begin
    temperature := temperature * r^i;                              { over-exponential }
    good_steps := 0;
    k := 0;
    repeat
        Choose randomly an edge e;
        Change randomly spring constant of e;
        Calculate G according to equation (12);
        if (G < G_min) then begin         { the system is now a better approximation }
            G_min := G;
            good_steps := good_steps + 1;
        end else begin
            Choose random number p ∈ [0, 1];
            if (p < e^((G_min - G)/temperature))             { take worse approximation }
                then G_min := G;
                else put back old spring constant of e;
        end
        k := k+1;
    until (k>nlimit) or (good_steps>glimit)
end
```

Figure 6: Simulated annealing algorithm.

A drawback of the method is the high sensitivity to the number of temperatures, the initial temperature, the reduction function and the number of good steps (glimit) allowed in each temperature. Although, we found generally applicable values for those parameters (e = number of edges):

Parameter	initial_temperature	r	nlimit	glimit
Value	[0.0001..0.001]	[0.97..0.99]	$e * 2$	e

The simulated annealing process converges if nearly no bad steps are done any more (due to temperature) and the improvement at each temperature is below some threshold. We used an over-exponential temperature reduction to get convergence.

Another possibility is to stop the algorithm after a specific number of temperatures (e.g. no_of_temperatures = 2*e) as done in Figure 6. In this case, the time complexity of the algorithm is $O(e^2)$.

6 Extension to 3-D

Because equations (2) and (11) are formulated independently to the dimension, the method can be extended to 3-D without general changes. Instead of optimizing the four situations of Figure 4, now we have to consider nine basic loads (Figure 7).

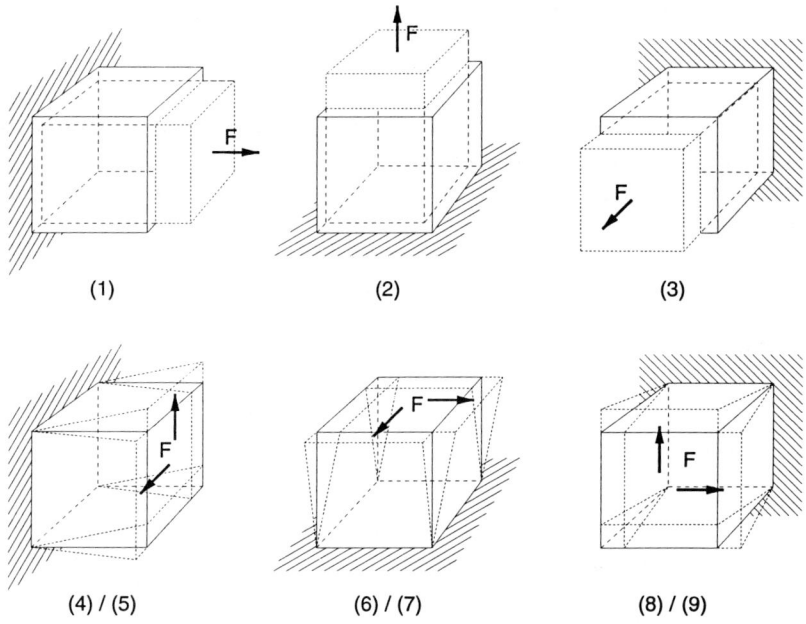

(1)   (2)   (3)

(4) / (5)   (6) / (7)   (8) / (9)

Figure 7: Basic loads in three dimensional space.

Reference values can be obtained similar to the 2-D method demonstrated in section 5.1. The annealing process works the same way as shown in Figure 6.

Some more effort is needed to calculate the Voronoi regions (now polyhedrons) within the mass point iteration. The number of edges obtained by the Delaunay triangulation is $O(n)$ if working in 2-D, but $O(n^{\frac{3}{2}})$ in three dimensional space (cf. [12]). This is of interest because the optimization has quadratic time complexity.

7 Results

In the upper part of Figure 8, initial displacements of a system with 25 nodes and connection structure 1 (see Figure 3(b)) are shown, in the lower part the system is optimized. The constants for horizontal, vertical and diagonal springs rsp. are set to the same value, which is convenient for homogeneous bodies and reduces optimization effort. The same system with all constants optimized separately is shown in Figure 9.

Rectangular cells are useful to simulate anisotropic behaviour. This can be seen in Figure 10, where different elasticities in x and y direction are modeled.

An inhomogeneous material is simulated in Figure 11, the results are yet in need of improvement, but demonstrate the capability of the optimization.

Figure 12 shows the influence of Voronoi iterations on homogeneity and optimization quality of a nodal approximation.

8   Conclusion and Future Work

Spring mass systems are often used for real time simulation of complex deformable objects. Our method allows the generation of systems with definite mechanic behaviour. We found a way to obtain an adequate mass distribution and simulated homogeneous materials as well as inhomogeneities and anisotropies. Systems up to some hundred points were optimized successfully. For large systems the optimization is computational expensive but this has to be done only once.

Besides the full implementation of the 3-D case, we are working on frequency analysis. This is a promising approach because natural frequencies give some more information about the dynamic behaviour of deformable systems. Natural frequencies ω_i can be obtained by solving the eigenvalue problem

$$(\mathbf{K} - \lambda \mathbf{M})\mathbf{u} = 0. \tag{13}$$

The frequencies are derived by $\lambda_i = \omega_i^2$. Once again we have the advantage that $\mathbf{M}$ is diagonal, what makes efficient calculation methods applicable.

Frequency analysis is to be inserted into our optimization process in order to obtain nodal systems with good equilibrium and natural frequency approximations.

In addition, natural frequencies can be used to find very efficient integration methods for specific systems and situations. No stepsize control is needed if the highest natural frequencies are integrated with respect to the sampling theorem. This can be used in virtual reality applications like surgery simulation or virtual sculpting, for which our optimization process as well is of high interest.

References

1. E.H.L. Aarts and P.J.M. van Laarhoven. *Statistical cooling: A general approach to combinatorial optimization problems*. Philips Journal of Research, (40):193–226, 1985.

2. K.-J. Bathe and E.L. Wilson. *Numerical methods in finite element analysis*. Prentice-Hall, 1976.

3. W. Boehm and H. Prautzsch. *Numerical methods*. AK Peters Wellesley, 1993.

4. D.E. Breen, D.H. House, and P.H. Getto. *A physicially-based particle model of woven cloth*. The Visual Computer, (8):264–277, 1992.

5. H. Delingette, G. Subsol, S. Cotin, and J. Pignon. *A craniofacial surgery simulation testbed*. Research report 2199, Institute National de Recherche en Informatique et Automatique, 1994.

6. O. Deussen and Chr. Kuhn. *Echtzeitsimulation deformierbarer Objekte über nodale Modelle*. in: Th. Strothotte and P. Lorenz, Hrsg., Proc. Integration von Bild, Modell und Text. ASIM Mitteilungen No. 46, University of Magdeburg, 1995.

7. J. Eisley. *Mechanics of elastic structures*. Prentice Hall, 1989.

8. Xiaochun Gao, Zhiying King, and Qixian Zhang. *A hybrid beam element for mathematical modelling of high-speed flexible linkages*. Mech. Mach. Theory, 24(1):29–36, 1989.

9. G.E. Kirsch. *Die Fundamentalgleichungen der Theorie der Elastizität fester Körper, hergeleitet aus der Betrachtung eines Systems von Punkten, welche durch elastische Streben verbunden sind*. VDI-Zeitschrift, 1868.

10. U.G. Kühnapfel, B. Neisius, H.G. Krumm, and M. Hübner. *CAD-Based simulation and modelling for endoscopic surgery*. Endoscopic Surgery, 1993.

11. G.S.P. Miller. *The motion dynamics of snakes and worms*. Computer Graphics, 22(4):169–173, 1988.

12. F.P. Preparata and M.I. Shamos. *Computational geometry.* Springer-Verlag New York, 175 Fifth Avenue, New York, New York 10010, USA, 3 Auflage, 1990.

13. D. Terzopoulos and K. Waters. *Analysis and synthesis of facial image sequences using physical and anatomical models*. IEEE Transactions on Pattern Analysis and Machine Intelligence, 1993.

14. P.J.M. van Laarhoven and E.H.L. Aarts. *Simulated annealing, theory and applications*. Reidel Publishing, Dordrecht, 1987.

15. K. Waters. *A physical model of facial tissue and muscle articulation derived from computer tomography data*. Visualization in Biomedical Computing, pp. 574–583. SPIE, 1992.

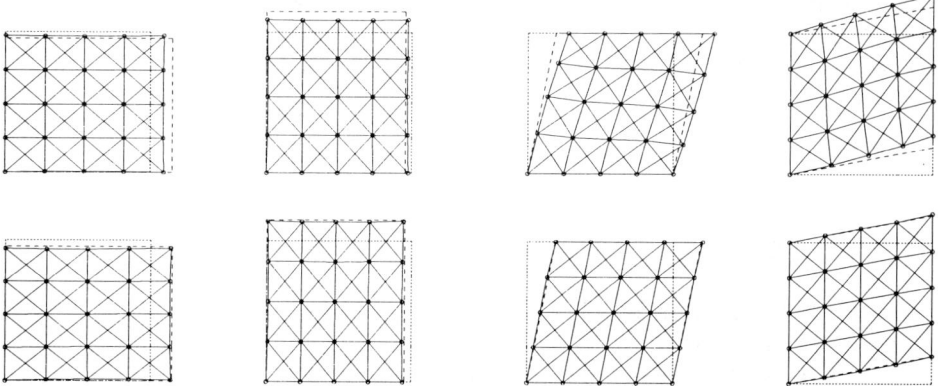

Figure 8: Initial (first line) and optimized displacements of a system with 25 nodes and connection structure 1. Stiffnesses for horizontal, vertical and diagonal springs are set to the same value ($G_{1:6:18} : 2.8 \rightarrow 0.55$)

42

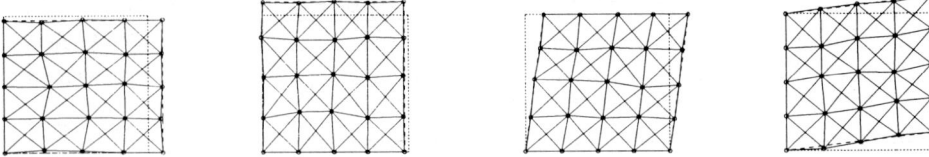

Figure 9: If all spring constants are optimized separate (which is to be done for inhomogeneous bodies) the system approximates the given deformations ($G_{1:3:15}$: 2.3 → 0.6) but has some irregularities within the grid.

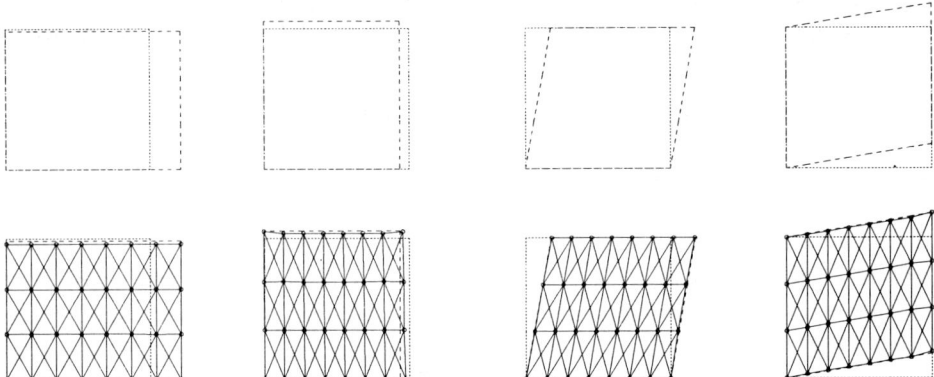

Figure 10: Modeling anisotropic behaviour with rectangular cells ($G_{1:3:15}$: 10.5 → 0.48). The system has different elasticities in x and y-direction, thus the deformations due to the test loads are different.

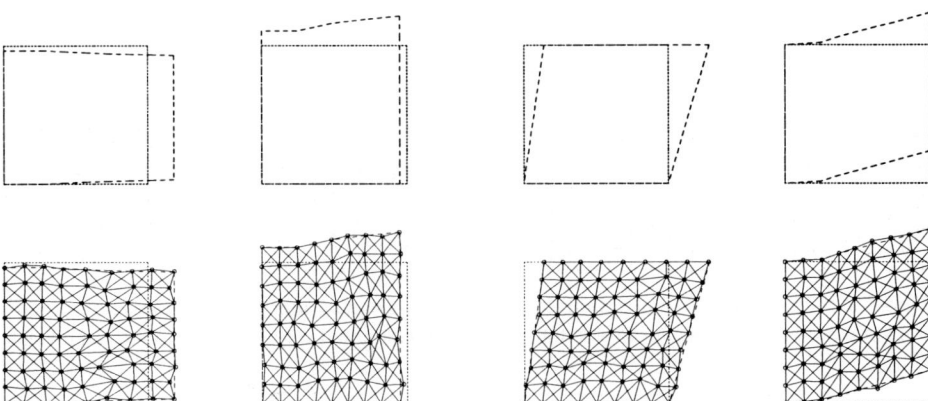

Figure 11: Simulation of an inhomogeneous material. The Young's modulus of the left third of the plate is twice as high as the right part. In the upper part of the figure the initial approximation of the spring/mass system was omitted. The lower part shows the optimized system.

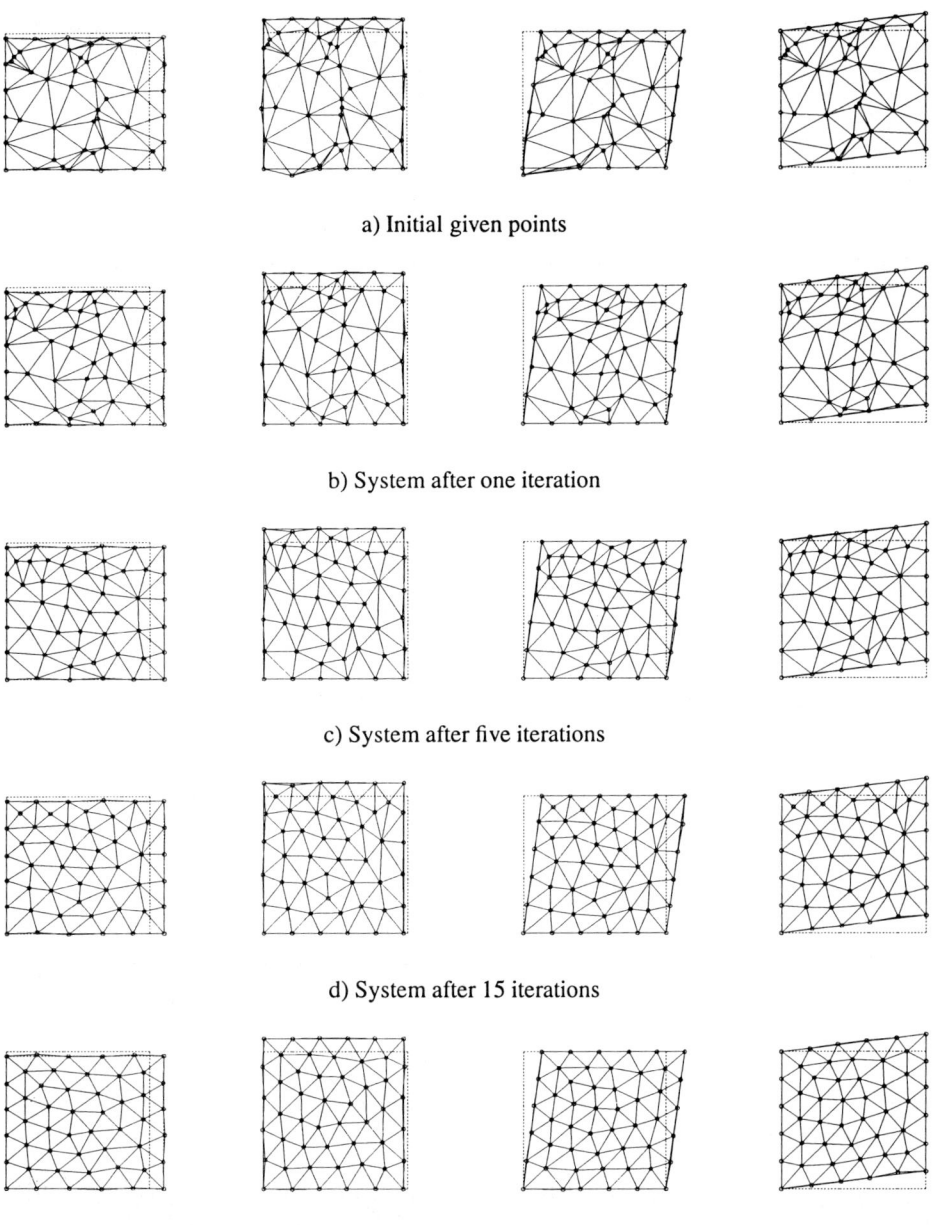

a) Initial given points

b) System after one iteration

c) System after five iterations

d) System after 15 iterations

e) System after 50 iterations

Voronoi iterations	0	1	5	15	50
$G_{1:3:15}$ before optimization	8.6	7.8	7.6	6.0	6.1
$G_{1:3:15}$ after optimization	0.45	0.47	0.44	0.42	0.37

Figure 12: Optimized displacements with different number of preceding Voronoi-iterations. The The starting quality raises more than the quality after the optimization with 100 temperatures.

Evolutionary identification of cloth animation models

Jean LOUCHET†‡, Xavier PROVOT‡, David CROCHEMORE†

† ENSTA	‡ INRIA
Laboratoire d'Electronique et	projet SYNTIM
d'Informatique	Rocquencourt
32 boulevard Victor	B.P. 105
75739 PARIS cedex 15	78153 LE CHESNAY cedex
France	France
+33-1-45 52 60 75	+33-1-39 63 54 38

e-mail: louchet@bora.inria.fr   provot@bora.inria.fr

Abstract

This paper presents an application of evolutionary genetic techniques to the identification of internal parameters of a mass-spring physically-based animation model.

A physical model of fabrics is first presented. It uses a mass-spring mesh and an inverse dynamics procedure in order to model the non-linear elasticity of fabrics.

A method to identify the internal parameters of the model from geometric data is then presented. It is based on a cost function which measures the difference in behaviour between the reference and the model, and an evolutionary minimisation algorithm.

Keywords

Physically-based modelling, animation, simulation, evolutionary algorithms.

1 Introduction

Cooperation between the processes of vision and image synthesis has been widely studied from the viewpoints of 3-D geometry and photometry, proving the mutual benefit of such an approach to both domains and leading to viewing vision as the process of *building synthesizable models*.

Here, while still adopting this philosophy of implementing image analysis techniques to fulfil the modelling needs of computer graphics, we shall focus on the problems of modelling motion and deformation of fabrics in image synthesis.

In order to be able to reproduce the behaviour of a cloth object, e.g. a flag in the wind, it is necessary to build the animation model itself, before using it to create images. To be visually realistic, these models should be identified from real world images. Thus, we may see modelling in computer graphics, as the process of *creating identifiable models*.

In the first part of this paper, we shall describe a system we devised to build visually realistic animations of fabrics, using a mass-spring physically based model.

In the second part, we present a method to identify such a model from given geometric data. Present results show the algorithm's ability to recover parameters from synthetic cloth animations.

2 A Mass-Spring cloth model

We are using the model described in [P95] which has proved to be more realistic than classical elastically deformable models used by Terzopoulos in [TPBF87] and by Thalmann in [CYMT92]. The linear elasticity of the elastic models used by the latter, leads indeed to unrealistic deformations of cloth objects which are successfully controlled in [P95] with a minimal increase in the computation cost.

Breen's particle systems [BHW94] have not been used to model the dynamic behaviour of cloth objects, and the computation time needed for such a system is much greater than that of the model we use. A reasonable computation time is required in order to use evolutionary algorithms.

2.1 The mesh

Our elastic model is a mesh of $m \times n$ virtual masses, each mass being linked to its neighbours by massless springs of non-zero "natural length" (i.e. length at rest). The links between neighbours are:

- springs between masses [i, j] and [i+1, j], or between masses [i, j] and [i, j+1], referred to as "structural springs" (types 0 and 1);
- diagonal springs between masses [i, j] and [i+1, j+1], or masses [i+1, j] and [i, j+1], referred to as "shear springs" (types 2 and 3);
- double-length springs between masses [i, j] and [i+2, j], or masses [i, j] and [i, j+2], referred to as "flexion springs" (types 4 and 5).

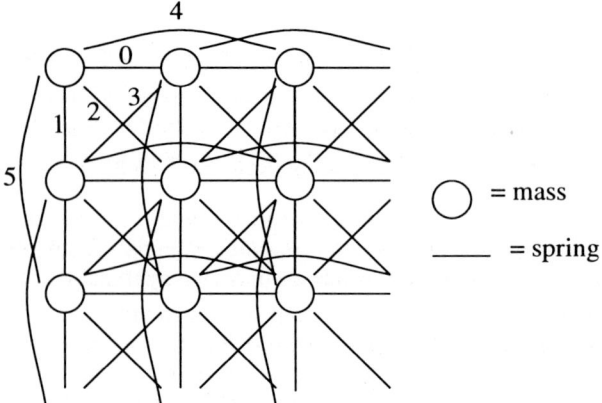

Fig. 1. The periodic mesh of masses and springs used in our model.

Shear springs are introduced in order to give the fabric a shear rigidity and prevent it from excessive and unrealistic distortion in its own plane.

"Flexion" double-length springs are under stress when flexion occurs in the cloth and therefore have a three-dimensional role. They may even be used to introduce preconstraints into the fabric and provide it with an extra degree of angular stiffness. For example, planar rigidity will be obtained by introducing type 5 springs with a natural length greater than twice the natural length of type 1 springs.

2.2 A Dynamical Model

The system considered is a mesh of $m \times n$ masses, each mass being located at time t on the point $P_{i,j}(t)$, where $i = 1... m$ and $j = 1... n$.

The evolution of the system is governed by the fundamental law of dynamics:

$$\vec{F}_{i,j} = \mu \vec{\gamma}_{i,j}$$

where:

μ is the mass of each point,

$\vec{\gamma}_{i,j}$ its acceleration,

$\vec{F}_{i,j}$ the force applied to point $P_{i,j}$,

$\vec{F}_{i,j}$ can be divided into internal and external forces.

The internal force results from the tensions of the springs linking $P_{i,j}$ to its neighbours:

$$\vec{F}_{int}(P_{i,j}) = - \sum_{(k,\, l \in R)} K_{i,j,k,l} \left[\vec{L}_{i,j,k,l} - l^0_{i,j,k,l} \frac{\vec{L}_{i,j,k,l}}{\|\vec{L}_{i,j,k,l}\|} \right]$$

where:

- R is the set of all ordered pairs (k, l) such that $P_{k,l}$ is linked to $P_{i,j}$
- $\vec{L}_{i,j,k,l} = \overrightarrow{P_{i,j}P_{k,l}}$
- $l^0_{i,j,k,l}$ is the natural length of the spring between $P_{i,j}$ and $P_{k,l}$
- $K_{i,j,k,l}$ is the stiffness of the spring between $P_{i,j}$ and $P_{k,l}$

The external forces depend on the types of loads we wish the model to be exposed to. Typical loads will be gravity, a viscous damping and a viscous interaction with an air stream (or wind).

Let $\vec{g}$ be the gravity; the weight of $P_{i,j}$ is given by:

$$\vec{F}_{grav;i,j} = \mu \vec{\gamma}_{i,j}$$

Viscous damping is modelled by:

$$\vec{F}_{visc;i,j} = -C_{visc}\vec{v}_{i,j}$$

where C_{visc} is a damping coefficient, and $\vec{v}_{i,j}$ the velocity of $P_{i,j}$.

The role of damping is to model a first approximation of the mechanical energy dissipation.

Finally, a viscous fluid moving at a uniform velocity $\vec{u}_{fluid}$ applies onto the surface of a body moving at a velocity $\vec{v}$, a local force

$$\vec{F}_{visc} = C_{visc}\left[\vec{n}.\left(\vec{u}_{fluid} - \vec{v}\right)\right]\vec{n}$$

where $\vec{n}$ is the normal vector to the surface. In the discrete case,

$$\vec{F}_{visc}(P_{i,j}) = C_{visc}\left[\vec{n}_{i,j}.\left(\vec{u}_{fluid} - \vec{v}_{i,j}\right)\right]\vec{n}_{i,j}$$

where $\vec{n}_{i,j}$ is the unit normal on the surface at the point $P_{i,j}$.

2.3 Time Integration

The elements described above allow us to compute the resulting force $\vec{F}_{i,j}(t)$ applied to the point $P_{i,j}$ at time t. The fundamental equation of dynamics can therefore be explicitly integrated through time by a simple Euler method:

$$\begin{cases} \vec{\gamma}_{i,j}(t + \Delta t) = \frac{1}{\mu}\vec{F}_{i,j}(t) \\ \\ \vec{v}_{i,j}(t + \Delta t) = \vec{v}_{i,j}(t) + \Delta t\,\vec{\gamma}_{i,j}(t + \Delta t) \\ \\ \vec{P}_{i,j}(t + \Delta t) = \vec{P}_{i,j}(t) + \Delta t\,\vec{v}_{i,j}(t + \Delta t) \end{cases}$$

where Δt is a chosen time-step.

2.4 Inverse dynamics constraints and deformation rates

In a classical mass-spring model, large deformations often occur locally in the mesh. This behaviour, caused by the fact that all the springs are linear springs, does not fit with the behaviour of real clothes. In order to prevent these unrealistic deformations, we devised an ad-hoc inverse dynamics procedure to the most deformed (or "super-elongated") springs in order to reduce their elongation.

At each given time step, the numerical integration is achieved using equation (2). Then the deformation rates of all springs are computed.

If the deformation rate of a spring is greater than a critical given deformation rate τ_c (e.g. 0.1), then an inverse dynamics procedure is applied to the two ends of the spring so that its deformation rate exactly equals τ_c . This means that we want the length of the springs not to exceed their natural length by more than 10%. For more details, this procedure is described in [P95].

Thus, in a single computation, all the springs with a deformation rate exceeding τ_c after the numerical integration are adjusted to a more "reasonable" and realistic deformation rate.

3 Identifying a physical model of cloth from its motion

3.1 Introduction

The fabric model above uses (in the case of homogeneous fabrics) equal masses, and 6 different spring types. Each spring being described by three parameters, the cloth is described by a total of 18 parameters.

In a first approach to the identification problem, in order to reduce the algorithmic cost of analysis, we have partly simplified this general model, making the assumption that the fabric is isotropic and all the springs share a common stiffness value.

The simplified model contains 5 parameters (instead of 18):

- the springs' stiffness,
- the elongation rate,
- natural lengths of springs 0 and 1,
- natural lengths of springs 2 and 3,
- natural lengths of springs 4 and 5.

3.2 The cost function

The basic idea is to define and optimise a cost function which measures, for any set of model parameters, the difference between the behaviour predicted using these parameters, and the actual behaviour of the cloth.

Such a general cost function could be:

$$f(parameters) = \sum_{time} \sum_{i,j} \left[(x_p - x_r)^2 + (y_p - y_r)^2 + (z_p - z_r)^2 + \Delta t^2 \left((vx_p - vx_r)^2 + (vy_p - vy_r)^2 + (vz_p - vz_r)^2 \right) \right]$$

where

$x_r, y_r, z_r, vx_r, vy_r, vz_r$ are the actual (recorded) positions and velocities of particles;

$x_p, y_p, z_p, vx_p, vy_p, vz_p$ are the positions and velocities of particles as predicted by the model.

Δt is an arbitrary coefficient. In practice, Δt will be of the same order of magnitude as the time step chosen in the animation.

In order to prevent a quick divergence between actual and predicted coordinates, which would result in the cost function being extremely sensitive to the parameters values and therefore difficult to optimise, positions and velocities will be predicted by the model using actual positions and velocities at the preceding time step, rather than values predicted over several time steps.

The major problem with this cost function is its computational cost (about 1 minute on a Sparc10), remembering this cost function will have to be calculated several thousand times in the identification process. Therefore we have defined a new "small" cost function, which only involves the last time step in the sequence, rather than all the time steps. Experience shows it is sufficient in practice to give good estimates of parameters (see section 3.4).

3.3 An evolutionary strategy

Evolutionary Strategies play an increasing role in the optimisation of functions of several variables, especially in cases where a mathematical characterization of the function to be optimised is not easily obtainable ([G89], [K92]). Their main characteristics are generally a good noise resistance and their ability to escape multiple local minima. However, on convex domains, more classical methods are preferable on both points of view of precision and computational load. Experience shows [L94] that in similar cases of identification of complex physical animation models, it is advisable to use first an evolutionary strategy and then, if necessary, refine the results using a convex optimisation algorithm.

Here, the optimisation process will involve a *population*, the *individuals* of which are tentative sets of model parameters. An individual is a n-uple of real numbers.

The population will be randomly *initialised*, then evolve using three random basic processes controlled by the cost function values: a *selection* process, a *mutation* process and a *crossover* process.

The aim of the algorithm is to make the population converge to a final population in which the most performing individuals will be as close as possible to the optimal solution of the problem.

Selection

At each generation, individuals are sorted according to their cost function values. The selection process is guided by *ranking* rather than by the cost function value in itself. We chose to keep the 50% most performing individuals unchanged, the remaining 50% are deleted and replaced by new individuals created by the mutation (20%) and crossover (30%) processes.

Mutations

At each generation, 20% new individuals are created through mutations of randomly chosen parameters among those from the 80% most performing individuals at the preceding generation.

Crossover

At each generation, 30% new individuals are created through uniform crossover. For each new individual to be created, we choose a number of parents equal to the number of model parameters, among the 50% most performing individuals in the preceding generation.

Initialising

The population is initialised with random values for all the parameters. However, in order to increase the algorithm's efficiency, natural spring length values are chosen around the average length values observed on the reference data.

3.4 Experimental results

We tested the algorithm in the case of a simulated cloth hanging from two corners, with different parameter values. Our reference trajectory is computed using a simulation with fixed parameters. We are testing if our evolutionary algorithm can converge toward the fixed parameters of the reference.

Fig. 2. A hanging cloth obtained with our model

In order to check the suitability of the cost functions, we calculated their theoretical values using the simplified 5-parameter model in a neighbourhood of the reference values.

The following diagrams (Figures 3 and 4) show variations of theoretical cost functions, in function of spring stiffness K and maximum elongation rate

τ_c, for two parameter sets; spring natural lengths are fixed to their reference values.

The accuracy of the new (small) cost function appears to be good in the absence of noise, in spite of the fact it is based on only one frame from the synthetic animation. In fact, this is compensated by the large number of occurrences of identical springs in different elongation states. This should be true with any position of the cloth, except its initial state where all spring lengths equal their natural length and therefore give no information about spring parameter values.

The small cost function is generally very sensitive to the maximum elongation rate. This sensitivity may be explained by the fact the last image in the animation corresponds to a state where most springs are far from their rest position and where many of them are close to their maximum elongation rate.

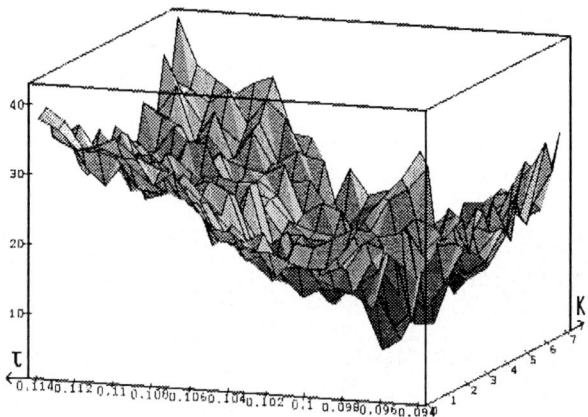

Fig. 3. Cost function for a reference trajectory computed with the fixed parameters $K = 4$ and $\tau_c = 0.1$.

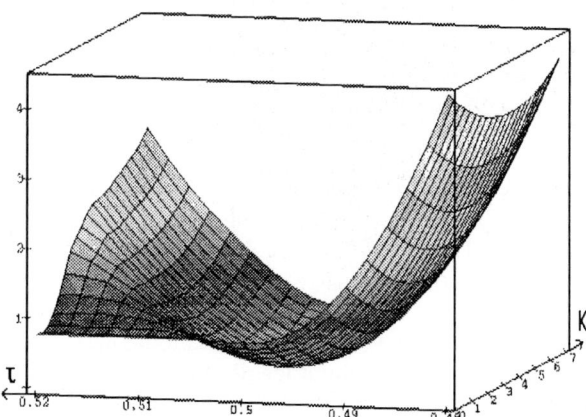

Fig. 4. Cost function for a reference trajectory computed with the fixed parameters $K = 4$ and $\tau_c = 0.5$.

In most cases, convergence is obtained after about 50 to 100 generations and gives results in good accordance with the reference. In some cases, the theoretical cost function suffers from apparent numerical stability problems, as it can be seen above in Figure 3, but this only results in a less accurate identification.

The listing below shows the values of parameters of the 10 best individuals in a 100 individual population, after 49 generations, in typical good and bad situations generated by the evolutionary algorithm, with a 17×17 mesh. The first line shows the reference values which were not known by the algorithm.

```
              /   101   /   123   /   145   /   K      /  tau    /  cost   /
reference       0.093750 0.132583 0.187500 4.000000 0.500000 0.000000

candidate 95:0.093985 0.133019 0.187111 3.938169 0.497108 0.024182
candidate 12:0.093985 0.133019 0.187111 3.938169 0.497108 0.024160
candidate 65:0.093984 0.133019 0.187083 3.938169 0.497108 0.024137
candidate 31:0.093984 0.133019 0.187111 3.938169 0.497108 0.024133
candidate 82:0.093984 0.133019 0.187109 3.938169 0.497108 0.024130
candidate  4:0.093984 0.133019 0.187106 3.938169 0.497108 0.024129
candidate 26:0.093887 0.133019 0.187111 3.906064 0.497108 0.022811
candidate 57:0.093960 0.133019 0.187107 3.926550 0.497108 0.022180
candidate 39:0.093954 0.133019 0.187108 3.927238 0.497108 0.021845
candidate 88:0.093984 0.132705 0.187083 4.084211 0.497108 0.014619
```

In the other (bad) case:

```
              /   101   /   123   /   145   /   K      /  tau    /  cost   /
reference       0.093750 0.132583 0.187500 4.000000 0.500000 0.000000

candidate 70:0.086170 0.132648 0.200459 0.363856 0.630850 0.650783
candidate 47:0.086170 0.132094 0.201230 0.370355 0.630850 0.650390
candidate 43:0.086170 0.132654 0.199978 0.369424 0.630850 0.649559
candidate 95:0.086170 0.132671 0.200991 0.386130 0.630850 0.648277
candidate 74:0.086170 0.132671 0.197468 0.386130 0.630850 0.646357
candidate 73:0.086170 0.132667 0.199857 0.394229 0.630850 0.645847
candidate  7:0.086170 0.132667 0.198607 0.394229 0.630850 0.645059
candidate  1:0.086170 0.132670 0.199827 0.400431 0.630850 0.644962
candidate 40:0.086170 0.132668 0.199821 0.406031 0.630850 0.644202
candidate 51:0.086170 0.132671 0.200991 0.435233 0.630850 0.642728
```

In the first case, the cost of 0.014 corresponds to an average error per frame of about one twentieth of the springs' natural length and gives very small visual differences with the original sequence (Figure 5, middle column).

In the second case, the cost function has been trapped into a local minimum and the number of generations was not sufficient to get a correct identification; the cost of 0.64 corresponds to a quadratic average error per frame on particles' positions slightly less than half the structural springs' natural length. In such a case, the model identified gives an important difference with the original animation as it can be seen in Figure 5, right column. This means that the criterion used to stop the evolutionary algorithm should be based on the cost function values rather than the number of generations.

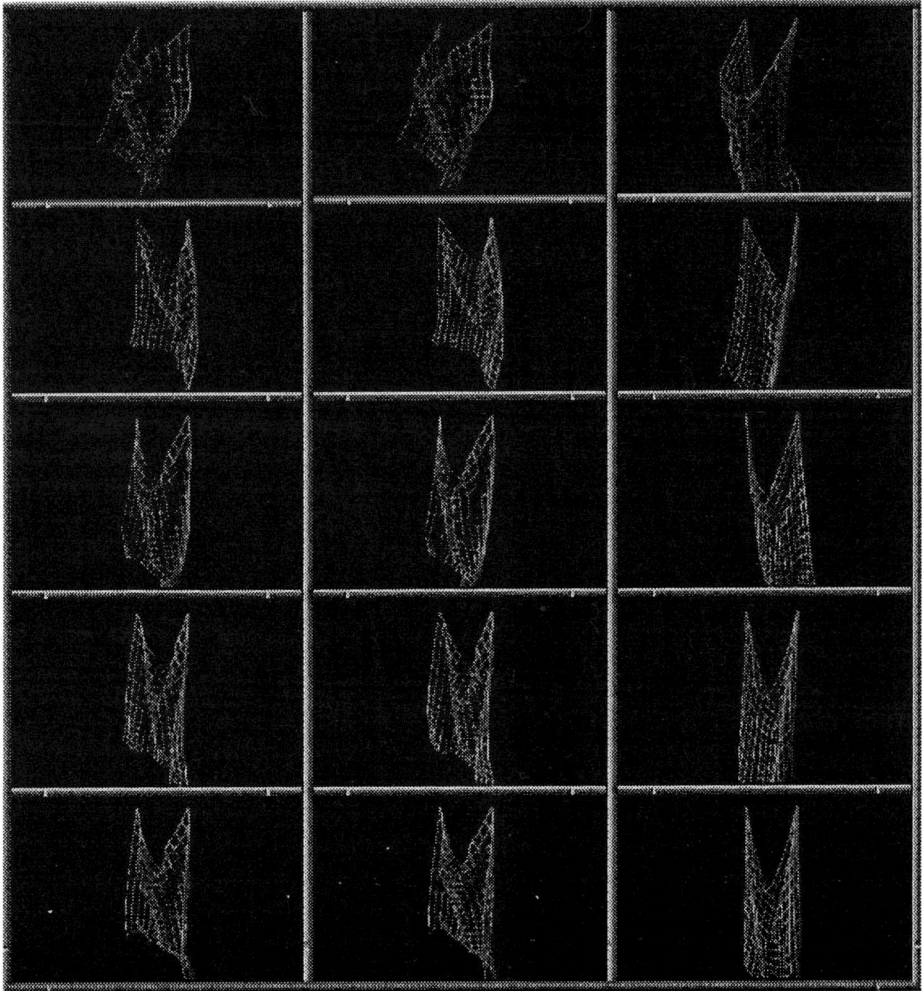

Fig. 5. The original animation (left column), and two reconstructions of the animation using different identification results (centre column: cost = 0.014; right column: cost = 0.642).

4 Conclusion

These first encouraging results demonstrate the use of computer-generated 3D geometric data to identify physical parameters. To apply this method to real images, it will be necessary, first to implement low-level vision algorithms to locate reference points on the cloth, then to adapt the cost function in order to identify parameters from 2-dimensional data (projections of 3D positions) extracted from real cloth images.

The given example shows the transferability of the model identification general method described in [L94], to a simplified cloth model using a reduced set of parameters. The main differences lie in the introduction of a non-linearity factor to prevent hyperelastic behaviours, and the existence of multiple occurrences of identical springs. The main consequence of which is the introduction of "short" cost functions based on single frames, made necessary by the otherwise excessive calculation cost. The number of parameters used in the model is not a critical issue in the identification process; in the general case, [L94] showed that the number of generations needed to converge is theoretically independent of the number of parameters, and that the calculation cost is about proportional to the number of parameters involved. Present research aims at verifying this in the application to cloth identification, using more complex models.

References

[AG85] W.W. Armstrong, M.W. Green, "The Dynamics of Articulated Rigid Bodies for Purposes of Animation", Proc. of Graphics Interface, 1985.

[BHW94] D. Breen, D. House, M. Wozny, "Predicting the drape of woven cloth using interacting particles", Proc. Siggraph 94, Computer Graphics, 1994, pp. 365-372.

[CYMT92] M. Carignan, Yang Ying, N. Magnenat-Thalmann, D. Thalmann, "Dressing Animated Synthetic Actors with Complex Deformable Clothes", Proc. Siggraph 92, Computer Graphics, 1992, Vol. 26, No. 2, pp. 99--104.

[G89] D. A. Goldberg, "Genetic Algorithms in Search, Optimization and Machine Learning", Addison-Wesley 1989.

[K92] J. Koza, "Genetic Programming", MIT Press, 1992.

[L94] J. Louchet, "An Evolutionary Algorithm for Physical Motion Analysis", British Machine Vision Conference, York, Sep. 1994.

[NM93] J. Thomas Ngo, Joe Marks, "Spacetime constraints revisited", proc. Siggraph 93, Computer Graphics, pp. 343-350.

[P95] X. Provot, "Deformation Constraints in a Mass-Spring Model to describe Rigid Cloth behavior", Graphics Interface 1995, Québec, April 1995.

[TPBF87] D. Terzopoulos, J. Platt, A. Barr, K. Fleischer, "Elastically Deformable Models", Proc. Siggraph 87, Computer Graphics, 1987, Vol. 21, No. 4, pp. 205-214.

Collision and Self-Collision Detection :
Efficient and Robust Solutions
for Highly Deformable Surfaces

Pascal VOLINO and **Nadia Magnenat THALMANN**
MIRALab, C.U.I., University of Geneva
CH-1211, Switzerland
(E-mail : `thalmann@uni2a.unige.ch` ; `pascal@cui.unige.ch`)

Abstract

We present an efficient algorithm for detecting self collisions, as well as some techniques for evaluating collision inside-outside orientation in a robust way. As presented in [VOL 94], we detect collisions using a hierarchical algorithm that takes advantage of curvature properties giving us full power of hierarchical algorithms for self-collision situations. Determining the collision orientation may become a complex problem dealing with complex collisions reulting from highly deformable surfaces. We use collision remnance and consistency correction for computing collision orientation in a robust way, for accurate collision response in simulations involving highly deformed and wrinkled surfaces.

Keywords :   Collision detection, self-collision, geometrical regularity, automatic hierarchisation, adjacency detection, surface orientation, consistency.

1. Introduction

Mechanical simulation of soft surfaces usually require collision detection to be performed, for avoiding the simulated objects to penetrate themselves or each other. For instance, cloth simulation require avoiding cloth-to-body penetration, but also cloth-to-cloth collisions, for instance between wrinkles.

Collision detection is often very time consuming. Dealing with discretized surfaces, it consists in computing which couples of polygons are interpenetrating. The simulation algorithm then calculates the appropriate interaction response that will correct the surface deformation accordingly.

Several algorithms have been proposed for handling efficiently collision detection, some suited to parametrical surfaces ([BAR 90], [VHE 90], [DUF 92],

[SNY 93]), others based on rasterization ([SHI 91]), shortest distance tracking ([LIN 93], [MOO 88]), voxelistation or octree ([LAF 91], [YAN 93]), hierarchisation ([WEB 92]).

As we intend to cope with highy deformed surfaces, like those obtained for surface wrinkling, we need an algorithm that keeps being very efficient for self-collision detection. Using some geometrical considerations based on curvature, we have successfully extended a hierarchical algorithm to get very fast self collision evaluation on discretized surface animations. [VOL 94] includes a detailed presentation of the algorithms and the resulting efficiency.

For getting appropriate collision response, penetration orientation has to be computed for the detected collisions. Quite trivial when handling surfaces that have a well-defined inside-outside orientation (bodies, closed surfaces, ...), this problem becomes ambiguous for general situations considering surfaces that do not contain any orientation information (wrinkling fabric, ...). Techniques have been developed for computing orientation in a robust way using remanance and consistency, in order to get a very robust simulation system that can handle complex situations involving wrinkling.

2. Efficient self-collision detection

Usual collision detection algorithms are rather inefficient for handling self-collisions because of adjacency : Two adjacent subareas are virtually "colliding" by contact along their common borders, and the algorithms will spend time focusing on them. For instance, dealing with polygonisations, they will consider each edge separating polygons as potential collision areas between these polygons.

We intend to speed up self-collision detection by taking advantage of adjacency, using some geometrical properties in order to skip collision detection within some areas or between adjacent areas.

2.1. Self-collisions and curvature

It is quite evident that a very smooth and regular surface will not show many self-intersections, at least at short ranges. In fact, the only causes of self-intersection are the following:

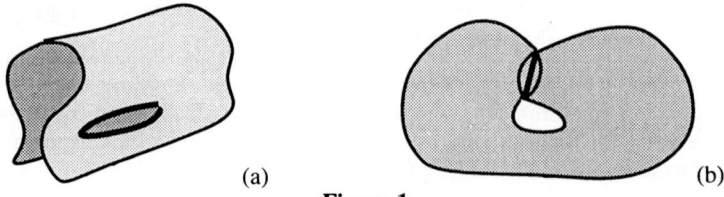

(a)   (b)

Figure 1
Self-collision occurring because of curvature (a) or contour shape (b)

(a) - The surface is curved enough for making a "loop" and hitting another part of the surface.

(b) - The contour of the surface has such a shape that a minimal fold will bring superposition and collision of the surface.

A more formal formulation of this geometrical property would be :

* Let S be a continuous surface in the Euclidean space delimited by one contour C.

if :

- There exists a vector V for which N.V > 0 at (almost) every point of S (N being the normal vector of the surface at the considered point)

and :

- The projection of C on a plane orthogonal to V along the direction of V has no self-intersections

then :

- There are no self-collisions on the surface S.

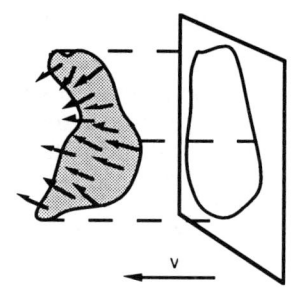

Figure 2
Geometrical conditions
for no self-collision

We take advantage of this property in two different ways, as described below:

2.1.1. Self-collision into a surface area

(I) - If can be found an area for which (a) there exists a vector that has positive dot product with the normals of every triangle of the area and if (b) the 2D projection of its contour along this direction does not intersect itself, then we need not look for self-intersections within that area.

This has great impact : We can check for normals in O(n) time (see 2.2.2), and test a 2D contour for collisions (that should contain at most O(sqrt n) elementary segments) also in an efficient way (see 2.2.3). That means that we can discard big areas from self-collision detection in O(n) time. Furthermore, normal calculation is a task that has often to be performed for many other reasons, like rendering or mechanical calculation, and the collision-specific calculation time is therefore reduced by this amount.

2.1.2. Collision between two surface areas

(II) - if can be found two areas that are adjacent (connected by at least one vertex), then if (a) there exists a vector that has positive dot product with the normals of every triangles of both areas and if (b) the 2D projection of their contours along this direction do not intersect each other, then we need not look for intersections between these two areas.

By this, we can also efficiently discard intersection tests between two adjacent subparts of our surface. Adjacency test may be performed in O(log n) time (see 2.2.1).

2.2. *Efficient implementation using a hierarchical algorithm*

Hierarchical algorithms are well known solutions for reducing worst-time computations to O(n log n) when dealing with a huge set of objects, such as all the polygons of a discretized surface. Still, even considering O(n) average time can be heavy computation, for example if a self-collision algorithm focuses on each edge of a polygonisation, even when the surface contain only sparse collisions.

We extend the traditional hierarchical collision detection algorithm in order to take advantage of the geometrical properties mentioned above, in order to get full efficiency of the algorithm even for self-collision detection, that is a computation time in average proportional to the number of colliding polygons.

Thus, we use respectively the (I) and (II) properties for skipping self-collisions within one area of the hierarchy, or between two areas if they are adjacent.

Three practical problems still remain :

2.2.1. *Adjacency storage and evaluation in a hierarchical surface*

Brute force storage of every adjacent subsurfaces around every subsurface in the hierarchy wouldn't lead to efficient storage space, nor to acceptable adjacency evaluation time.

Instead, we only store the vertices separating adjacent subsurfaces *of highest level* in the hierarchy around each subsurfaces. This computation may be performed in O(log n) time. The number of such vertices is in average constant whatever the hierarchy level of the subsurface (around 6).

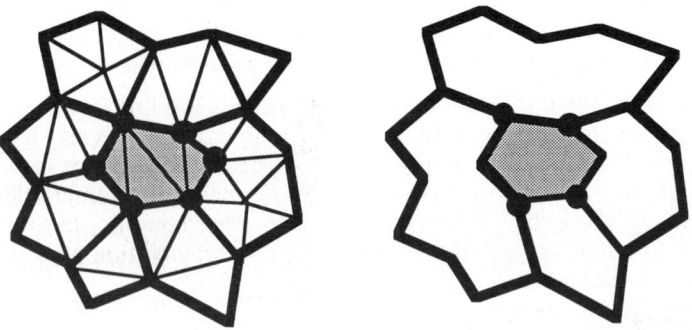

Figure 3
Storing adjacencies: vertices to be stored around a subsurface

We can then prove that two given subsurfaces are adjacent (i.e. have at least one common vertex) if and only if there is at least a common vertex in their stored vertices. The number of them being in average constant, the evaluation time is in average constant.

59

2.2.2. Curvature criteria evaluation in a surface polygonalisation

We find a common direction yielding positive dot product with the normals of every polygon of a discretized surface using direction sampling : For instance, we can use a set of 14 unit vectors oriented to the vertices and face middles of a cube. For each polygon we evaluate which vectors give positive dot product with the normal, and we propagate this information up in the hierarchy tree. We then can evaluate quickly if the common direction can be found by looking at the remaining sample vectors in the hierarchy.

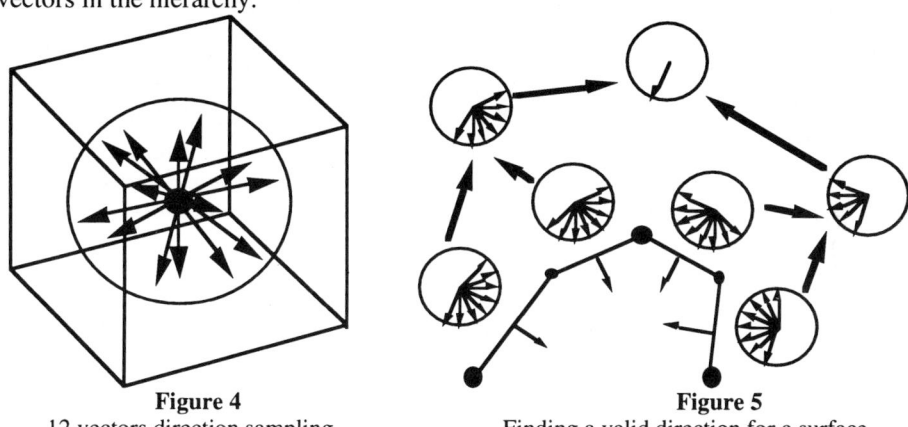

Figure 4
12 vectors direction sampling

Figure 5
Finding a valid direction for a surface

2.2.3. Evaluating collisions in the contour projection.

This can be performed rather efficiently by taking advantage of the already existing bounding box hierarchy. However, practical tests have shown that this criteria as almost never decisive, and can be skipped for all non-pathological collision situations involving acceptable surface shapes and hierarchisation.

Figure 6
Collision and self collision detection

3. Robustness and orientation consistency

Once collisions are detected, correct response has to be computed in order to provide the collision feedback. For instance, collision between surfaces animated using physically based algorithms have to yield mechanical contact interaction.

Dealing with mechanical surfaces, an important difficulty bay be to compute the correct collision orientation: As a given element may be detected to be geometrically close to a surface, shall we consider this element at the correct side of the surface (where it has always been and should remain), or at the other side (oops, it has crossed the surface, lets put it back)? Except for some closed surfaces like body skin, balls, that have an already predefined inside-outside orientation and for which the "normal" position of other objects is outside, collision situations can become very ambiguous when two deformed surfaces interpenetrate: At which side of each surface should the other surface be considered, and thus, how to compute the collision interaction orientation correctly?

In order to get a robust system for which collisions are always computed in a consistent way, several techniques have been implemented.

3.1. Collision remnance

This first technique is quite easy to implement : Once detected, a collision is stored in a structure and tracked during the animation according to the positions of the concerned objects. In-out orientation is updated according to the moves of the objects, such as when the conserned elements cross.

Any detected collision remains in the structure for a given time even if it is not actually occurring, providing extra robustness when two object parts in contact are scattered by any kind of simulation artifact.

3.2. Orientation consistency tracking

Remanance is a quite simple technique for maintaining the consistency of an initially correct situation. However, the system should also be able to recover from an initially inconsistent situation, or a situation that has become inconsistent after some severe simulation trouble.

The basic idea of this technique is to keep track of all the collision areas of the scene. Thus, we group every detected collisions that are part of the same "contact region", and we compute the "most probable" orientation for this collision region by considering statistically the individual collision orientations. Then, the common collision orientation is given for every collision.

The most important difficulty is to track efficiently the collision regions. We use an incremental process, based on the labeling of the collisions handled by the remanance mentioned above, using neighborhood walking along the colliding surfaces.

If any ambiguous and inconsistent collision situation happens, the colliding surfaces will then "choose" the most probable collision orientation, and each individual collision within the considered area will then behave in a consistent way.

Combined with remanance this orientation consistency correction gives us a very robust system, able to recover most of the inconsistencies concerning colliding non oriented surfaces.

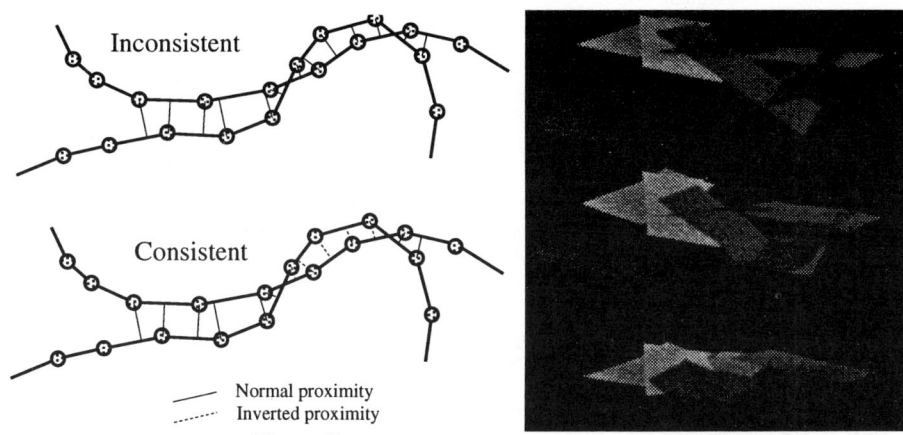

--- Normal proximity
------- Inverted proximity

Figure 7
Consistent and inconsistent collision orientations.

Figure 8
Consistency correction
n a set of intersecting falling surfaces.

3.2.1 - Implementing collision consistency correction

Collisions are of two kinds:

* **Proximities**: Elements from two different surface regions that are separated by a distance smaller than a given detection distance. They can be vertex-polygon, edge-edge, and more marginally vertex-edge and vertex-vertex proximities.

* **Interferences**: Elements from two different surface regions (an edge and a polygon) that are interpenetrating each other. They reveal that the surface regions are crossing each other.

Each element of the surface mesh data structure contains a list of the collisions in which it is involved (including remnant collisions).

A proximity is represented by a couple of elements, one from each colliding surface region, and a distance, which represents the distance of the two concerned elements. Positive distance means that the elements are at the right side of each other, and negative means they should cross for being at the right side.

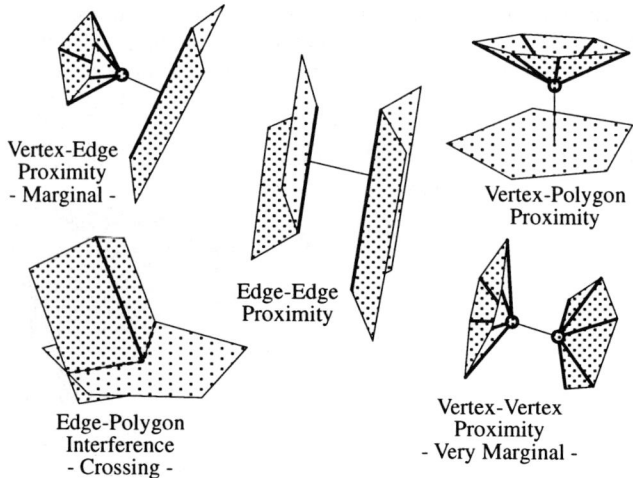

Figure 9
Different kinds of collisions.

In case surface orientation information is lacking, collision detection returns only positive distance collisions, assuming the surfaces are at the correct side of each other. However, if interferences are detected as well (i.e. edges crossing polygons), we then know that the situation is inconsistent and some collision orientations have to be reversed.

The first task is to group the detected collisions into sets characterizing collision regions. A collision region between two surfaces is the area where the two surfaces are "in contact", according to the collision detection distance. The second step is to reorient all the collisions of a given region so that they all behave in the same way, according to some statistical considerations.

The labeling process is performed by the following algorithm:

```
LabelCollision(coll,group) (
      if coll is not yet labelled (
            label coll to group
            for every col in the neighborhood of coll (
                  LabelCollision(col,group)
            )
      )
)

LabelAllCollisions() (
      while exists coll not yet labelled (
            create a new group
            LabelCollision(coll,group)
      )
)
```

Two collisions are considered as neighbors if their elements are neighbors. We find all the neighbor collisions of a given collision by scanning all the collisions concerning the neighboring elements of both collision elements.

Then, for each group, we compare the surface orientation and collision the orientation of each collision in it. By numbering how many collision push in which direction of the surfaces, we consider the majority direction, and we force every collision of the group to that direction. While not being the most reliable criteria (considering collisions in the border of the group is certainly better), the majority criteria has shown to give good results for the mechanical simulations that have been tested, as in those cases only a small amount of crossings occur.

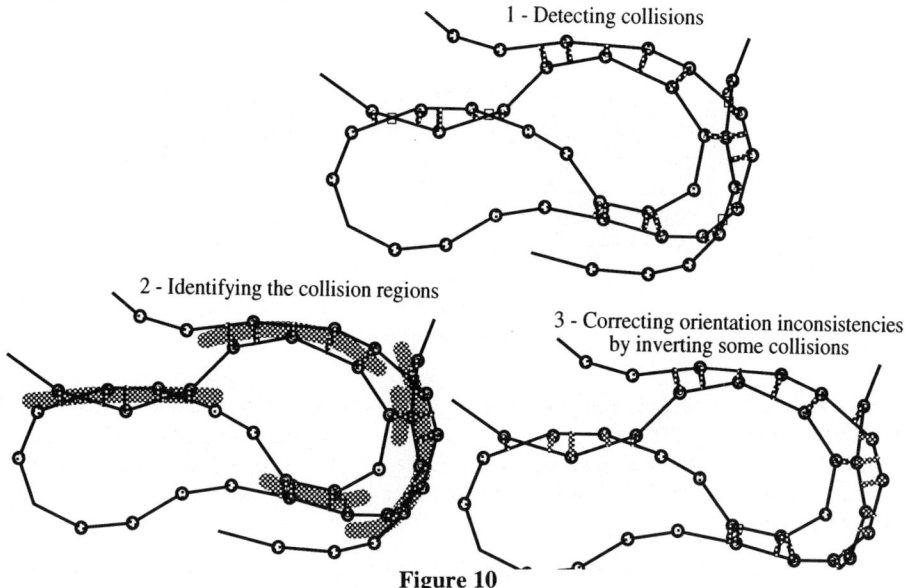

Figure 10
The collision orientation consistency correction process.

Some future work will consider maintaining consistency between different collision groups, as they may interfere each other when some elements get involved into several collisions.

4. Results and conclusion

The collision detection algorithm has been tested on various situations, from detecting self-collisions on a sphere up to complex collision situations involving wrinkling cloth. The result is quite obvious : We now get an average self-collision detection time proportional to the number of colliding elements. In situations like Figure 5, less than 10 % of the detection time is spent for cloth self-collisions. We obtain full power from the hierarchical algorithm, which is now not fooled by all the fake collisions resulting from adjacent elements.

Orientation consistency detection improves drastically simulation robustness for non oriented surfaces. As shown by Figure 4, a mechanical simulation on an initially

64

inconsistent (interpenetrating) set of surfaces yields a consistent result. Each surface have been forces to "choose" the most probable side for each ambiguous collision.

The combination of our self-collision detection algorithm and the collision orientation consistency correction yields us a very efficient and robust system for simulating highly deformable surface. This can be included in a powerful cloth software, able to handle severe mechanical contexts and complex wrinkling situations. Way is then open for complex cloth simulation systems, that may include actors putting on and off cloth, or any other situation beyond the simply worn cloth situation.

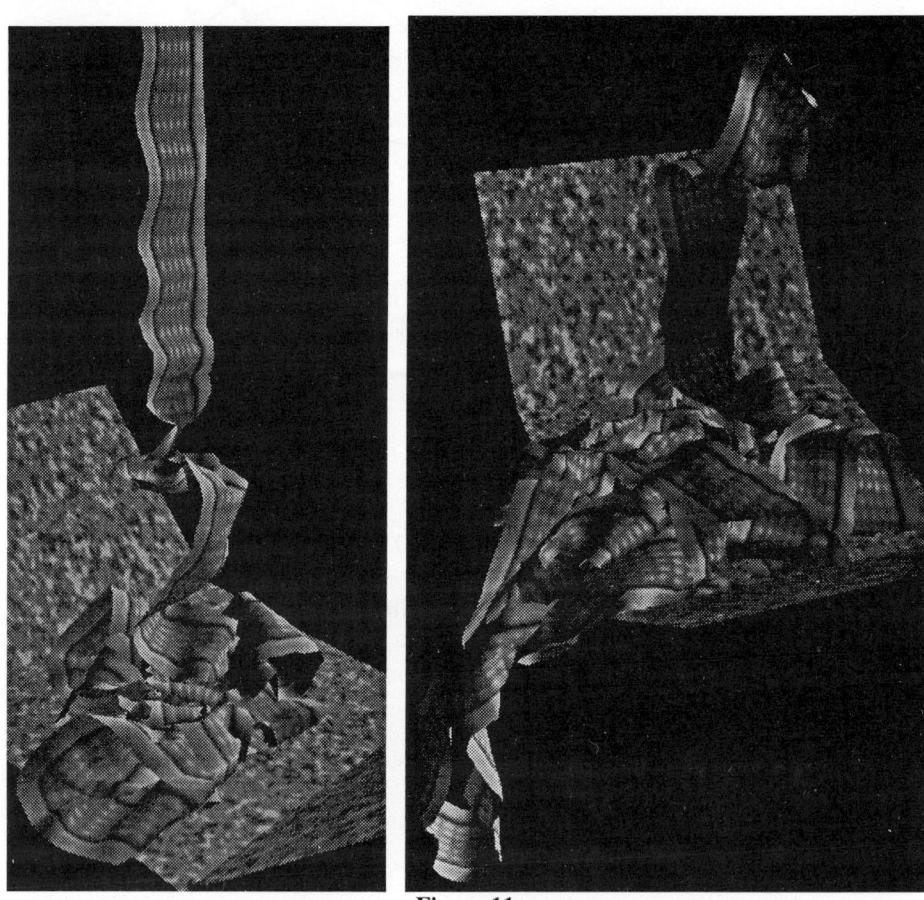

Figure 11
Complex collisions: The crumpling ribbon

Acknowledgements

This work is supported by the Swiss National Foundation and the European ESPRIT HUMANOID 2 project. Special thanks to all the people that have contribued to it.

Bibliography

[BAR 90] : **D. Baraff**, *"Curved Surfaces and Coherence for Non-Penetrating Rigid Body Simulation"*, Computer Graphics, 24(4), pp 19-28, 1990.

[BAR 92] : **D. Baraff, A. Witkin**, *"Dynamic Simulation of Non-Penetrating Flexible Bodies"*, Computer Graphics, 26(2), pp 303-308, 1992.

[CAN 91] : **J.F. Canny, D. Manocha**, *"A new approach for Surface Intersection"*, International journal of Computational Geometry and Applications, 1(4), pp 491-516, 1991.

[DUF 92] : **T. Duff**, *"Interval Arithmetic and Recursive Subdivision for Implicit Functions and Constructive Solid Geometry"*, Computer Graphics 26(2), pp 131-138, 1992.

[LAF 91] : **B. Lafleur, N.M. Thalmann, D. Thalmann**, *"Cloth Animation with Self-Collision Detection"*, Proc. of the IFIP conference on Modeling in Computer Graphics, pp 179-187, 1991.

[LIN 93] : **M.C. Lin, D. Manocha**, *"Interference Detection between Curved Objects for Computer Animation"*, Models and techniques in Computer Animation (C.A. proceedings 1993), pp 43-55, 1993.

[MOO 88] : **M. Moore, J. Wilhelms**, *"Collision Detection and Response for Computer Animation"*, Computer Graphics, 22(4), pp 289-298, 1988.

[SHI 91] : **M. Shinya, M.C. Forgue**, *"Interference Detection through Rasterisation"*, The journal of Visualisation and Computer Animation, 4(2), pp 132-134, 1991.

[SNY 93] : **J.M. Snyder, A.R. Woodbury, K. Fleisher, B. Currin, A.H. Barr**, *"Interval Methods for Multi-Point Collisions between Time-Dependant Curved Surfaces"*, Computer Graphics annual series, pp 321-334, 1993.

[VHE 90] : **B. Von Herzen, A.H. Barr, H.R. Zatz**, *"Geometric Collisions for Time-Dependant Parametric Surfaces"*, Computer Graphics, 24(4), pp 39-48, 1990.

[VOL 94] : **P. Volino, N. Magnenat Thalmann**, *"Efficient Self-Collision Detection on Smoothly Discretised Surface Animations using Geometrical Shape Regularity"*, Computer Graphics Forum (EuroGraphics Proc.), 13(3), pp 155-166, 1994.

[WEB 92] : **R.C. Webb, M.A. Gigante**, *"Using Dynamic Bounding Volume Hierarchies to improve Efficiency of Rigid Body Simulations"*, Communicating with Virtual Worlds, (CGI proceedings 1992), pp 825-841, 1992.

[YAN 93] : **Y. Yang, N.M. Thalmann**, *"An Improved Algorithm for Collision Detection in Cloth Animation with Human Body"*, Computer Graphics and Applications (Pacific Graphics proceedings 1993), 1, pp 237-251, 1993.

[ZYD 93] : **M. Zyda, D. Pratt, W. Osborne, J. Monahan**, *"Real-Time Collision Detection and Response"*, The journal of visualisation and Computer Animation, 4(1), pp 13-24, 1993.

Editors' Note: see Appendix, p. 226 for coloured figures of this paper

Efficient Collision Detection for General CSG Objects

Michael Zeiller, Werner Purgathofer, Michael Gervautz

Technical University of Vienna, Institute of Computer Graphics
Karlsplatz 13/186, A-1040 Vienna, Austria

Abstract. A complete method to detect collisions among objects modeled with constructive solid geometry within a computer animation system is introduced. In contrast to existing methods the CSG objects may be constructed from arbitrary kinds of primitives, e.g., polyhedral primitives or primitives with curved surfaces. Collision detection is performed in three stages. Bounding volumes and spatial subdivision are used to reduce the complexity of the CSG objects for detailed analysis. In those regions that are partially covered by both objects an exact collision test for those small parts of the CSG objects that are inside the region is performed. To be able to deal with general CSG objects an adaptive collision detection algorithm for CSG objects containing curved primitives is presented.

1 Introduction

Computer animation models various changes of objects over time, but its major concern is to model their movement. If the motion shall appear very realistic, it has to be simulated due to physical laws which is well known as dynamic simulation [15]. A body moves under the influence of forces and torques which cause linear and angular accelerations. The dynamic equations of motion are set up and the state (including position and orientation) of the body is derived for each time step. In a realistic simulation the moving bodies are not allowed to interpenetrate other bodies. They cannot move around freely, but have to obey certain constraints. We have to detect whether two bodies collide and respond to the collision.

Collision detection can be performed in two major ways [2]. Continuum methods view the problem of determining a collision between two instants of time t_0 and t_1 as a single, continuous function of time. They solve the problem of computing the time and location when two bodies come into contact in the given time interval [6, 7]. For dynamic simulation the usability of continuum methods is limited since they presuppose the motion path of the bodies which is actually computed by the simulation. Discrete methods that analyze a series of instants of time $t_0 < t_0 + \Delta t_1 < t_0 + \Delta t_2 < ... < t_0 + \Delta t_n < t_1$ are more popular. For each time step $t_0 + \Delta t_i$ these methods are given the state of the bodies and determine whether they interpenetrate or are in contact. They are based on a geometric analysis since two bodies A and B collide if their surfaces intersect, i.e., their intersection is not empty ($A \cap B \neq \emptyset$, null-object detection NOD) [9, 14]. Coherence-based methods increase the efficiency of discrete methods by taking similarities between the current and previous time steps into account [1, 11].

Most of the existing algorithms for collision detection work on rigid bodies of polyhedral shape. The majority of them is based on detecting vertices inside the other body or edges that intersect the other body. However, this paper deals with bodies modeled with constructive solid geometry. Tilove presents a collision detection algorithm for CSG objects using null-object detection [16]. He reduces the CSG representation to the null set by determining redundancy of primitives. Cameron detects collisions among CSG objects using three stages [4]. First he creates a set of bounding volumes called S-bounds around the nodes of the CSG tree. In the next stage he splits the problem into simpler subproblems using spatial subdivision. Finally, he generates a set of sufficient points that are classified regarding to the objects being tested. While these algorithms are restricted to CSG objects constructed from polyhedral primitives, Duff's algorithm, which uses interval arithmetic, deals with primitives described by implicit functions [7]. In contrast to these methods (except [7]), the collision detection algorithm presented in this paper is designed for general CSG objects that are made up of arbitrary kinds of primitives, particularly primitives bounded by planar faces or curved surfaces [18]. Thus, it is not restricted to polyhedral CSG objects, but it can be applied to CSG objects that are made up of curved primitives.

Section 2 gives a short outline of the proposed collision detection method made up of three stages. Stage one is presented in section 3, stage two in section 4 and stage three in section 5. Section 6 covers the calculation of collision point and collision time. Section 7 discusses the improvement of the proposed method by applying coherence. Finally, results are presented in section 8.

2 Outline of the method

The moving bodies and the entire scene in a dynamic simulation can be modeled in various ways. Constructive solid geometry is a flexible and powerful way of representing objects, especially if primitives are not restricted to be polyhedra, but may consist of curved surfaces as well [12]. Throughout the rest of this paper we refer to CSG objects as objects constructed by the regularized set operations union (A∪B), intersection (A∩B), and difference (A–B), which are represented by a binary tree structure. Arbitrary kinds of objects can be used as primitives. They may either have polyhedral shape or have a curved surface like quadrics.

Dynamic simulation computes the state of moving objects at consecutive time steps. At each of these time steps the collision detection algorithm has to be applied to each pair of CSG objects. Consequently, the basic algorithm is a discrete method. If a collision has been detected, one of the well-known methods for collision response has to be applied, but this is beyond the scope of this paper [2, 14].

Detecting a collision among two CSG objects can be performed in two ways. The CSG objects can either be converted to a boundary representation which is then used for collision detection or collision detection is performed directly on the CSG representation. The first approach requires a conversion task for the entire objects which becomes very complex if primitives have curved surfaces. A BREP approximation is usually impracticable for such objects because an accurate approximation requires a tremendous amount of polygons. In the second approach collision detection is applied to the CSG representation. This is much more complicated to do than for a BREP, but the detailed analysis of the objects' surfaces can be restricted only to those small regions where a collision is likely to occur. The method proposed in this paper is based on the latter technique.

The proposed method consists of three stages which is similar to [4]. It is based on the principle to eliminate as many objects as possible from further consideration by fast tests and to perform an exact analysis only for those parts of the objects where a collision is likely to occur. In the first stage bounding volumes are used to reject those pairs of objects where even the bounding volumes do not overlap. S-bounds provide an efficient means to handle this problem for the intersection test of two CSG objects [5]. If the resulting bounding volume is empty, the objects do not collide. Otherwise, we have to continue with stage two.

The bounding volume of the S-bounds test restricts the region of interest where a collision may take place. Spatial subdivision is used in the second stage to reduce the complexity of the CSG objects inside this region for further analysis. The bounding volume is adaptively decomposed into cells until a configuration is obtained where it can be decided whether there is an intersection, there is no intersection, or there is no profit from another subdivision.

If stage two ended up with some cells that cover parts of both objects, a third stage providing an exact (within tolerances) solution is performed. The cells may be partially covered by single primitives or by entire CSG structures. Due to the two preprocessing stages these CSG structures are (hopefully) very small and cover only a fraction of the original CSG objects we started with. If only a single primitive of each CSG object interferes the cell (which happens most often), a localized collision detection for the two primitives is performed. Pairs of polyhedra are tested with a localized version of a BREP collision detector. Curved primitives (and mixed pairs) are analyzed by an iterative collision detection algorithm that is based on an approximation by outer and inner bounding polyhedra. They are adaptively refined and repeatedly tested until a definite decision, whether the exact shapes collide, can be made or the tolerance is reached. To determine whether two CSG objects consisting of more than one primitive interpenetrate inside a cell null-object detection is used. This localized NOD algorithm deals with CSG objects consisting of polyhedral and curved primitives. Similarly to pairs of curved primitives curved CSG objects are iteratively tested by repeatedly applying polyhedral NOD to outer and inner bounds of their shape.

3 Bounding volumes

Complex and time consuming null-object detection tests shall not be performed on the entire CSG objects. A collision will only affect a small part of an object's surface and in most cases no collision will occur. An efficient means of accelerating computations on arbitrary kinds of objects are bounding volumes which provide an approximate solution to a given problem much faster. At each time step the dynamic simulation computes the new states of the CSG objects that have to be analyzed for collision. The bounding volumes enclosing the entire objects are updated and used as a first estimate whether they collide. For many configurations this test will be sufficient. If the bounding volumes of two objects do not overlap, these objects cannot collide and they are rejected from further consideration. Otherwise, they have to be analyzed in more detail.

In CSG modeling a hierarchy of bounding volumes can be established, i.e., in each node there exists a bounding volume that encloses the corresponding subtree. In this first stage we are using S-bounds that have proved to be very efficient bounds for null-object detection [4, 5]. Two CSG objects A and B collide if their intersection S=A∩B is not the null set. A new temporary CSG object S is created that is the intersection of the two objects A and B and the S-bounds algorithm is applied to it [4]. Spheres and axis-aligned boxes are used as bounding volumes. The reduction of the bounding volumes will be significant, because in collision detection the original objects are apart from each other in most cases. If this intersection object S is null-bounded (Fig. 1 left), then the objects A and B do not collide and we ca stop testing them. Otherwise, the S-bounds overlap and the CSG objects are likely to intersect (Fig. 1 right).

In the latter case collision detection has to continue and take a closer look at the objects themselves. However, we can still gain from the S-bounds test. A potential intersection can only take place inside the common region (i.e., bounding volume in root node of S) and everything outside can be ignored in the further NOD test. Consequently, the complexity of the CSG objects can be significantly reduced by removing those subtrees that have empty bounds.

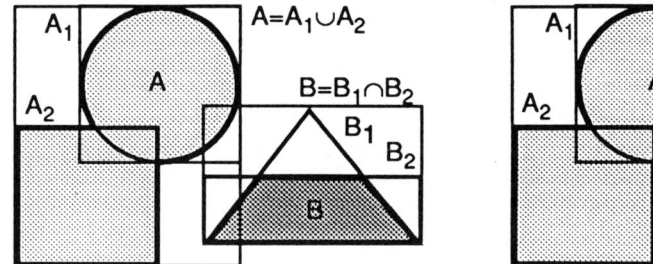

Fig. 1. Empty (left) and non-empty S-bounds (right) in 2D

4   Spatial subdivision

Pruned CSG objects of low complexity are immediately passed to stage three. However, occasionally the pruned CSG objects may still be too complex to perform NOD efficiently. For such objects spatial subdivision is performed in stage two. The NOD problem is spatially split into a number of subproblems. The CSG trees will get smaller when the region gets smaller and the NOD problem can be dealt with more easily. A popular strategy for spatial subdivision is based on divide-and-conquer. For a given region and a CSG tree it decides dynamically whether to conquer the problem (i.e., easy decision or direct NOD) or to perform another subdivision. Two major problems arise in this stage: One task is to decide whether the region shall be further subdivided or not. The other task is to perform the subdivision and to determine those parts of the CSG object S that lie inside the subregions.

The axis-aligned bounding box associated with the root node of the intersection CSG object S is recursively decomposed into eight octants of the same size. We are interested to know whether a cell is completely inside (*full*), partially inside (*partial*), or outside (*empty*) according to a CSG object [8]. If a cell is classified as *empty*, we do not have to consider it any further. If it is classified as *full*, we can stop, too, because we have discovered a region of space that is covered by both objects. Thus, a collision is found. If a cell is partially covered, it has to be decided whether to tackle the NOD problem or to perform another subdivision. This decision depends on the complexity of the CSG tree, i.e., the number and type of primitives, and the level of subdivision based on an estimation of the cost of an additional step of subdivision. It has to be ensured that the overall cost is not increased by splitting the NOD problem into several subproblems. If the CSG tree consists of only two primitives or a minimum size of a cell is reached, collision detection continues with the next stage.

5 Exact collision detection

In the previous stages the size of the regions of interest and the complexities of the CSG objects within these regions have been reduced considerably. The complexity of the NOD problem has decreased, but the basic question still has to be solved: Given a region of space and two CSG objects A and B, do they collide in this region? Since we have created an intersection CSG object $S=A \cap B$, the question has been reformulated as: Does this intersection object represent the null set? Due to the preprocessing of stage one and two it is very likely that the CSG tree of S consists of only two primitives, each of them belonging to one of the two original CSG objects A and B. They can be tested directly whether they collide inside the cell (section 5.1). If the CSG tree consists of more than two primitives, the entire CSG object has to be analyzed whether it represents the null set (section 5.2).

The spatial subdivision resulted in a number of cells with associated CSG trees. We have to test all cells for NOD, but we can stop immediately after the first intersection has been detected. Cells with CSG trees constructed from few primitives (ideally two) will be tested before cells with more primitives. The next subsections will show that it is preferable to test CSG trees constructed from polyhedral primitives before testing CSG trees with curved primitives.

5.1 Pairs of primitives

If the intersection object S consists only of two primitives, both objects A and B that are tested for collision inside the given cell are represented by a single primitive. There is no need to perform null-object detection on CSG structures and collision detection is performed directly on the primitives. The CSG objects can be constructed from arbitrary kinds of primitives. They may be polyhedra or they may have a curved surface like quadrics or other parametric curved objects. Various kinds of curved primitives may be used provided that a polyhedral approximation can be generated. The primitives should be convex, otherwise they have to be decomposed into a collection of convex parts. The following pairs of primitive types have to be tested: polyhedron–polyhedron, polyhedron–curved object, curved object-curved object.

5.1.1 Pair of polyhedral primitives

We use a modified version of Moore and Wilhelms' collision detection method to test two polyhedral primitives [14]. This algorithm is based on a point test and proceeds in three steps. Step one is a test to find vertices of polyhedron A inside polyhedron B and vertices of B inside A. Step two tests whether an edge of A penetrates B or an edge of B penetrates A. Step three tests for the rare case of perfectly aligned faces. Since this collision test may only be applied inside a cell, a localized version is used where only vertices and edges that are inside the cell are tested for interference.

5.1.2   Pair of polyhedral and curved primitive

The collision test for a polyhedral and a curved primitive inside a cell is similar to the localized collision test for two polyhedra. Whether a vertex of the polyhedron is inside the curved object can be determined easily. The penetration of an edge of the polyhedron with the curved object is tested by intersecting it with the curved surface. Furthermore, the faces of the polyhedron have to be tested against the curved object whether they intersect its surface. A single point of the curved object has to be classified against the polyhedron to determine the rare case that it is entirely enclosed by the polyhedron. Only a local collision test may be performed inside the cell, thus, all vertices, edges, and faces have to be clipped at the cell boundary.

5.1.3   Pair of curved primitives

There exist several ways to test two objects bounded by curved surfaces for collision. Exact methods use either algebraic approaches based on algebraic equations or geometric reasoning based on the shape, location and orientation of the objects [13]. Approximate methods represent the curved objects with planar facets that are used for intersection testing. Others use subdivision based on interval arithmetic like Duff [7], hierarchically refined bounding volumes like Von Herzen et al. [17], or simply test a set of significant points like Essa et al [10]. We have decided to use the more general approach based on a polyhedral approximation since it can be applied to various kinds of objects and is not restricted to special shapes [18]. However, the accuracy of the result depends on the quality of the approximation. A coarse approximation is easy to test, but gives inexact answers with high tolerances. On the other hand a fine approximation provides results of high accuracy, but is very costly. Since we require accurate results, we have developed a new adaptive refinement technique based on the boundary evaluation method of Beacon et al. that uses inner and outer sets [3].

Outer and inner bounding polyhedron. The curved objects are circumscribed by an enclosing outer bounding polyhedron (OBP) and are inscribed by an inner bounding polyhedron (IBP). The OBP is of arbitrary shape and encloses the curved surface as close as possible. The IBP has similar shape and structure and is enclosed by the curved surface. Together they make up an interval inside which the exact boundary of the object lies (Fig. 2 left). While testing these bounds are refined by replacing each polygon by smaller polygons that fit more tightly to the surface (Fig. 2 right). The number of facets constantly increases, but the thickness of the interval decreases.

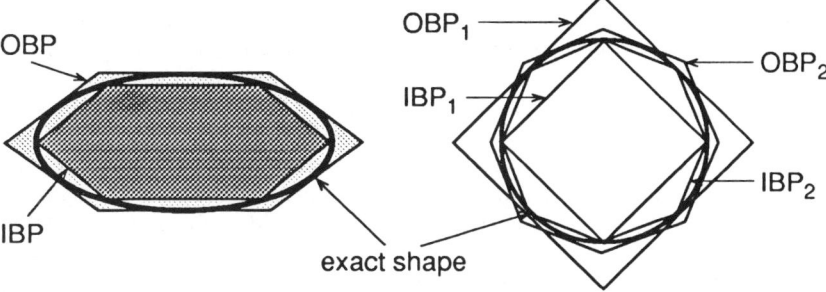

Fig. 2. Outer and inner bounding polyhedron (in 2D)

Collision detection with bounding polyhedra. The new collision detection algorithm for curved objects using an outer and inner bound proceeds as follows [18]:

- At first the outer bounds are tested for collision.
- If the OBPs of two curved objects do not intersect, the objects themselves cannot intersect as well. There is no collision and testing stops.
- Otherwise, the IBPs are tested for collision.
- If they intersect, the curved objects have to intersect as well. There is a collision and the collision point is determined.
- Otherwise, no decision can be made. The approximation has to be refined and the test is repeated.

Testing continues until a definite decision can be made that the approximated objects intersect or do not intersect, or the required tolerance has been reached. If the thickness of the interval between the outer and inner bound is less than a given tolerance, the objects are assumed to intersect. Let us consider the following example (Fig. 3): In a given region two curved primitives A and B shall be tested for collision. Let $\overline{A}$ denote the OBP of A and $\underline{A}$ the IBP of A, $\overline{B}$ and $\underline{B}$ are defined respectively. $\overline{A}$ and $\overline{B}$ intersect (Fig. 3 left), but $\underline{A}$ and $\underline{B}$ do not intersect (Fig. 3 right). No correct decision can be made, yet. The OBPs and the IBPs of A and B are replaced by a better approximation and the process is repeated.

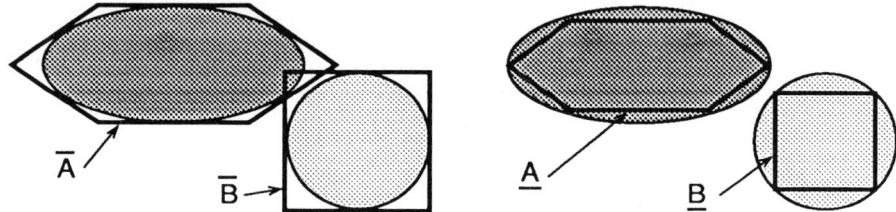

Fig. 3. Collision test with outer and inner bounds in 2D

Two outer bounds and two inner bounds are tested for collision with a modified version of the collision test for pairs of polyhedra (section 5.1.1) that also determines the intersecting polygons (to make up the region of interest, see below). Computations can be speeded up by testing the outer or inner bound of one object against the exact shape of the other object. Testing may be more complex (section 5.1.2), but it converges faster.

Refinement: To apply this method of collision detection to any kind of curved primitives outer and an inner bounding polyhedra that can be refined easily have to be created. In the actual implementation we have restricted the curved primitives to natural quadrics (sphere, cylinder, cone), but arbitrary shapes can be used as long as an OBP and IBP can be generated. The initial approximation for a sphere is an icosahedron, whose equilateral triangular faces are decomposed into four equilateral triangles in each iteration. A cylinder is initially approximated by a hexagonal prism and a cone is approximated by a hexagonal pyramid. In each refinement step each face is split into two halves. If the primitives have been nonuniformly scaled (e.g., sphere changes to ellipsoid), the bounding polyhedra can be generated before scaling or the approximation tries to cope with the nonuniform curvature.

In each step of refinement the length of the edges is (nearly) bisected and the thickness of the interval between the outer and the inner bounding polyhedron is reduced to one quarter. In R steps of refinement we gain a precision of $1/2^{2R}$ (e.g., 5 steps for a precision of 10^{-3}). Thus, the cost of this algorithm depends on the required precision of the result.

The number of bounding polygons constantly increases while the thickness of the interval decreases. However, the number of polygons that really have to be considered in the collision test stays nearly the same throughout the refinement because the relevant region of interest ROI shrinks with the same order of magnitude. Only those polygons of the OBP that intersect and their related polygons of the IBP have to be refined and considered in the next step. The region of interest shrinks with each iteration to a half in each dimension and the number of polygons in it and the computational cost of each step stays nearly constant (Fig. 4).

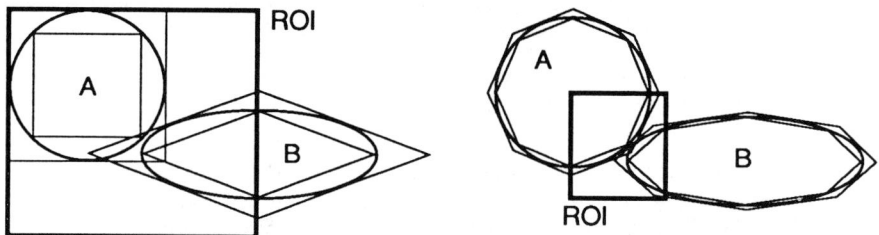

Fig. 4. Refinement of bounds and region of interest in 2D

5.2 Null-object detection

If the reduced CSG objects A and B still consist of more than one primitive, null-object detection on these CSG objects is performed. Although this is similar to the initial problem, preprocessing in stage one and two ensures that the number of primitives which still have to be considered is rather small. Two CSG objects do not collide if their intersection S represents the null set. Existing NOD methods are restricted to CSG objects made up of polyhedral primitives. Tilove presents a NOD algorithm that determines primitive redundancy [16]. Cameron performs an exhaustive test by generating a sufficient set of points on the boundary of A and B which are then classified against S [4].

The proposed new method for general CSG objects including curved primitives is based on locally evaluating the boundary of the intersection CSG object S=A∩B. The intersection has to be empty if the boundary of S is empty. Boundary evaluation for collision detection has to generate candidate edges and faces which are then classified with respect to the intersection S whether they belong to S or not. If there exist some elements (points, lines, curves, faces) that are contained in the boundary, the intersection object S is not empty and consequently there is a collision. Since stage three of the proposed method for general CSG objects is performed inside a cell of interest, a localized version of boundary evaluation is sufficient. CSG objects made up entirely of polyhedral primitives are treated differently from those containing curved primitives.

5.2.1 CSG objects with polyhedral primitives

Since boundary evaluation is based on the generate-and-test paradigm, the main task is to create a sufficient set of candidates that are classified afterwards. There exist various methods that can be applied to CSG objects constructed entirely from polyhedral primitives. The proposed method considers only edge segments as candidates which follows [16]. These edges are either derived from the edges of primitives or by pairwise intersection of the faces bounding the primitives. To get a localized boundary test the candidate edges are clipped at the cell boundary before classification.

All candidates (straight lines) are classified with respect to the CSG object by set membership classification [16]. If the classification of an element determines that none of its subsets is contained in the boundary of S or inside it, then this element neither contributes to the object's boundary nor interferes its interior. If at least one element inside or on the boundary of S is found, then S is not empty and there is a collision. Otherwise, the CSG objects A and B do not collide.

5.2.2 CSG objects with curved primitives

Boundary evaluation for CSG objects that are (at least partially) constructed from curved primitives is much more complicated. A set of candidates cannot be derived efficiently because the intersection curves of surfaces are difficult to compute (see e.g., [13] for quadrics) and would have to be classified against the intersection object S. Since the proposed collision detection method is designed for general CSG objects, a boundary evaluation algorithm is required that can deal with arbitrary kinds of curved primitives. A boundary evaluation method that meets the requirements for NOD for the aims of collision detection most closely is the ISOS method that approximates curved primitives by outer and inner bounding sets [3].

Outer and inner bounding polyhedron. To test CSG objects with curved primitives for NOD they are approximated by outer and inner bounding polyhedra as in section 5.1.3. An outer bounding polyhedron for the entire CSG object S can be created by replacing the positive primitives (i.e., subtracted an even number of times in the CSG tree) of S with their OBPs and the negative primitives with their IBPs. Consequently we get an inner bounding polyhedron of the CSG object by replacing the positive primitives with their IBPs and the negative primitives with their OBPs. Again, this leads to an interval inside which the exact boundary of the CSG object lies.

NOD with bounding polyhedra. The new null-object detection algorithm for curved CSG objects proceeds similarly to the collision test for curved primitives [18]:
- The polyhedral NOD test (section 5.2.1) is applied to the outer bound of the CSG object S.
- If the test of the OBP determines a null object, the CSG objects A and B do not collide and testing stops.
- Otherwise, the inner bound of S is tested by polyhedral NOD.
- If NOD of the IBP determines that it is not null, the objects A and B collide and the collision point is determined.
- Otherwise, no decision can be made, yet. The approximation has to be refined and the test is repeated until a decision can be made or the tolerance is reached.

Example: In a cell two CSG objects A and B shall be tested for collision, thus, NOD is applied to $S=A\cap B$. Let $\overline{S}$ denote the OBP of S and $\underline{S}$ the IBP of S. If $\overline{S} = \overline{A} \cap \overline{B}=\varnothing$, A and B definitely do not collide and we can stop. Otherwise we have to test $\underline{S}=\underline{A}\cap\underline{B}$. If $\underline{S}\neq\varnothing$, then A and B definitely collide and we can stop, too. If $\underline{S}=\varnothing$ and $\overline{S}\neq\varnothing$ we cannot make a correct decision, yet. The OBPs and the IBPs in $\overline{S}$ and $\underline{S}$ are replaced by a refined approximation and the process is repeated. In Fig. 5 $A=A_1\cup A_2$ and $B=B_1-B_2$ are tested. $\overline{S}\neq\varnothing$ and $\underline{S}=\varnothing$ and another iteration has to be performed.

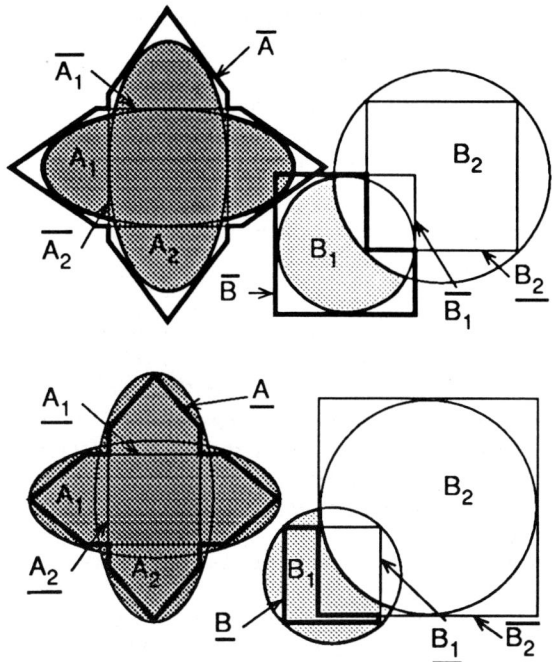

Fig. 5. Outer and inner bound of CSG objects

Refinement. Like the NOD test for polyhedral primitives these tests on the outer and inner bounds have to be performed locally inside the given cell. Refining the bounding polyhedra works similarly to the collision test of curved primitives (see section 5.1.3). The OBPs and IBPs of each primitive are individually replaced by a refined bounding polygon and then they are combined to make up the refined OBP and IBP of S. Besides the cost of polyhedral NOD, the overall cost is determined by the required precision (i.e., the number of iterations) of the detected collision.

Although the number of polygons of the bounds increases, the number of polygons under investigation stays nearly constant because the region of interest shrinks, too. Convex surfaces collide at a single collision point, but the union and difference operation of CSG modeling may cause non-convex surfaces even if all primitives are convex. This may result in several collision points. In this case the ROI does not shrink. Such configurations have to be detected and are solved by point sampling.

6 Collision point and collision time

The collision test described above determines whether two objects intersect at a given time or not. To be able to respond to the collision correctly the collision time and the collision point have to be determined. If there is no intersection at time t_0, but there is an intersection at the next time step $t_0+\Delta t$, then a collision has occurred in the time interval $[t_0,t_0+\Delta t]$. We do not consider multiple collisions and assume that there is only one collision point. If there is a single interpenetrating vertex, it is taken as the collision point, otherwise the point of greatest interpenetration is chosen. If the precision of the result is sufficient, i.e., the amount of interpenetration and/or the time interval are very small, testing stops. Otherwise, we compute a more precise collision time by binary search.

7 Improvements

This method, as it has been presented above, belongs to the discrete methods for collision detection. Although coherence-based methods have shown to be more efficient, they are usually more complex to design and cannot be applied to all collision problems [1, 11]. However, the computational cost of this discrete method may become quite remarkable in certain configurations, especially when two curved objects are nearly in contact. Its performance can be increased by exploiting temporal coherence that arises from the fact that the state of the objects changes only very little between two successive time steps of the dynamic simulation.

Coherence might be used to incrementally compute the collision region based on S-bounds. However, since this is a fast test, the benefits of coherence are limited. Spatial subdivision is much more costly, thus being a better target for optimization. The subdivision tree of the current time step can be reused in the next time step. It will not change significantly, but those cells which have to be subdivided once more or those which can be merged have to be determined and processed accordingly.

The highest profit of coherence can be gained in null-object detection when objects are very close. When curved primitives are involved, an iterative collision test is applied. If two objects are nearly in contact, but do not collide, the approximation by outer and inner bounds of the other time steps can be reused for the exact collision test instead of calculating them from scratch. The approximation has to be updated to cover the correct surface parts by extending it to the nearby regions and/or by refining the polygonal approximation. If a previous time step is analyzed (to compute the collision time), chances are high that polyhedral NOD can be applied straightforward to the actual set of outer and inner bounds. Application of coherence to this collision detection method is currently under investigation.

8 Results

The collision detection method proposed in this paper has bee implemented in a testbed system for animating general objects modeled by CSG [19]. The primitives currently supported are the Platonic solids (tetrahedron, cube, etc.) and the natural quadrics (sphere, cylinder, and cone). The simulation results prove the aim of the design to obtain a fast decision if objects are far apart and to require more time the closer the objects get.

Most profit in performance is gained by the bounding volume and S-bounds test in stage one. Especially S-bounds are really fast and reject most candidate pairs even if they are comparably close. In stage two spatial subdivision has been limited to level 2 or 3. There is not much gain in further subdivisions because its cost dramatically increases and the complexity is seldom reduced. Various simulations have shown that null-object detection in stage three is either applied to pairs of primitives or to very small CSG objects S (typically 3 or 4 primitives) in most cases. Larger CSG objects have to be tested only very seldom. The computational cost of NOD depends on the type of primitives (polyhedral vs. curved) involved, the number of iterations in the case of curved primitives and the location of contact.

Table 1 presents the runtime data of two approaching CSG objects at some significant instants of time. Object A consists of 19 primitives: 9 cylinders, 8 cubes, 2 spheres. Objects B is made up of 5 primitives: 3 cones, 2 cylinders. The objects are steadily approaching, thus reducing the minimum distance between them. Fig. 6 shows a detail of the test scene near the collision region. The primitives involved in the collision are one cone of B and two cubic primitives of A that make up an intersection edge due to a difference operation. Computing the S-bounds requires two passes to determine that the collision region is empty and 3 passes to determine a non-empty collision region that contains 2 polyhedral (P) and two quadric (Q) primitives. When the objects are very close, NOD has to be performed after 2 levels of subdivision. The last column indicates relative timings in ticks (e.g., 1/200 seconds on a 486/DX-2 CPU) to compare the efficiency of the different stages.

Table 1. Runtime data for approaching objects of test scene

distance	S-bounds	spatial subdivision	NOD	collision?	time
1.0	no intersection (2)	–	–	NO	3
0.8	no intersection (2)	–	–	NO	3
0.6	no intersection (2)	–	–	NO	3
0.4	no intersection (2)	–	–	NO	3
0.2	no intersection (2)	–	–	NO	3
0.1	intersection (3) 2 P, 2 Q	no intersection (1) 1 *partial*, 8 *empty*	–	NO	186
0.07	intersection (3) 2 P, 2 Q	no intersection (1) 1 *partial*, 8 *empty*	–	NO	185
0.04	intersection (3) 2 P, 2 Q	no intersection (1) 1 *partial*, 8 *empty*	–	NO	186
0.01	intersection (3) 2 P, 2 Q	no intersection (1) 1 *partial*, 8 *empty*	–	NO	186
0.007	intersection (3) 2 P, 2 Q	no intersection (1) 1 *partial*, 8 *empty*	–	NO	188
0.004	intersection (3) 2 P, 2 Q	no intersection (1) 1 *partial*, 8 *empty*	–	NO	187
0.001	intersection (3) 2 P, 2 Q	unknown (2) 6 *partial*, 18 *empty*	NOD (2 P, 1 Q) 78 edges, level 0	NO	368
0.0	intersection (3) 2 P, 2 Q	unknown (2) 6 *partial*, 10 *empty*	NOD (2 P, 1 Q) 727 edges, level 2	**YES**	697
-0.001	intersection (3) 2 P, 2 Q	unknown (2) 6 *partial*, 10 *empty*	NOD (2 P, 1 Q) 702 edges, level 2	**YES**	669

78

Fig. 6. Detail of a test scene

10 Conclusion

A new method to detect collisions among general objects modeled by constructive solid geometry is proposed. In contrary to other methods there is no limitation on the type of primitives being used. To speed up the computation and to avoid expensive calculations for each time step it consists of three stages. The first stage uses bounding volumes and the second stage uses spatial subdivision to reduce the complexity of the collision detection problem. However, the initial problem still may have to be solved which is done by null-object detection. Curved primitives are approximated by outer and inner bounding polyhedra. Due to an adaptive refinement of the approximation the computational cost of this test is kept low. This approach can be applied to all types of curved primitives since it should be possible to create the approximation very easily. This method supports results of variable precision depending on the requirements of the user. Inaccurate results can be achieved very fast, whereas precise results require several iterations at a higher cost.

Acknowledgment

We would like to thank Florian Zwerina for his help on implementing this method.

References

1. Baraff, D.: Curved Surfaces and Coherence for Non-penetrating Rigid Body Simulation. Computer Graphics, Vol. 24, No. 4, pp. 19-28, August 1990.
2. Baraff, D.: Non-penetrating Rigid Body Simulation. State of the Art Reports of EUROGRAPHICS '93, Eurographics Technical Report Series, 1993.
3. Beacon, G., Dodsworth, J., Howe, S., Oliver, R., Saia, A.: Boundary Evaluation Using Inner and Outer Sets: The ISOS Method. IEEE Computer Graphics & Applications, Vol. 9, No. 2, pp. 39-51, March 1989.
4. Cameron, S.: Efficient Intersection Tests for Objects Defined Constructively. The International Journal of Robotics Research, Vol. 8, No. 1, pp. 3-25, February 1989.
5. Cameron, S.: Efficient Bounds in Constructive Solid Geometry. IEEE Computer Graphics & Applications, Vol. 11, No. 3, pp. 68-74, May 1991.
6. Canny, J.: Collision Detection for Moving Polyhedra. IEEE Transactions on Pattern Analysis and Machine Intelligence, Vol. PAMI-8, No. 2, pp. 200-209, March 1986.
7. Duff, T.: Interval Arithmetic and Recursive Subdivision for Implicit Functions and Constructive Solid Geometry. Computer Graphics, Vol. 26, No. 2, pp. 131-138, July 1992.
8. Elber, G., Shpitalni, M.: Octree creation via C.S.G definition. The Visual Computer, Vol. 4, No. 2, pp. 53-64, July 1988.
9. Hahn, J.: Realistic Animation of Rigid Bodies. Computer Graphics, Vol. 22, No. 4, pp. 299-308, August 1988.
10. Essa, I., Sclaroff, S., Pentland, A.: A Unified Approach for Physical and Geometric Modeling for Graphics and Animation. Computer Graphics Forum, Vol. 11, No. 3, pp. 129-138, 1992.
11. Lin, M., Canny, J.: Efficient Collision Detection for Animation. Proceedings of Third Eurographics Workshop on Animation and Simulation, Eurographics Technical Report Series, September 1992.
12. Mäntylä, M.: An Introduction to Solid Modeling. Computer Science Press, 1988.
13. Miller, J.: Analysis of Quadric-Surface-Based Solid Models. IEEE Computer Graphics & Applications, Vol. 8, No. 1, pp. 28-42, January 1988.
14. Moore, M., Wilhelms, J.: Collision Detection and Response for Computer Animation. Computer Graphics, Vol. 22, No. 4, pp. 289-298, August 1988.
15. Thalmann, D.: Dynamic Simulation as a Tool for Three-dimensional Animation., In: Magnenat-Thalmann N., Thalmann D. (eds.): New Trends in Animation and Simulation, John Wiley&Sons, pp. 257-272, 1991.
16. Tilove, R.: A Null-Object Detection Algorithm for Constructive Solid Geometry. Communications of the ACM, Vol 27, No. 7, pp. 684-694, July 1984.
17. Von Herzen, B., Barr, A., Zatz, H.: Geometric Collisions for Time-Dependent Parametric Surfaces. Computer Graphics, Vol. 24, No. 4, pp. 39-48, August 1990.
18. Zeiller, M.: Collision Detection for Complex Objects in Computer Animation. PhD thesis, Technical University of Vienna, Austria, 1994.
19. Zwerina, F.: Collision Detection for CSG Objects. Diploma thesis, Technical University of Vienna, Austria, 1994.

All You Need Is Force:
a constraint-based approach for rigid body dynamics in computer animation

Kees van Overveld and Bart Barenbrug

Department of Mathematics and Computing Science, Eindhoven University of Technology
PO Box 513 ; 5600 MB Eindhoven, the Netherlands

Abstract. Over the last few years, simulating the motion of linked articulated rigid bodies based on classical rigid body dynamics has become a valuable paradigm for making realistic 3-D computer animations. Although several operational methods for dynamical simulation have been developed, in general these are both conceptually and computationally complex. To inspire further research in devising alternative and possibly simpler schemes for dealing with articulated rigid bodies, this paper discusses an alternative approach to rigid body dynamics which is based on (conceptually much simpler) point mechanics. Geometric constraints, e.g. the requirement that the distance between two points should be conserved, take the form of additional algebraic equations. We propose to solve these algebraic constraints in concert with the numerical integration. First, we give a general formulation of such a scheme. Next, we describe a preliminar implementation on the basis of a very naive numerical solver for ODE's (ordinary differential equations).

1 Introduction

(The first few paragraphs of this introduction have appeared earlier, in a different context, in [8])

The mathematical theory of rigid body dynamics has been developed over the past 200 years by Euler, Lagrange, Poincelet and others. One of the main applications of this theory was the quantitative description of motions of celestial bodies. This meant that the theory had to be formulated such that numerical results could be obtained without having to rely on elaborate numerical calculations: sophisticated analytical methods were used instead.

What if computers and numerical methods would have existed in the 18th century?

An interesting question then is whether this would have changed the appearance of the theory, i.e. if the theory would emphasise numerical methods rather than analytical techniques. As a consequence, would the collection of canonical applications of the theory comprise more examples in the context of the motion of composite mechanisms and articulated systems, rather then (symmetrical) tops and celestial bodies?

Let us elaborate a bit on this speculation.

Much of the mathematical complexity of rigid body dynamics is due to the introduction of angle coordinates rather than Cartesian coordinates: the geometry of $O(3)$ (the space of three-dimensional rotations) is much more complicated than the geometry of $E(3)$ (the three dimensional Euclidean space). This reflects itself in the occurrence of torques and angular momenta, resulting in coupled nonlinear ODE's in the angular velocities[1].

Now suppose instead that rigid objects were described as a collection of N point masses, whose locations were represented by points in a $3N$-dimensional Euclidean space (like a gas consisting of N molecules). Its phase space, which also contains the velocities of the points, therefore would be $6N$-dimensional. The rigidity of the object then might be assured by extending this system with a sufficient number of geometrical constraints. Since the state vector of a rigid object has 12 components (3 coordinates of the centre of gravity, 3 components of the translation vector, 3 Euler angles and 3 components of the angular velocity vector), the number of scalar constraints would be $6N$-12. These constraints could e.g. state that the distances between appropriate point-pairs has to be invariant and hence that the relative velocity component in that direction vanishes. (We will call these constraints length constraints; one length constraint therefore adds effectively two scalar constraints, so in this case $3N$-6 length constraints are needed).

By this manipulation, we have replaced a problem of differential geometry in $E(3) \times O(3)$ by a simpler problem in $E(3N)$ together with $3N$-6 length constraints. The differential equations of the latter problem are trivial when compared with the differential equations of the former problem: they take the form $F = m\ddot{x}$ for each of the point masses, whereas the original problem gives rise to the Euler equations of a rotating rigid body ([2]).

In other words, we have exchanged a great deal of analytical complexity by numerical complexity. Of course, such a manipulation would not have made sense in the 18th century, without the availability of numerical methods and computers to implement these, so it is obvious that the classical textbook theory has not been developed along these lines.

Nowadays, however, computers and efficient numerical algorithms are available, so an alternative development of rigid body dynamics, with a larger emphasis on these numerical algorithms is possible.

Now the major motivation of the current work can be stated as follows: we want to investigate the applicability of the alternative formulation of rigid body dynamics, based on point-mass mechanics enhanced with additional constraints, such as the length constraints introduced above.

Even though a definitive implementation should use more sophisiticated numerical methods, the results of our preliminar implementation already show the potential merits of our scheme. One of the consequences of our scheme is that, to keep the structure of the ODE's as simple as possible, rigidity is also treated as a constraint, thus avoiding the necessity of introducing angular momentum and torque. As a result, we arrive at a particular transparent representation where both linked rigid objects, collision handling, point and line hinges and point-to-curve (PTC) constraints all are dealt with in

---

[1] See [2] for a treatment of classical rigid body mechanics, and [1], [9], [5], [4], [10], [6] for the application of classical rigid body mechanics to computer animation.

the same formal context. We will also study the qualitative and some quantitative merits of such methods. We stress, however, that the primary claim of this paper is NOT that point-mass based mechanics is in some way a better way to do rigid body mechanics than the classical Euler-type mechanics; it rather aims at provoking a discussion on the issue of whether computer based simulations should be founded on the same theoretical formulations as developed in the pre-computer era, OR that some aspects of classical theories might profit from minor re-structuring in order to provide a smoother transition from theory to computer simulation.

In section 2, the numerical scheme in its general setting is presented which will be used throughout this paper. Next a toy implementation of this scheme is introduced which consists of taking the Euler midpoint method as ODE solver, since this gives rise to straigthforward mathemetical manipulations. In 2.1, the scheme is introduced for the examples of a point mass which collides with a plane, and for a swinging pendulum. The constraints here arise from the requirement that the point mass does not penetrate the collision plane, and the conservation of the length of the pendulum, respectively. In 2.2, we study constraints that express the rigidity of an object; this gives rise to our formulation of rigid body dynamics. In 2.3 we study the coupling of two rigid bodies via a PTP constraint. This constraint gives rise to additional forces, and in the canonical formulation, to additional torques as well. We show how such torques can be eliminated, so that our original representation, based on forces only, still holds. A slightly more complicated interface between two rigid objects is the line hinge; it is discussed in 2.4. Section 2.5 discusses collision response based on constraint forces for articulated rigid objects. Point-to-curve constraints, e.g. needed for modelling moving beads on a curved string, or roller coasters, are the topic of 2.6. In section 3 we assess some quantitative properties of our algorithm which allow comparison with the standard methods. Section 4 summarises our results and concludes the paper.

2   Rigid Body Dynamics = Point Dynamics + Constraints

Consider a dynamical system with state vector $\phi = \phi(t)$, given by the evolution equation $\dot{\phi} = f(\phi; F)$ where $F = F(t)$ is the combined vector of all (*a priori* unknown) internal reaction forces in the system. The system should satisfy the algebraic constraints $c(\phi) = 0$ at all times. Suppose we have a numerical method N to give an estimate for $\phi(t + h)$, given $\phi(t)$ and $F(t)$ (and possibly the values of $\phi(t_i)$ at earlier time points $t_i < t$). Since $F(t)$ is *a priori* unknown we cannot compute $\phi(t + h) = N(\phi(t); F(t))$ right away. Therefore we adopt the assumption that the reaction forces $F(t)$ change slowly over time. That is $F(t) = F(t - h) + \delta F$ with δF in some sense small. We introduce an iterative scheme where in each step the estimate for δF, and hence for $F(t)$ (and hence the estimate for $\phi(t + h)$) will be improved. The values for $F(t)$ and $\phi(t + h)$ will be labeled by superscript k to distinguish the several subsequent estimates, so $\phi^k = N(\phi; F^k)$; and $\phi^{k+1} = N(\phi; F^{k+1})$ is supposed to be a better estimation for $\phi(t + h)$ than ϕ^k. Without a superscript, ϕ is short for $\phi(t)$. We start the iteration by taking for δF the value 0, so $F^0(t) = F^\infty(t - h)$. Next the algorithm looks as follows:

$$F^0(t) := F^\infty(t - h);$$
$$\delta F(t) := 0;$$
$$\phi^0 := N(\phi; F^0);$$
$$k := 0;$$

do

    compute improved estimate for δF

    $$F^{k+1} := F^0 + \delta F;$$
    $$\phi^{k+1} := N(\phi; F^{k+1});$$
    $$k := k + 1;$$

until convergence

$$\tag{1}$$

Notice that we have not explained how $\delta F = \delta F(\phi^k)$ should be obtained. It goes without saying that here the algebraic constraint $c(\phi) = 0$ comes into play. Indeed, assume that $c(\phi) = 0$ holds for $\phi(t)$. It should hold as well for $\phi(t+h)$. If we demand it to hold for ϕ^k then we get

$$
\begin{aligned}
0 = c(\phi^k) &= c(N(\phi; F^k)) \\
&= c(N(\phi; F^{k-1} + \delta F)) \\
&= c(N(\phi; F^{k-1}) + \frac{\partial N}{\partial F}\delta F + \cdots) \\
&= c(N(\phi; F^{k-1})) + \frac{\partial c}{\partial N}\frac{\partial N}{\partial F}\delta F + \cdots \\
&= c(N(\phi; F^{k-1})) + \frac{\partial c}{\partial F}\delta F + \cdots
\end{aligned}
\tag{2}
$$

This gives rise to the Newton-like method for computing δF^k:

$$\delta F^k = -(\frac{\partial c}{\partial F})^{-1} c(N(\phi; F^{k-1}))$$

This is the suggested scheme in the most general setting. In order to demonstrate how it works, we choose a naive numerical method N, namely the Euler midpoint method. Also, we will make use of additional knowledge of the structure of the constraints $c = 0$ to avoid the explicit computation[2] of the Jacobians $\frac{\partial c}{\partial F}$.

A differential equation of the form

$$F(t) = m\ddot{x}(t) \tag{3}$$

can be solved numerically by observing that

$$\ddot{x}(t) = \frac{x(t + h) + x(t - h) - 2x(t)}{h^2} + O(h^2)$$

---

[2] Observe, however, that an explicit computation of $\frac{\partial c}{\partial F}$ would not even be that expensive since every constraint component of c typically depends on very few components of F, so the Jacobian consists of small blocks.

so

$$x(t + h) = 2x(t) - x(t - h) + h^2 \ddot{x} + O(h^4). \tag{4}$$

Therefore an assignment to $x(t + h)$ should be:

$$x(t + h) = 2x(t) - x(t - h) + h^2 F(t)/m.$$

Given $x(t)$ and $x(t-h)$ and $F(t)$, the function N in our scheme, using this Euler method, is $N(x(t), x(t - h), F(t)) = 2x(t) - x(t - h) + h^2 F(t)/m$.

2.1 Mechanical Systems without Internal Structure: a Colliding Mass Point and a Swinging Pendulum

Consider a point mass moving in the positive x-direction with location $x(t)$ with uniform velocity. For $x = x(t_0)$, an impenetrable wall, perpendicular to the x-axis, blocks the motion of the point mass, so for $t = t_0$ a collision takes place. In a fully *inelastic* case, the point mass would come to a full stop due to an infinitely large force that works during an infinitely short time interval. In our discretised model, we assume that a finite, constant force works during the entire time interval of length h from t_0 to $t_0 + h$. So

$$x(t_0) = x(t_0 + h) = 2x(t_0) - x(t_0 - h) + h^2 F/m$$

and hence

$$F = m \frac{x(t_0 - h) - x(t_0)}{h^2}.$$

In this (trivial) example we see how evaluating a geometric constraint of the form $c(x(t+h)) = 0$ may serve to compute a constraint force at time t.

A less trivial example is a physical pendulum. Here $x(t)$ is the location of a point mass in $\Re^3$ that moves while keeping its distance to a given point, say the origin, constant. The motion equation reads

$$F(t) + G = m\ddot{x}(t),$$

and the numerical scheme is

$$x(t + h) = 2x(t) - x(t - h) + h^2(F(t) + G)/m.$$

The force G is a known gravity force; $F(t)$ is an *a priori* unknown reaction force that is induced by the constraint $c(x) = (x(t), x(t)) - l^2 = 0$. Rather than computing $(\frac{\partial c}{\partial F})^{-1}$, we proceed as follows: we can evaluate this constraint at $t + h$ which gives a quadratic equation in the magnitude of F. Since the direction of F is known ($F(t)$ is parallel to $x(t)$), this completely defines the reaction force.

2.2 Rigidity is a constraint.

We consider a 3-dimensional rigid object with total mass M and inertia tensor I. Assume that this object is composed of a large number of point masses, labeled with i, with locations $x_i(t)$ and masses m_i. These point masses have fixed relative positions with respect to each other since the object is rigid, so they can be written as $x_i = c + \sum_j \rho_{ij} B_j$

where c is the centre of gravity; B_j, with $j = 0, 1, 2$, are basis vectors for some body fixed frame, and ρ_{ij} are fixed coefficients expressing the relative position of x_i with respect to the frame $\{B_j\}$. Assume for the moment that c is in rest, so the object is only rotating round c. The kinetic energy then can be written either as $E_{kin} = \frac{1}{2}I\omega^2$ or $E_{kin} = \sum_i \frac{1}{2}m_i\dot{x}_i^2$. Elaborating the second expression gives

$$
\begin{aligned}
E_{kin} &= \sum_i \frac{1}{2}m_i(\dot{x}_i, \dot{x}_i) \\
&= \sum_i \frac{1}{2}m_i \sum_{jk} \rho_{ij}\rho_{ik}(\dot{B}_j, \dot{B}_k) \\
&= \frac{1}{2}\sum_{jk} \gamma_{jk}(\dot{B}_j, \dot{B}_k),
\end{aligned}
\tag{5}
$$

$$\tag{6}$$

where $\gamma_{jk} = \sum_i m_i \rho_{ij}\rho_{ik}$. Now suppose for the moment that γ is diagonal, then

$$
E_{kin} = \frac{1}{2}\sum_j \gamma_{jj}(\dot{B}_j, \dot{B}_j).
\tag{7}
$$

This means that if we consider the $B_j = B_j(t)$ as generalised coordinates, the associated Euler equation takes the form (see [2]):

$$
F_j = \gamma_{jj}\ddot{B}_j.
\tag{8}
$$

The force F_j in the left hand part is not defined yet; it will follow from the rigidity constraints to be discussed below. We see that for coordinates B_j, the motion equation 8 takes exactly the form of 3 when we consider γ_{jj} as generalised mass parameter. Also note that, due to the assumption of diagonality of γ, the motion equations for each of the three B_j are un-coupled. From now on we will assume that rigid bodies posses a body fixed frame with base vectors B_j such that γ is diagonal. This base can be found by diagonalising the inertia tensor of the object. For convenience we scale each of the B_j such that the corresponding γ_{jj} reduces to unity, say $|B_j| = \beta_j$, so the remaining motion equations are

$$
F_j = \ddot{B}_j.
\tag{9}
$$

Forward integration, ignoring F yields

$$
B_j(t + h) = 2B_j(t) - B_j(t - h)
\tag{10}
$$

and similarly for the centre of gravity:

$$
c(t + h) = 2c(t) - c(t - h).
\tag{11}
$$

A rigid object has six degrees of freedom (location and orientation). Our representation has twelve (the four vectors c, B_0, B_1 and B_2; assuming an object of dimension 3). So we have to impose some additional constraints that ensure that the generalised coordinates remain an orthogonal base. Using j, j' and j'' to distinguish the three base vectors we must take care that:

- $(B_{j'}, B_{j''}) = 0$, for all j

- $|B_j| = \beta_j$, for all j

The forward integration 10 of the generalised coordinates might violate these constraints, so we need to compute the values of the forces F_j from 9. We derive the F_j using Lagrange multipliers. The directions of these forces are defined beforehand: for the orthogonality, the correction on B_j has a component in the direction of $B_{(j+1)mod3}$ and one in the direction of $B_{(j+2)mod3}$. For the length constraint, the correction forces are directed along the base vector that is to be corrected. So again we can avoid to compute the Jacobian $\frac{\partial c}{\partial F}$. The *a priori* unknown magnitudes of the correction forces are represented by Lagrange multipliers. For each orthogonality constraint, we introduce the multiplier Λ_j (enforcing the constraint $(B_{j'}, B_{j''}) = 0$; note the antisymmetric naming convention for the indices. For each length constraint, we introduce the multiplier λ_j (enforcing $|B_j| = \beta_j$). Adding the appropriate terms to the motion equations of the generalised coordinates yields for B_j: (we assume the factors h^2 to be included within the values of the multipliers)

$$B_j(t + h) = 2B_j(t) - B_j(t - h) + (\Lambda_{j'} B_{j''} + \Lambda_{j''} B_{j'} + \lambda_j B_j)(t) \qquad (12)$$

From the condition that the rigidity constraint should also be satisfied for time $t + h$, we can derive equations for the values of the multipliers. In the case of the pendulum in section 2.1, we found a quadratic equation for the multiplier that could be solved without iteration; here we find six coupled quadratic equations. This means that we now have to resort to the iterative method as explained in section 2, but rather than computing and inverting the Jacobians $\frac{\partial c}{\partial F}$ we make use of the geometric meaning of the reaction forces to find linearised approximations of their magnitudes in a straightforward manner.

In the absence of any other constraint (see sections 2.3, 2.4, 2.5, 2.6) this iterative method converges extremely fast. In practice, the number of iterations is fixed to about 3 or 4.

2.3 Coupled Rigid Bodies Require Dealing with Point-to-point Constraints

In case a rigid objects moves subject to an external force F (scaled such that the factor h^2 is taken into account), we have to have a device for translating F into a set of equivalent forces on the centre of gravity and the B_j, since these are the only coordinates of our representation. The effect of F on the centre of gravity c is trivial: $F = m\ddot{c}(t)$. If F works on a given point p_i, one of the points x_i of the rigid object, it causes a torque, $(p_i - c) \times F$. The effect of this torque is going to be accounted for by introducing 3 forces, F_{Bj} on the B_j. So we have

$$\sum_j F_{Bj} = 0 \qquad (13)$$

and

$$\sum_j B_j \times F_{Bj} = (p_i - c) \times F \qquad (14)$$

This does not completely determine the F_{Bj}: we have room for additional requirements on the F_{Bj}. We may demand the F_{Bj} to be such that the rigidity constraints are still satisfied:

$$|B_j + F_{Bj}| = \beta_j; \tag{15}$$

$$(B_{j''} + F_{Bj''}, B_{j'} + F_{Bj'}) = 0. \tag{16}$$

Choosing the F_{Bj} such that they don't affect the rigidity constraints up to first order in the F_{Bj} means that the rigidity correction from section 2.2. converges fast.

If we linearize these equations, assuming the the F_{Bj} to be small we get

$$(B_j, B_j) + 2(B_j, F_{Bj}) = \beta_j{}^2; \tag{17}$$

$$(B_{j''}, B_{j'}) + (F_{Bj'}, B_{j''}) + (F_{Bj''}, B_{j'}) = 0. \tag{18}$$

Using 13, 14, 17, and 18, we can compute matrices A_j such that $F_{Bj} = A_j F$. The computation of the A_j is explained in [3].

(The linearity condition is not necessarily true. In the case of F being the force due to a PTP constraint, however, we again use the argument that F varies gradually, and a iterative approach is used to find *increments* in F_{Bj} between the previous and the current value, that *are* expected to be small. If F is an external force that is allowed to vary significantly over time, it is split in a number of small components that are accounted for subsequently within one time step.)

Applying a force F to an object means that for that object we have to do the following assignments:

$$c := c + \frac{1}{m} F \tag{19}$$

and for each j:

$$B_j := B_j + A_j F. \tag{20}$$

Note that in the derivation of the torque distribution matrices A_j, the rigidity constraints were linearised. The rigidity constraint mechanism, which works in parallel with the PTP constraint mechanism, thanks to the iterative approach, is used to restore the rigid shape of the object again, thus correcting for the ignored non-linearity.

Using these formulae, also the effect (=the displacement) of a force on one of the vertices of that object can be calculated. Using the definition of the ρ_{ij}, we have:

$$p_i := (c + \frac{1}{m} F) + \sum_j \rho_{ij}(B_j + A_j F)$$

$$:= p_i + M F, \tag{21}$$

where $M = (\frac{1}{m} I + \sum_j \rho_{ij} A_j)$.

So also the displacement of an arbitrary vertex due to the application of a force to a given location of a rigid body can be expressed using a 3×3 matrix.

So far we assumed that F was a *known* force. The same observations, however, hold for an *a priori* unknown force, such as the force in a PTP hinge (constraint). Let the two vertices that are connected via a PTP constraint be distinguished by the superscripts k and l: they belong to two different rigid objects. The matrices M for the corresponding vertices of these objects are M^k and M^l, respectively. The location of a vertex after application of the correcting PTP constraint force, F_{ptp} is denoted by a tilde (˜). We then have:

$$\tilde{p}^k = \tilde{p}^l, \text{ so}$$
$$p^k + M^k F_{ptp} = p^l - M^l F_{ptp}, \text{ and hence}$$
$$p^l - p^k = (M^k + M^l) F_{ptp} \qquad (22)$$

The point to point error in the absence of F_{ptp}, $p^l - p^k$ is known, as is matrix $M^k + M^l$, so the reaction force F_{ptp} can be calculated from 22 as $F_{ptp} = (M^k + M^l)^{-1}(p^l - p^k)$.

Although we didn't compute $M^k + M^l$ via differentiation of the constraint equation $(p^l - p^k = 0)$ with respect to F_{PTP}, this matrix does play the role of the Jacobian $\frac{\partial c}{\partial F}$.

Note that in the presence of more than two coupled rigid objects, we arrive at a coupled set of constraint force equations. As previously, the combined effect of several of such forces may be accounted for by means of iteration. Alternatively, all linearised equations may be grouped together and be solved simultaneously by means of a standard LU-decomposition method.

2.4 A Pair of Point-to-point Constraints Removes Two Degrees of Freedom

Consider two rigid objects. They are coupled with two PTP constraints, so effectively they share a line hinge. This means that (1) they have only one relative DOF left (rotation round the line through the two point pairs), as opposed to 3 relative DOF in the case of one PTP constraint; and (2) the two PTP reaction forces may contain components along this line of arbitrary, mutually opposite, magnitudes. This means that the approach from 2.3 does not work. We have to be careful to avoid the undetermined force components growing beyond boundaries, thus making the computation instable.

Let the point to point reaction forces be denoted by F_1 and F_2. If the the pair (F_1, F_2) satisfies the line hinge constraint, then so will the pair $(F_1 + \lambda e, F_2 - \lambda e)$ for any λ with e being the hinge vector, since the effects of the added terms are exactly opposite. To avoid growth of such components, we must find a way to minimize them. This can be done by forcing the components of both reaction forces in the direction of e to be the same. This yields:

$$(F_1 + \lambda e, e) = (F_2 - \lambda e, e), \text{ so}$$
$$\lambda = \frac{(F_2 - F_1, e)}{2(e, e)} \qquad (23)$$

Replacing F_1 by $F_1 + \lambda e$ and F_2 by $F_2 - \lambda e$ with λ from 23 solves the problem.

2.5 Collision Forces Result from Constraints

When a vertex of a rigid object collides with a collision plane, this plane exerts a reaction force onto that vertex that prevents the vertex from crossing the collision plane (and perhaps causes the vertex to bounce off the surface). In case of a completely inelastic collision, the result of the reaction force (which we assume to be directed perpendicular to the collision plane) is that the velocity of the vertex perpendicular to the collision plane is zero after the collision. This observation can be used to calculate the reaction force.

Let n be the normal of the collision plane, and the reaction force λn (for a yet unknown λ). Let $p(t)$ be the location of the colliding vertex at the current time stamp, and $p(t + h)$ the location at the next time stamp as it would be without application of a reaction force (so $p(t)$ and $p(t + h)$ lie at opposite sides of the collision plane). The position of the vertex after application of the reaction force will be denoted by $\tilde{p}(t + h)$ ($= p(t + h) + M\lambda n$, using 21). The (discrete) new velocity of the vertex is then given by $\tilde{p}(t + h) - p(t)$. Let, for vectors v and w, $[v]_w$ denote the component of v in the direction of w. The observation that the new velocity of the vertex perpendicular to the collision plane is zero after the collision force is applied then yields:

$$
\begin{aligned}
0 &= [\tilde{p}(t + h) - p(t)]_n \\
&= [p(t + h) + M\lambda n - p(t)]_n \\
&= [\frac{(p(t + h) + M\lambda n - p(t), n)}{(n, n)}]_n \\
&= (p(t + h) - p(t) + M\lambda n, n) \\
&= (p(t + h) - p(t), n) + \lambda(Mn, n),
\end{aligned}
\tag{24}
$$

and hence

$$
\lambda = -\frac{(p(t + h) - p(t), n)}{(Mn, n)},
\tag{25}
$$

which again was obtained without explicitly computing $(\frac{\partial c}{\partial F})^{-1}$.

So using this constraint we can find the reaction force λn for a completely inelastic collision. This force operates upon the point p, and the method from section 2.3 is used to account for the effect of this force on the entire rigid object. For an elastic collision, we only have to enlarge the reaction force (to cause the vertex' speed to be 'reflected' by the collision plane), so for an arbitrary collision we have a reaction force of $(1+\gamma)\lambda n$ for an elasticity coefficient γ which is zero for complete inelasticity and one for a completely elastic collision. Note that a more sophisticated approach should take the precise time point for the collision into account. We make a mistake here of at most h, which may cause some aliasing effects if h is relatively large.

2.6 Computing the Constraint Forces for a Point-to-curve Constraint

Consider a point p, which may be a point from a rigid object, which is constrained to move along a curve g, $g : \Re \rightarrow \Re^3$. The force between p and g may be modeled by a PTP constraint where one of the two points is an *a priori* unknown point on the curve, say $g(s)$. To account for the movement along the curve, s should be modified each frame.

Let the change in s be δ. Then δ represents the velocity along the curve. If p would move uniformly, the assignment $s := s + \delta$ would suffice to describe p's motion.

After the new position $g(s + \delta)$ is calculated, the required reaction force F_{ptp} that pulls p to $g(s + \delta)$ can be computed based on the PTP constraint.

(Notice that we cannot simply write that the direction of F_{ptp} is directed along $g(s + \delta) - (2p(t) - p(t - h))$, since pulling on $p(t)$ also causes a torque, and hence an angular acceleration to operate on the object. Instead we have to apply the method from section 2.3, using the M-matrix.)

Assume a given value for δ. Then in general the resulting F_{ptp} will contain both a normal component and a tangential component. Let the latter component be $\lambda \frac{d}{ds} g(s)$. Assume the case of a friction-less contact between p and g. Then F_{ptp} can only be perpendicular to the curve. So if we find a F_{ptp} with $\lambda \neq 0$, the starting value for δ was wrong, and a correction is e.g. $\delta := \delta - \kappa\lambda$ for some positive κ. In this manner, again an iterative algorithm is obtained to find the appropriate value for δ. This iterative process is executed in parallel with the algorithms for rigidity, PTP constraints, line hinges and collision response as explained in sections 2.2-2.5: all these algorithms work by improving the estimates for the corresponding reaction forces, and when they all converge the total collection of all reaction forces is known such that all constraints are being met.

The curve parameter s should stay within the domain of g. The current implementation in our animation system is such that, when this isn't the case, the PTC constraint is cancelled automatically. This causes e.g. a roller coaster vehicle to fly off the track in a physically correct way when it reaches the end. An animator can always ensure that the vertex doesn't leave the curve by placing collision planes on its extremes.

3 Some Quantitative Properties of The Algorithm

The algorithms dealing with constraints as outlined above have been implemented in the Eindhoven computer animation system WALT ([7]. To asses the numerical properties of the algorithm, some experiments were performed.

Experiment 1

In the first experiment the configuration consisted of one object (a cube with sides of length 2), zero gravity, and two equal forces (working in opposite directions) working on two different point-masses of the cube. These forces cause the cube to rotate with precession. During the first 1000 frames (approximately 50 full rotations) the rotational energy of the cube was measured. It follows that after the forces have accelerated the cube, all energy in the system is preserved within 4 digits of accuracy. No energy is lost during the orthogonalisation and preservation of the length of the base vectors. For this experiment there were only two iterations for the rigidity constraints per frame.

Experiment 2

Next, a PTP constraint was added to keep one vertex of a cube fixed in space. Gravity is introduced to cause a swinging motion of the cube. Again, there were only two iterations for the rigidity constraints per frame and now also only two iterations per frame for the PTP constraints. For this configuration, we found that the value of the orthogonality-preserving multiplier oscillates in a completely periodic fashion between + and - 3.1×10^{-6} and the value of the length-preserving multiplier varies in the same phase between

0 and 2.3×10^{-3}.

The magnitude of the PTP force consists of a constant contribution of about 0.09 due to gravity and a varying centripetal force with magnitude between 0 and 0.1 which depends on the instantaneous angular velocity. The error in the PTP constraint does not exceed 4.1×10^{-12}, which is probably due to numerical quantisation in the internal representation of real numbers. We also measured the total energy of the system. The observed dissipation of about 0.4% per 1000 iterations is chiefly due to the truncation error of the assignment 4.

To further explore this energy-loss, the loss of energy was also measured as a function of the number of iterations for the PTP constraints (with this number varying between 1 and 100). The value of the energy-loss turned out to be independent of the number of iterations. Also the maximum PTP-error was measured as a function of the number of iterations. Only in case of one iteration this value is significant (0.003). For larger numbers, the error is masked by the errors of the internal representation of the reals (it is of order 10^{-12} or smaller).

Experiment 3

Next, the configuration of experiment two was expanded with another cube connected to the first cube by a PTP constraint. Again, gravity causes a (chaotic) swinging motion of the two coupled cubes.

For this configuration, the maximal PTP error as a function of the number of iterations decreases exponentially from 3.6×10^{-4} for 7 iterations to $< 10^{-6}$ for 15 iterations.

The energy-loss of the system is also measured as a function of the number of applied iterations. It turns out that after approximately 15 iterations no further accuracy gain is obtained.

In figures 1 and 2 two animation fragments can be seen of somewhat more complex systems. Figure 1 models an articulated beach chair tumbling of the stairs which demonstrates the interplay between rigidity constraints, line hinges and collision response. An example of the combination of rigidity, PTC constraints and line hinges can be seen in 2 where a constellation of two linked rigid objects slides from a curved rail. Note that the topmost object is connected via two PTC constraints to the rail. The colour plates show some stills from the tumbling articulated beach chair sequence.

4 Discussion; Summary

We propose a method to implement rigid body dynamics for computer animation based on two central ingredients:

rigidity is a constraint: several approaches for rigid body simulation are based on the notion of constraints to emulate e.g. the couplings between rigid components and hinges. We take this idea one step further to consider even rigidity proper as a constraint. This reduces the formal framework for the motion equations to point mass dynamics plus algebraic constraints.

use forces only: rigidness does not occur in our motion equations proper. This means that there is no need for angular coordinates, and hence angular momentum and

92

torque need not to be represented in the model. This results both in a straightforward mathematical treatment and a transparent implementation. Moreover, these forces can be simply visualised for instructive purposes. Also, if we impose a threshold value on the applied PTP-forces, it is straightforward to have objects break apart if internal reaction forces become too large.

A less central ingredient is

use iteration: The iterative method with about 10 iterations gives sufficient performance to achieve a frame update rate of about 20 frames/second in on a sun SPARC station 10 for systems with several tens of constraints. This number of iterations is sufficient to preserve all rigidity constraints, PTP constraints and PTC constraints within visible accuracy (equivalent to about 10^{-2} relative accuracy) in all cases except fierce collisions where temporary deformations may be visible.

References

1. William Armstrong and Mark Green. The dynamics of articulated rigid bodies for purposes of animation. *The Visual Computer*, 1:231–240, 1985.
2. V.I. Arnold. *Mathematical Methods in Classical Mechanics* . Springer Verlag, New York, 1989.
3. B. Barenbrug. Using a constraint driven approach to dynamic simulation of rigid body movements in computer animation. Master's thesis, Eindhoven University of Technology, April 1994.
4. Ronen Barzel and Alan H. Barr. A Modeling System Based On Dynamic Constraints. *Computer Graphics (Proc. SIGGRAPH 88)*, 22(4):179–188, August 1988.
5. Paul M. Isaacs and Michael F. Cohen. Mixed methods for complex kinematic constraints in dynamic figure animation. *The Visual Computer*, 4(6):296–305, 1988.
6. Mathew Moore and Jane Wilhelms. Collision Detection and Response for Computer Animation. *Computer Graphics (Proc. SIGGRAPH 88)*, 22(5):289–298, August 1988.
7. C.W.A.M. van Overveld. The generalised display processor as an approach to real time interactive 3-D computer animation. *The Journal of Visualisation and Computer Animation*, 2:16–25, 1991.
8. C.W.A.M. van Overveld. A simple approximation to Rigid Body Dynamics for Computer Animation . *The Journal of Visualisation and Computer Animation*, 5:17–36, 1994.
9. Jane Wilhelms, Matthew Moore, and Robert Skinner. Dynamic animation: interaction and control. *The Visual Computer*, 4(6):283–295, 1988.
10. A. Witkin, M Gleicher, and W Welch. Interactive dynamics. *Computer Graphics ACM SIGGRAPH; special issue on 1990 symposium on interactive 3D graphics*, 24(2):11–21, March 1990.

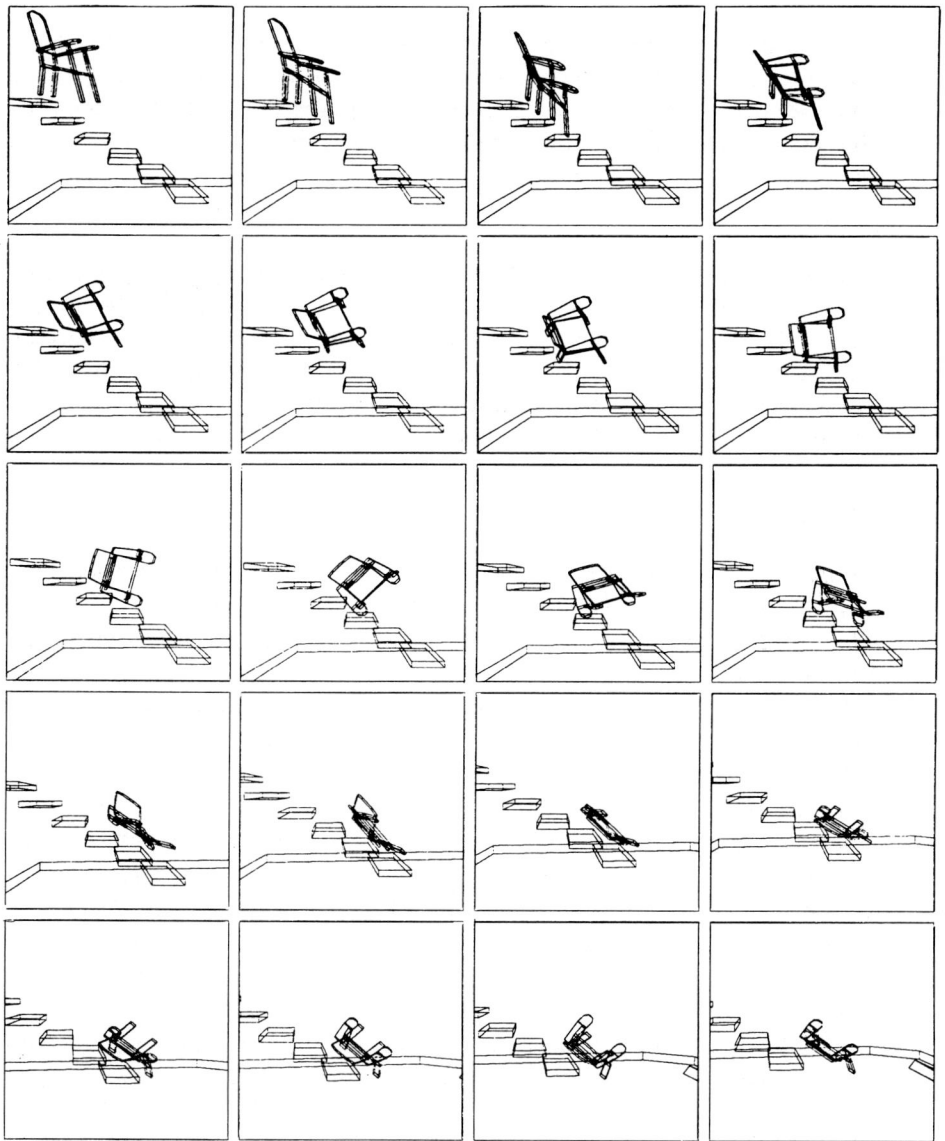

Figure 1. A tumbling articulated beach chair

94

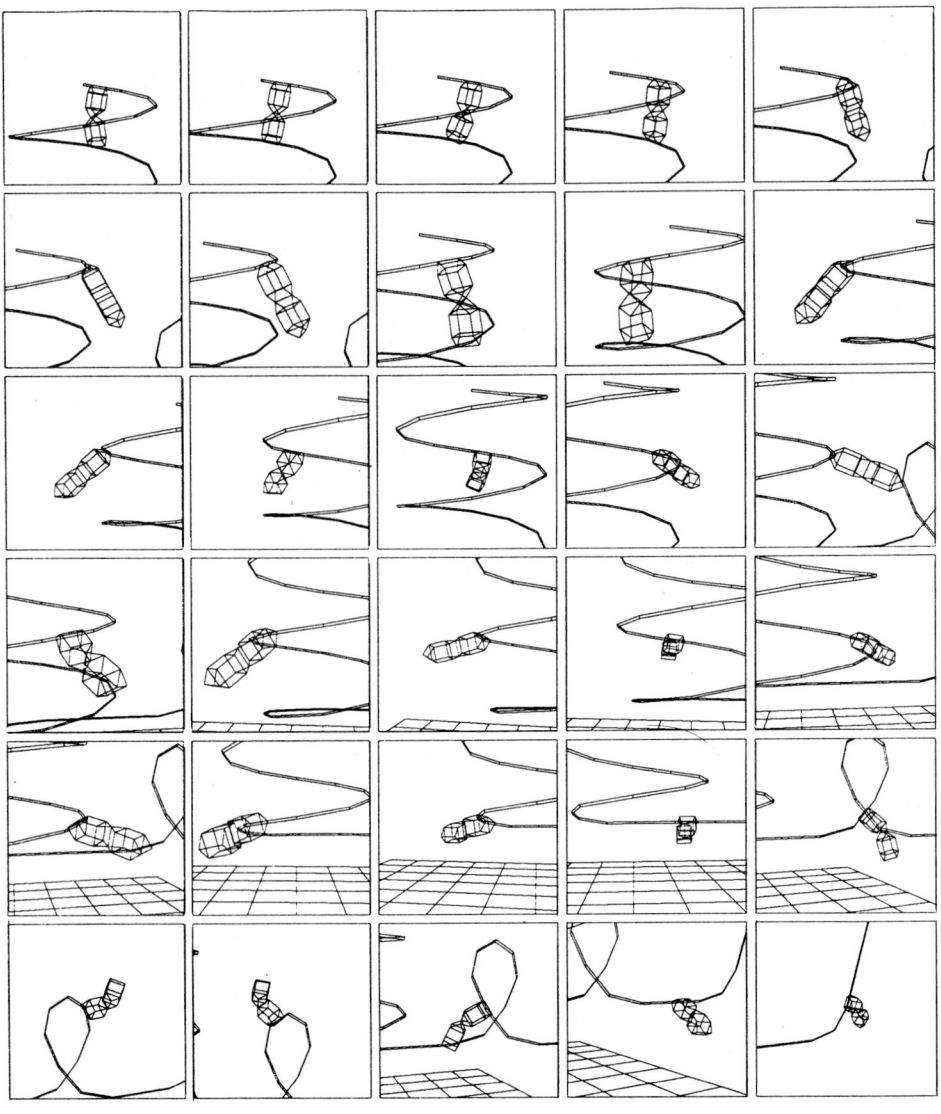

Figure 2. A simple roller coaster

Editors' Note: see Appendix, p. 227 for coloured figure of this paper

Part II:
Animating Biological Objects

Animated Texels

Fabrice Neyret

INRIA, Syntim Project
B.P. 105, 78153 Le Chesnay Cedex, France
Fabrice.Neyret@inria.fr
http://www-rocq.inria.fr/syntim/research/neyret

Abstract.

Volumetric texturing is a method dedicated to modeling complex repetitive geometries, such as grass, fur or foliage, by storing a volumetric sample to be mapped
on a surface. This representation is effective in a ray-tracing environment, giving
images with low aliasing at low cost. We show here that it can be extended to get
an easy way of animating complex repetitive geometries, like the effects produced
by the wind in a wheat field, or fur motions.

1   Introduction

Complex repetitive geometries such as grass, hair, foliage, fur, forest and so on are
a major component of the natural world, very important for the realism of synthetic
images. Many representations exist to model such objects, such as particle systems
[10, 11], L-systems [9], growing models [3], hypertextures [7], volumetric textures
[4, 5].

Animating these objects is also a very important point for realism, and is also hard
to model with classical geometric representations. One has to figure out the effects
of the wind in a wheat field, or in a foliage, the motion of a moving animal's fur,
etc. Representations dedicated to complex geometry have been generally studied for
static scenes, excepted particle systems that are re-generated at each frame. But particle
systems use an ad-hoc description based on thin trajectories, and an ad-hoc lightning
incompatible with ray-tracing. Ray-tracing is however necessary for the realism, as
shadows are important for the appearance of complex objects. Furthermore, ray-tracing
can handle most of the other object representations.

In this article, we present a method for easily modeling animated complex repetitive
geometries, in a ray-tracing context. The purpose is to handle a wide class of shapes,
and to control the animation at a global scale. This method is based on volumetric
texture representation (see section 3) and space animated deformations (see section 2).
It is detailed in section 4.

2   Animating Complex Geometry

Two dedicated kinds of approach have been previously used to give realistic animation in the scope of the 'natural look': physical or pseudo-physical models (e.g. waves on the ocean), and particles systems (e.g. waterfalls). The results are impressive, but the methods cannot be reused so well: both are monolithic, as there is no separation between the model and its animation (and even its rendering, for particles systems). It is thus difficult to introduce and animate a given usual shape in this way. Moreover, both methods take the control of the 'simulation'. As a result, it is difficult for the user to specify precisely and interactively the motions.

Another point concerns the integration of a complex object in a whole scene: a rendering algorithm can produce an integrated image of the scene if it can handle the various kinds of objects that are present. The dedicated rendering used for particles systems prevents from integrating them in a classical 3D scene (this is generally done by image composition), thus forbidding interaction like shadows.

To model a wide class of animated complex geometries in an integrated context, one has thus to keep the generality and the interactivity of the usual tools and representations, and to make the model usable by a classical rendering algorithm (e.g. ray-tracing).

Many methods can be used to animate usual objects. Space deformation approaches [2, 1] have interesting properties in the scope of complex objects, especially if they deal with bounding volumes:

• no information is needed about the object structure (e.g. skeleton) so that the surface description is sufficient,
• collisions are considerably more easy to deal with as one has only to be aware of collisions between bounding volumes,
• self-collisions are avoided if the resulting space is not self-intersecting,
• animation specifications are easy to describe interactively, with few parameters.

The other animation approaches are not adapted so well: an explicit description of the motion of each part of the objects would be complex to specify for the user, physical models and particle systems are hard to control interactively and use ad-hoc representations dedicated to animation, using articulated models needs too much degrees of freedom in the scope of complex geometry.

Therefore, space deformation methods seem to be a good approach to animate easily complex repetitive geometry. But usually such methods operate on classical geometric data (e.g. facets, patches), which are seldom used to model complex geometry and may be costly for a large database, where a great amount of useless facets are transformed in any case (moreover, a complex object can have more facets than visible pixels). We adapt the approach in order to deal with a more efficient representation than classical geometry.

3 Modeling Complex Geometry

We propose to use the volumetric textures representation instead of classical geometry. Volumetric textures can represent geometry with every 3D effects and have interesting properties to model complex repetitive objects concerning efficiency and aliasing as described in [5], and work in a ray-tracing context. Volumetric texturing, first introduced by Kajiya et al [4], is based on the mapping of a volumetric 3D sample called *reference volume* over a surface (e.g. a lawn covering a hill, or fur on an animal). This allows to separate the specification of the local aspect of the geometry (e.g. weed blades) and the specification of its large scale shape (e.g. hill): one needs not to explicitly build each detail of the complex object everywhere it lays.

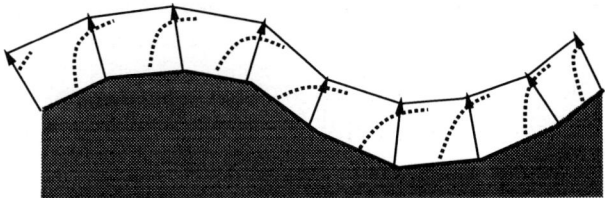

In our representation [5], the reference volume is encoded by an octree of voxels, in a multiscaling purpose. Each voxel contains a density of occupation, and a simplified reflectance model which simulates the piece of surface that is supposed to occupy this area of space. This model represents the normal distribution of the piece of surface (that otherwise would have been represented by several small facets), and can be filtered like density in order to obtain the rougher resolutions of the octree. This allows a correct and efficient multiscale representation of the object encoded in the reference volume, which can be rendered with few aliasing using only one ray per pixel (other level of detail approaches like facets decimation do not preserve the reflectance, e.g. a corrugated iron sheet will be filtered into a flat object). Usual representations with facets need quite more information than what can be really seen (e.g. leaves on the trees in a forest), which implies extra cost concerning ray intersection, storage, aliasing and modelization work.

The repeated and deformed copies of the reference volume mapped over the underlying surface are called *texels*, which are thus a space deformation of the reference volume. Unlike usual deformation methods, no transformations of the objects are effectively computed (which may be very costly for complex geometry): the deformation is formal, being achieved at rendering time by converting the rays crossing the deformed area into the reference volume, thus directly using the objet description without having to modify it. This approach saves computation as a complex object can have more details than visible pixels. It also allows the use of representations that cannot be explicitly space-deformed (e.g. implicit functions, CSG) since no transformations are effectively computed.

This also simplifies the building of a scene without intersections: instead of dealing with collisions between all the represented objects (e.g. weed blades on a hill), the user has just to build a correct sample. Then the texel mapping imposes the deformations so that the texels lay upon a surface and stick to one another without overlapping.

4 Animating Texels

As explained in the previous section our complex geometry model is volumetric textures, defined by the mapping with space-deformations of a reference volume onto a surface. Animation of the model is done on the mapping parameters, mainly by controlling the vertical edges of the texels (initially normal to the underlying surface), which determines the texels' deformation: pressure on the four vertical edges of a texel defines the deformation of the box bounding the texel, which causes the deformation of its content as for FFD [12].

- For a deformable surface like a cloth object, the texels' 'thick skin' covering it naturally follows its deformation, as a continuous material. We study this case in subsection 4.1.

- Otherwise, on a rigid surface, explicit motions can be generated by a force field acting on the vertical edges, thus deforming the texels. We deal with this in subsection 4.2.

- Another animation way can be used with texels: in a cartoon-like approach, successive steps of a simple motion (like oscillations of leaves in foliage) can be sampled in few separated volumes, successively used along time. We consider this case in subsection 4.3.

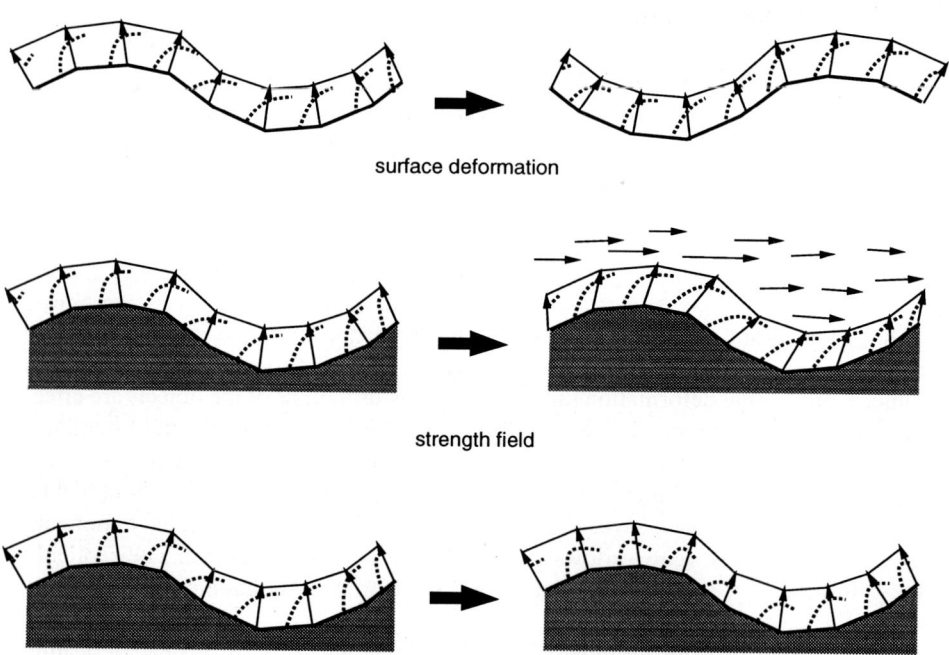

surface deformation

strength field

texel modification

Figure 1: The three ways of animating texels.

For a realistic animation, the three methods can be blended to take into account the different scales of motion: the fur on the skin of a running animal follows the deformation of the animated body, it makes waves according to acceleration and inertia, and maybe the pils locally oscillate a bit inside the texels. Similarly for a tree in the wind, the surface of each main branch associated to its bough is geometrically deformed, foliage waves with the wind, and leaves locally oscillate inside the texels.

4.1 Texels on an Animated Surface

In usual implementations, each texel sticks to a surface element which is a bilinear patch. The four vertical edges of the texel follow a vector stored at the four vertices, that can be equal to the normal or 'combed' in a given direction. A texel is thus a trilinear deformation of the cubic reference volume, and texels are naturally sticking to each others. (More complicated deformations may be used, but one has to be aware of the ray intersection cost while rendering.)

Texel animation is simply achieved by taking into account the new surface and normals at each time step. One has just to take care of the maximum curvature of the surface, which can bring to degenerated deformations when the curvature radius is near or less than the thickness of texels.

In figure 4 (see Appendix), a volumetric pattern representing a piece of scaffolding has been mapped onto a flag animated by a non-linear mass-spring model[1]. The texels thicken the flag, and follow continuously its deformations.

4.2 Texels Animated by a Force Field

The deformation of the texels can be explicitly controlled by the motion of the vertical edges: this motion can be generated by a force field (e.g. Laplace field [15], stochastic flow [13]) acting on the vertical edges, or by a dynamic scheme (e.g. mass-spring, elasticity [14]) linking the top of the vertical edges.

In figure 3 (see Appendix), we present a lawn in the wind. A texel contains 16 weed blades. The motion is generated by an animated force field acting on the normals. This field $\vec{F}(M, t)$ models a gust of wind combined with a random jittering, that are encoded by two separated fields. Given the propagation direction $\vec{F}/\|\vec{F}\|$, The wind intensity at point M is obtained by the wave propagation expression $f(2\pi \frac{\vec{F}.\vec{M}}{\lambda} - w.t)$ (the origin is arbitrary).

For the pure wind component, $f()$ is a continuous periodic function for which the chosen pattern has a sudden attack and a slow falling (see figure 2). The jittering component is built in the orthogonal direction of the wind, using for the intensity a fractal solid noise function as $f()$ in the propagation expression. *Solid noise*, usually used for solid texturing [6], gives a signal which is at the same time continuous, derivable, and pseudo-random. The pseudo-frequency of the noise function can be controlled, and is used to define a fractal function called *turbulence*, more realistic for both texturing and random motion. The resulting lightning and shadow waves increase the realism of the motion.

---

[1]Thanks are due to Xavier Provot [8] for his flag model.

102

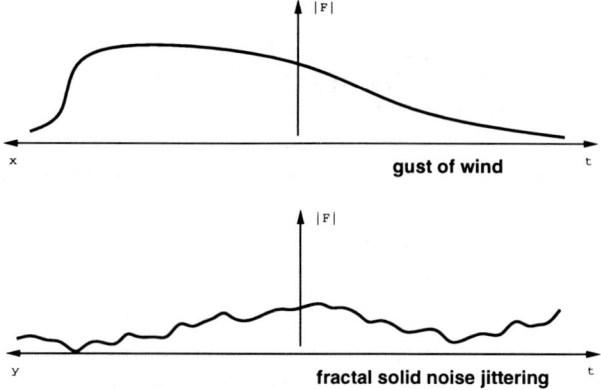

Figure 2: wind intensity in the x and y horizontal directions.

4.3 Animated Texels Content

Cartoon animation is based on switching sampled stages of a motion. This can also be used in 3D for simple or quick motions like oscillations of parts of the object encoded in the volumetric texture: some states are encoded in few separated volumes, successively used along the time (a single volume can also be modified after each step).

However, this increases the cost as additive storage or volume recomputation are needed. So it has to be used only for specific effects with very simple motions, like oscillations of leaves in foliage. This is also a way to break the regularity of the texel mapping: the phase of this loop animation can be randomly distributed along the surface.

5 Conclusion

Animated volumetric textures provide a tool adapted for animated complex repetitive geometries, which was not available before, and handle a wide class of repeated objects. This is done in a convenient way, at the scale adapted to the problem in the spirit of volumetric textures, and easily controlled in the spirit of space deformations.

The convenience is inherited from the different domains used to constitute the volumetric texture model:

- as a space deformation approach, animation can be easily interactively specified by the deformation of the bounding boxes, and intersection problems are limited to the intersection of the boxes.

- as a textural approach, the geometry encoded in texels sticks automatically to an underlying surface and follows its deformations.

- as a representation dedicated to complex repetitive geometry in a ray-tracing context, it can provide realistic results with low aliasing and low cost.

References

1. D. Bechmann. Space deformation models survey. *Computer & Graphics*, 18(4):571–586, July–August 1994.

2. Sabine Coquillart and Pierre Jancène. Animated free-form deformation: An interactive animation technique. In Thomas W. Sederberg, editor, *Computer Graphics (SIGGRAPH '91 Proceedings)*, volume 25, pages 23–26, July 1991.

3. Phillippe de Reffye, Claude Edelin, Jean Françon, Marc Jaeger, and Claude Puech. Plant models faithful to botanical structure and development. In John Dill, editor, *Computer Graphics (SIGGRAPH '88 Proceedings)*, volume 22(4), pages 151–158.

4. James T. Kajiya and Timothy L. Kay. Rendering fur with three dimensional textures. In Jeffrey Lane, editor, *Computer Graphics (SIGGRAPH '89 Proceedings)*, volume 23(3), pages 271–280, July 1989.

5. Fabrice Neyret. A general and multiscale method for volumetric textures. In *Graphics Interface'95 Proceedings*, May 1995.

6. Ken Perlin. An image synthesizer. In B. A. Barsky, editor, *Computer Graphics (SIGGRAPH '85 Proceedings)*, volume 19(3), pages 287–296, July 1985.

7. Ken Perlin and Eric M. Hoffert. Hypertexture. In Jeffrey Lane, editor, *Computer Graphics (SIGGRAPH '89 Proceedings)*, volume 23(3), pages 253–262.

8. Xavier Provot. Deformation constraints in a mass-spring model to describe rigid cloth behavior. In *Graphics Interface'95 Proceedings*, May 1995.

9. Przemyslaw Prusinkiewicz, Mark James, and Radomír Měch. Synthetic topiary. In Andrew Glassner, editor, *Computer Graphics (SIGGRAPH '94 Proceedings)*, pages 351–358, July 1994.

10. W. T. Reeves. Particle systems – a technique for modeling a class of fuzzy objects. *ACM Trans. Graphics*, 2:91–108, April 1983.

11. William T. Reeves and Ricki Blau. Approximate and probabilistic algorithms for shading and rendering structured particle systems. In B. A. Barsky, editor, *Computer Graphics (SIGGRAPH '85 Proceedings)*, volume 19(3), pages 313–322, July 1985.

12. Thomas W. Sederberg and Scott R. Parry. Free-form deformation of solid geometric models. In David C. Evans and Russell J. Athay, editors, *Computer Graphics (SIGGRAPH '86 Proceedings)*, volume 20, pages 151–160, August 1986.

13. Mikio Shinya and Alain Fournier. Stochastic motion - motion under the influence of wind. In A.C. Kilgour and L. Kjelldahl, editors, *Computer Graphics Forum (Eurographics '92)*, volume 11(3), pages 119–128, September 1992.

14. Demetri Terzopoulos and Kurt Fleischer. Modeling inelastic deformation: Viscoelasticity, plasticity, fracture. In John Dill, editor, *Computer Graphics (SIGGRAPH '88 Proceedings)*, volume 22, pages 269–278, August 1988.

15. Jakub Wejchert and David Haumann. Animation aerodynamics. In Thomas W. Sederberg, editor, *Computer Graphics (SIGGRAPH '91 Proceedings)*, volume 25, pages 19–22, July 1991.

Editors' Note: see Appendix, p. 228 for coloured figures of this paper

A study of basic tools for simulating metamorphoses of subdivided 2D and 3D objects.
Applications to the internal growing of wood and to the simulation of the growing of fishes.

O. Terraz[*], P. Lienhardt[**]

[*] LSIIT, URA CNRS 1871, Université Louis Pasteur, 7 rue René Descartes, 67084 Strasbourg Cedex, France. e-mail: terraz@dpt-info.u-strasbg.fr
[**] SIC (IRCOM, URA CNRS 356), Université de Poitiers, 40 av. du Recteur Pineau, 86022 Poitiers Cedex, France. e-mail: lienhard@matpts.univ-poitiers.fr

Abstract. Many topology-based animation methods have been proposed for simulating natural phenomena, as the growing of plants. These methods allow one to simulate metamorphoses, i.e. evolutions during which not only the shape, but also the constitution of objects are modified. Most studies deal with metamorphoses of topologically 1-and 2-dimensional objects, for simulating the growing of trees and vegetal organs (leaves, flowers). Few studies deal with metamorphoses of topologically 3-dimensional objects, and generally for very particular applications. In order to simulate metamorphoses of subdivided 2- and 3-dimensional objects, we have developed and experimented basic tools which generalize mechanisms defined for simulating evolutions of lower-dimensional objects. We describe this approach, and experiments about the simulation of the "internal" growing of a part of a tree, and about the simulation of the growing of (the external surfaces of) fishes.

Key-words : Animation, simulation of natural phenomena, metamorphoses, subdivisions of geometric spaces, image synthesis.

1.- Introduction

We are interested in simulating *metamorphoses* of real objects, i.e. evolutions which consist in deformations of object shapes, but mainly in strong modifications of object constitutions : for instance, new parts of a plant or an animal often appear during its growing.

For this purpose, we have studied and developed some basic tools [Terr94], and we are experimenting them for simulating natural phenomena as the internal growing of wood and the growing of fishes. The basic principles on which our work is based are not new, and they have been used in many methods, mainly topology-based ones [CL92], [FPB90], [Lien88], [PHM93], [PL90], [Reev83], [REFJP88] ; see for instance [HA92], [Luci91] and [FL94] for synthetic presentations of these works).

Topology-based methods share common basic principles, which are :
• Methods are based on a double discretization of time and space. A metamorphosis is handled as a discrete sequence of objects, each of them corresponding to a step of the animation. Natural objects are often structured ones: one can distinguish several parts having their own characteristics (anatomy, function, geometric or mechanical properties, etc). From a geometric point of view, such objects are subdivisions (i.e. partitions into cells: vertices, edges, faces, volumes). Moreover, higher-level parts of objects can be distinguished, i.e. "coherent" sets of cells, according to some property (for instance, animals or plants are structured into organs, etc.).
• Animations are controlled by scripts and scenarii. For simulating metamorphoses of a natural object, one can handle all its parts (i.e. cells, but also higher-level parts), each one having its own associated script. According to these scripts, the "states" of the parts will evolve, new parts will appear, other ones will disappear, etc. (note that a new part has to appear with its associated script). Main related problems are the following ones. Parts are strongly dependent: for instance, since they make a subdivision, the modification of a part often implies modifications of other parts. Since there usually exist many and many parts, it is not possible to associate a proper script with each of them. In fact, since objects are structured ones, it is often possible to conceive scripts for higher-level parts, which control lower-level parts (an alternative way consists in associating a single parameterized script with all low-level parts which correspond to a high-level one) : cf. hierarchies of particle systems, most studies about the simulation of the growing of vegetal trees, etc. A consequence is a strong reduction of the number of "active" parts and of the disparity of scripts (see for instance [Reev83], [PHM93], [REFJP88]).

Most topology-based animation methods have been developed in order to simulate metamorphoses of topologically 0- and 1--dimensional objects (corpuscular objects, trees, etc.). Less methods have been conceived for metamorphoses of surface-like objects: generally, these methods are specialized ones, for instance for simulating metamorphoses of vegetal leaves handled as particular subdivisions of planar surfaces [Lien88], [CL92]. And simulating metamorphoses of subdivided volumes is still more difficult[1] [FPB90]. In fact, the control of metamorphoses of such objects is more complex than for lower-dimensional objects. Encountered problems are due to the complexity of the objects[2], and to the fact that, if objects are intrinsically complex, the control of their metamorphoses is complex too. We think that it is necessary, for simulating many natural phenomena, to be able to simulate metamorphoses of topologically 3D objects. For instance, it is well-known that wood is composed by *age-rings*, new age-rings appear during the growth of a tree, increasing the thickness of trunk and branches. From a topological point of view, age-rings are volumes.

---

[1] Many methods simulate metamorphoses of "skeletons" of objects, but not metamorphoses of the objects themselves. For instance, Reynods models a set of birds by using particle systems in order to control the animation : each bird (i.e. a 3-dimensional object) is controlled through a representative point (i.e. a 0-dimensional object) [Reyn87].

[2] This is well-known in geometric modeling : many works still deal with modeling subdivisions of 3-dimensional spaces.

We have have tried to generalize classical mechanisms used in topology-based methods for simulating metamorphoses of various subdivided and structured 2D and 3D objects. Based upon a geometric model for representing subdivided 2- and 3-dimensional objects, we have developed a set of basic tools, on which an animation software has been conceived. More precisely, 2 and 3-dimensional generalized maps [Lien94] are used in order to represent subdivided 2- and 3-dimensional objects. The definition of generalized maps is based on a single type of basic elements on which 4 applications act, and all notions as cells, connected components, etc. are defined through a single notion of *orbit*. A general mechanism has been elaborated in order to structure generalized maps, providing thus a higher-level control of animations. It is in fact a simple generalization of the orbit notion, which has been easily implemented. Most examples handle objects which are structured using *filiation trees*. From a static point of view, a filiation tree corresponds to a skeleton of the modeled object; From a dynamic point of view, it corresponds to the growth directions of the object. This structure is a generalization of that used in other topology-based methods (cf. [CL92], for instance). Its main interest is the fact that the control of the metamorphosis of a 2- or 3-dimensional object mainly consists in controlling a metamorphosis of a 1-dimensional object. Scripts are often context-dependent and parameterized, main parameters being temporal ones, attributes associated with object parts, computed parameters.

Examples of simulations of metamorphoses of subdivided 2- and 3-dimensional have been realized. We present here a simulation of the (simplified) internal growing of wood and a simulation of the growing of (the external surfaces of) fishes, in order to explain our approach (other examples are discussed in [Terr94] and [TL93]). According to the classification of animation systems into levels [Zelt85], our approach is located at an animator level. In fact, an animation is controlled by a program. According to the classification of animation models [Luci91] [HA92], examples discussed here are based on internal behavioural models, based on a botanical study of the internal growing of wood and on the study of the anatomy of fishes.

So, we do not define here a new geometric model, and we do not define a new type of animation system. Although we insist about difficulties related to the topological dimension of objects, the field here is not geometric modeling : geometric models and operations have been defined for handling this type of objects, and this is not our goal here. The adressed problem is *control*. Due to the difficulties quoted above, a first basic question we try to answer to is the following one : is it possible to control metamorphoses of such complex objects, using classical mechanisms (i.e. scripts associated with parts of objects).

This work is based on previous ones. The geometric model is presented in detail in [Lien94], and it is compared with other geometric models in [Lien91]. An approach for simulating metamorphoses of subdivided planar surfaces (structured in a predefined way), applied to the simulation of the growing of vegetal organs, is discussed in [LF87] and [Lien88], and other applications are presented in [CL92]. A first experiment about the simulation of metamorphoses of non-natural surface-like objects is presented in [TL93].

Basic tools are described in section 2, and their use for the simulation of the interal growing of wood is explained. A more elaborated use of these mechanisms is presented in section 3, for simulating the growing of fishes. Conclusions and possible developments are discussed in section 4.

2.- Basic mechanisms of control: an application to the internal growth of wood

A short analysis of tree growth and wood structure is presented in section 2.1. The basic principles of our method are introduced in section 2.2, and first results of simulations are presented in section 2.3.

2.1.– Analysis of the "internal" growth of wood

Since several years, numerous studies deal with modeling vegetal trees and simulating tree growth [AK84], [Bloo85], [EVJA89], [Jaeg87], [PHM93], [RDB90], [REFJ88] (see also [Fran91] and [PL90] for a survey of these works). For instance, the approach of de Reffye and al. is the following. A vegetal tree is composed by axes (trunk, branches) and organs (leaves, flowers, fruits). Each axis is composed by nodes (where leaves and buds are inserted) and internodes (parts of the tree between two consecutive nodes) : cf. figure 1. Nodes and internodes are parts of growth units: a growth unit is a set of internodes which are created within a bud. Growth units are parts of axes: the trunk is the axis of order 1, main branches are axes of order 2, etc. The principle consists in simulating the activity of meristems, which are embryonic tissues, origins of the development of the plant and of its organs. A vegetal tree is modeled by a tree (in the meaning of graph theory), which is, from a topological point of view, a 1-dimensional object : a vertex (resp. an edge) is associated with each node (resp. with each internode). In fact, this tree models a "skeleton" of the vegetal tree. A 3-dimensional tree (in a topological meaning) is obtained by associating 3D shapes (cylinders, for instance) with edges.

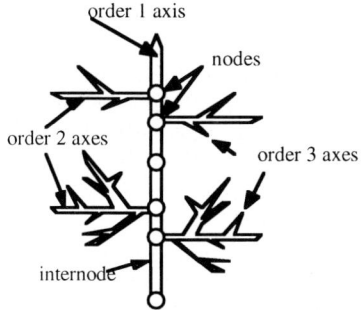

Figure 1.- Structure of a vegetal tree.

In order to simulate the "internal" growing of a vegetal tree, we consider that an axis is made of "woody piles" (i.e. age-rings : cf. figure 2.d). The length and the thickness of an axis are increased during its growing : new internodes (resp. new age-rings) appear, and their lengths (resp. their thicknesses) increase during time. Growth directions are represented in figure 2. Usually, age-ring thickness is not constant around the circumference of the axis.

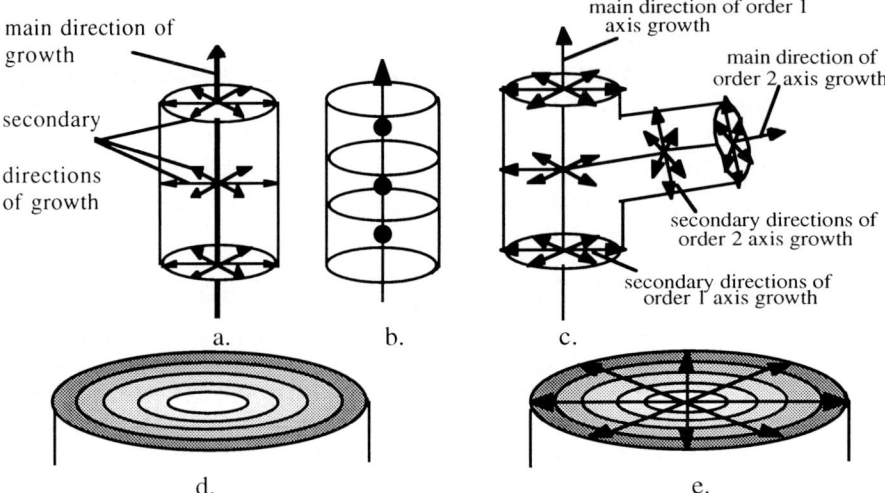

Figure 2.- Structure and growth directions of a trunk. a.– The main growth direction corresponds to the elongation of the trunk, due to the activity of a "main" meristem. Secondary growth directions correspond to the increasing of the trunk thickness, due to the activities of secondary meristems. b.– The trunk is a "pile" of internodes, here symbolized by a pile of cylinders. A 1-dimensional "squeleton" is added, where each vertex corresponds to an internode, an edge symbolizes adjacency between two internodes, and the arrow orientation symbolizes the order according to which internodes are created. c.- Growth directions in a part of a tree, composed by a part of a trunk on which a branch is inserted. d.– Internal structure (age-rings). e.– Growth directions correspond to thickness increasing, that is the order according to which age-rings are created.

From a geometric point of view, a pile of age-rings is, at a macroscopic level, a subdivided 3-dimensional object: the most internal part of the trunk (resp. age-rings around it) is approximately a cylinder (resp. full torii) [BJL93]. The trunk growth schematically consists in a sequence of creations of new volumes, adjacent to the previous ones (modification of the trunk structure) and in simultaneous modifications of geometric dimensions (length, thickness) of volumes.

2.2.– Method

The geometric model and basic construction operations are presented in section 2.2.1. Tools defined for controlling metamorphoses, and their application for simulating the growing of wood, are presented in section 2.2.2.

2.2.1.– Subdivisions of 3-dimensional spaces

For topology-based geometric modeling, a subdivided object is represented by a combinatorial model which describes its topology (intuitively its structure, i.e.

mainly the cells and their incidence relations), and by an embedding model which describes its location into the 3-dimensional euclidean space E^3 (intuitively its shape), its photometric embedding (its aspect), etc.

Topology. In order to represent the topology of 3-dimensional subdivisions, we use 3-dimensional generalized maps, or 3-G-maps [Lien94]. This model allows one to represent the topology of any subdivisions of any 3-dimensional manifolds, orientable or not, with or without boundaries. From a technical point of view, and due to the definition itself of G-maps, this model presents some advantages, simplifying the definition of tools and mechanisms which are useful for simulating metamorphoses of subdivided 3-dimensional objects, and for their implementation (cf. section 2.2.2).

Informally, a subdivision is a set of cells of different dimensions, on which boundary relations are defined. G-maps (and other topological models) model the topology of a subdivision by using a single type of basic elements (*darts*) on which applications are defined. According to Brisson's definition [Bris89], a dart corresponds to a 4-tuple (vertex, edge, face, volume) of incident cells, i.e. the face (resp. the edge, the vertex) is a part of the boundary of the volume (resp. of the face, of the edge). Four bijections α_i (for i = 0, 1, 2 or 3) act on these basic elements, and associate an other 4-tuple with each 4-tuple, such that the two 4-tuples differ by one cell. More precisely, the image of 4-tuple (s,a,f,v) is (s',a,f,v) (resp. (s,a',f,v), (s,a,f',v), (s,a,f,v')) by α_0 (resp. α_1, α_2, α_3), such that s' (resp. a', f', v') is the single vertex (resp. the single edge, the single face, the single volume) incident to the other cells of the 4-tuple (cf. figure 3, showing a 2-dimensional example).

All notions related to subdivisions (cells, connected components, orientation, etc.) are defined using a single *orbit* notion. The orbit of a dart, related to a set of applications, is the set of all darts which can be computed by applying *any* composition of these applications : cf. figure 3 (see [BDFL93] and [Lien94] for more details).

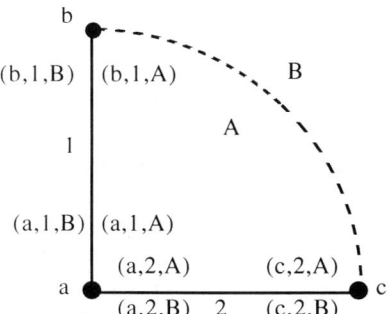

Figure 3. A subdivision of the plane : 3 vertices a, b and c, 2 edges 1 and 2, and 2 faces A and B are represented. Its topology is represented by a set of 3-tuples (vertex,edge,face), on which 3 bijections are defined. The image of (a,2,A) by bijection of index 0 (resp. 1, 2) is (c,2,A) (resp. (a,1,A), (a,2,B)). A vertex (resp. an edge, a face) is the set of 3-tuples which share this cell, i.e. the set of all 3-tuples which can be computed by applying any composition of bijections of indices 1 and 2 (resp. 0 and 2, 0 and 1).

110

Embedding. Here, 3-G-maps are linearly embedded into E^3, by associating a point of E^3 with each vertex. Embeddings of edges, faces and volumes is deduced from vertex embedding in a classical way (an edge is embedded as a segment, whose extremities are the points associated with the vertices incident to the edge, etc.). Photometric embedding is defined by associating photometric attributes with faces and edges : reflectance (diffuse, specular and ambient), emission, shininess, transparency.

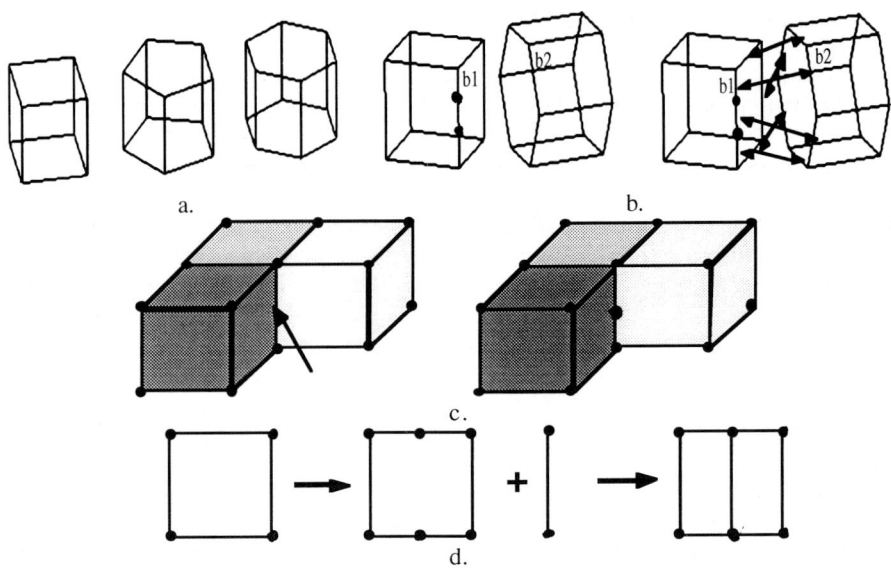

Figure 4.- In order to simplify, darts and applications are not explicitly represented. a.- Creating a volume, such that the degree of the extremity faces is 4, 5, 6. b.- Identification of non isomorphic faces. Left.– The two faces which have to be identified, and the two darts which are arguments of the operation. The initial degree of the face on the left (resp. on the right) is 4 (resp. 6). First step: The operation for splitting an edge is applied two times to the edge incident to dart b1. The faces are now isomorphic. Right.– Second step: Faces are identified. c. Splitting an edge. Left.– The arrow shows the edge which has to be split. Right.– Result of the operation. d. Splitting a face. Left.– Initial face. Middle.– Splitting edges and adding an edge. Right.– Result.

Basic operations. Numerous basic and higher-level operations have been defined for handling G-maps: cf. [BDFL93b], [Bori91], [Dufo91], [Duf2], [Lien94]. Here, only four simple and classical operations are used (cf. figure 4):
• *Creating a "cylindrical" volume.* The two bases of this cylinder are faces, such that the degree of each face is k (the degree of a face is the number of edges which belong to its boundary). These bases are referred as "extremity" faces, other faces being "lateral" ones. This operation is similar to an extrusion of a face of degree k. This operation creates two faces of degree k and k faces of degree 4: k is the parameter of the operation, and its result is a dart of an extremity face.
• *Identifying two faces.* First, this operation checks the degrees of the faces which have to be identified. If the faces are not isomorphic (if their degrees are not equal), the boundaries of the faces are modified by splitting edges (cf. following

operation). At last, the faces are identified (this is achieved by a simple modification of bijection α_3 for the darts of the faces). Two darts are the parameters of this application (one dart for each face).
• *Splitting an edge*, by inserting a vertex. One dart is the argument of the operation.
• *Splitting a face*. This operation consists in splitting two edges which are incident to a face, and in adding a new edge which extremities are the two new vertices. Two darts are the arguments of the operation.

An operation which *creates a volume on a face* is defined. It is a composition of basic operations. Given a dart incident to a face of degree k, it consists in creating a cylindrical volume, such that the degrees of the extremity faces are also k, and in identifying one of these extremity faces with the face incident to the dart.

In fact, for other experiments, other operations have been used, mainly the inverse operations of that described above. Implementation of embedded G-maps and of basic operations is detailed in [Terr94].

2.2.2.– Control of metamorphoses

• General mechanisms

Our approach, as other topology-based methods, is based on a double discretization according to time and space. Discrete time is symbolized by a global variable (the *clock*), increased at each step. A metamorphosis is modeled by a sequence of objects. Each object is a 3-dimensional subdivision structured into sub-objects, and attributes can be associated with sub-objects. Evolution is controlled by scripts associated with sub-objects.

Structure. Due to the definition of G-maps, we have developed a single mechanism, which allows one to define structures of objects into sub-objects of higher-level than cells. In fact, this mechanism is based on a simple generalization of the orbit notion :
• Attributes can be associated with darts or previously-defined sub-objects, for instance temporal attributes (e.g. the date of creation, and, consequenty, the age). Other attributes which have been experimented (order, filiation) are described below. These attributes can be applications defined on darts: for instance, applications which define the boundaries of G-maps can be easily deduced from bijections α_i [Lien94]. Since all sub-objects are formally defined as orbits of darts related to sets of applications, attributes which are associated with sub-objects are in practice associated with darts (with a *unique* representative dart for most cases : cf. [Terr94]).
• A set of sub-objects is defined by a selecting function (which usually cheks attributes of darts), and by a set of pre-defined applications. A sub-object is an orbit of a dart (which satisfies the selecting function) related to the set of applications. From a technical point of view, a single dart traversal operation (similar to a graph traversal) is employed in order to compute orbits (parameters are the names of applications and selecting function), simplifying thus the implementation.

Structure based on a filiation tree (growth directions)
We mainly use a structure based on the notion of *filiation tree*, which is quite a classical one for topology-based methods, used for instance by Chen et al. for

simulating metamorphoses of vegetal leaves [CL92] (the filiation tree corresponds to the "tree" of nervures of a leaf : the control of a leaf metamorphosis is mainly exerted through this tree). The idea is here similar. The main difference consists in the fact that, for leaves, the tree is explicit (nervures are composed by edges and vertices), though it is implicit here (relations between volumes are established during the growth, making a "tree of volumes". In fact, the filiation notion is here a relation between two volumes, such that the script associated with one volume implies the generation of the other one. As other relations between sub-objects, it is represented by an application which acts on darts. More precisely, the filiation relation is established when applying the operation for creating a volume on a face: it associates the darts of the initial face with the darts of the face which is created and identified with it. In order to warrant consistency when using a filiation tree, all volumes (the initial one excepted) have to be created by applying this operation. The name of the structure is due to the fact that we can deduce a tree (in the meaning of Graph Theory) by associating a vertex with each volume, and an edge with a set of two volumes related by filiation. More formally, a "filiation tree" is a connected component of the G-map composed by the set of all darts and by bijections α_0, α_1, α_2, and by the filiation application: cf. figure 5. Generally, each tree is oriented by distinguishing a root (i.e. one of its volume). Often, the initial object of a metamorphosis is composed by a single volume, which is root of the filiation trees of all generated objects.

Moreover, filiation trees are structured into axes of different order (each volume has an "order" attribute). Each connected component of the G-map composed by the set of all darts incident to volumes of a given order and by the bijections α_0, α_1, α_2, and by the filiation application, is an axis of this order. The tree being oriented, axes are oriented too. In order to simplify the control of metamorphoses (cf. below), axes have an *origin* face and an *extremity* face, other faces being *lateral* ones.

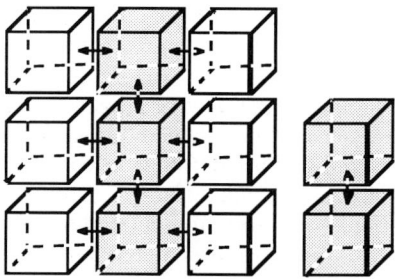

Figure 5.- Structure based on filiation trees. Eleven volumes have been created, and filiation relations are symbolized by arrows. This object contains two filiation trees. An order is associated with each volume (1 for the grey, 2 for the other ones) ; so the trees are structured into axes. Trees contain two axes of order 1 (one is composed by 3 volumes, the other by 2 volumes), and six axes of order 2 (each one being composed by a single volume).

Computing geometric embedding using filiation trees. The relative shape at one step, or deformations, are controlled by using a classical hierarchized mechanism, which is applied at each step of the animation.

Reference system.

As for particle systems [Reev83] and modular maps [Lien88] for instance, each volume has an associated reference system. More precisely, each volume has geometric attributes (3 angles, a translation ratio). Reference system (O,i,j,k) associated with a volume is computed, according to its associated attributes, by applying 3 rotations and a translation to the reference system (O',i',j',k') associated to the "father"-volume in the filiation tree (the three angles define rotations around axes (O',i'), (O',j'), (O',k'), and the translation ratio defines a translation along vector i).

Shape of the cell : default embedding.

Each volume has three associated scaling ratios h, h' and h", which implicitly defines its shape. Suppose that the volume is a cylindrical one, such that the degree of the extremity faces is dk. In order to compute the default embedding of the faces of the boundary of the volume, a reference system (O',i',j',k') is computed for each face, according to reference system (O,i,j,k) and scaling ratios h, h' and h". Reference systems associated with lateral faces are computed by varying a rotation angle around axis (O,i) in order to get a uniform distribution according to dk, and by applying at last a rotation around axis (O,j). Scaling ratios h' and h" are used in order to compute the origins of these reference systems. Scaling ratio h is used in order to compute the origins of the reference systems which are associated with extremity faces : cf. figures 6 and 7. If the volume is not a cylindrical one, its default embedding is computed in a similar way, by simple extensions of this technique.

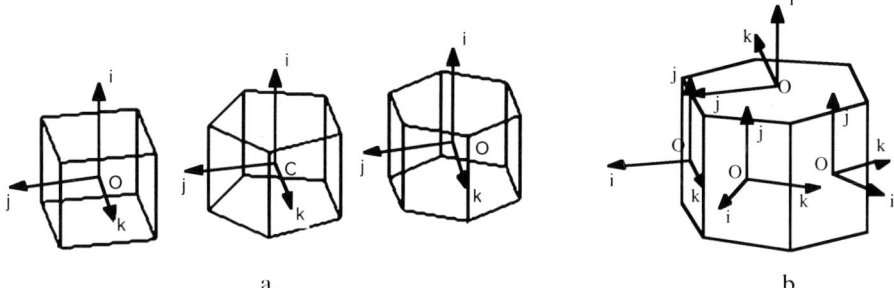

a.   b.

Figure 6.- a.– Default embedding of volumes, such that the degrees of their extremity faces are 4, 5, 6 (all scaling ratios are equal to 1). The reference system associated with the volume is represented. b.– Default embedding of a volume, such that the degree of its extremity faces is 6. The reference systems associated with the faces are represented.

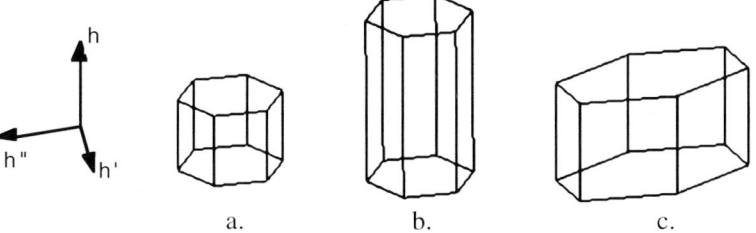

a.   b.   c.

Figure 7.- Default embedding of a volume (degree of its extremity faces is 6). a.– Scaling ratios are h = h' = h" = 1.   b.– h = 2, h' = h" = 1.   c.– h = 1.5, h' = 1, h" = 2.

114

Computing vertex coordinates.
The final location of a vertex is computed as the barycenter of the corresponding points associated with its incident volumes (computed at the previous step): cf. figure 8. For most experiments, all points are taken into account when computing the barycenter. Sometimes, points are selected according to an attribute associated with incident volumes. It is thus possible to define, for a face or a volume, an embedding which depends on the shape (i.e. the default embedding) of an other volume (cf. figure 8.c).

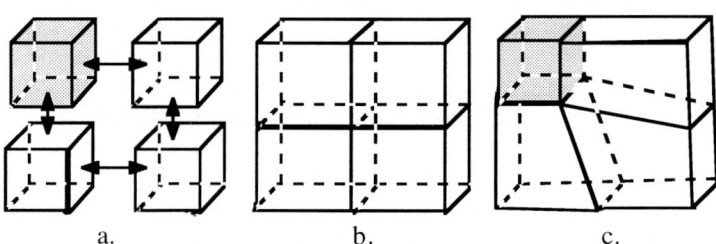

a.   b.   c.

Figure 8.– Computing the embedding of a vertex. a.– Four volumes and their default embeddings. Arrows symbolize adjacency relations between volumes along faces. b.– Vertices are embedded at the barycenters of all corresponding points of default shapes of adjacent volumes. c.– Only the points computed for the grey volume are taken into account for computing the location of its incident vertices.

Scripts.

The script associated with a (sub-)object "describes" its evolution according to time. Thus, a script mainly defines a high-level operation, composed by lower-level topological and embedding operations, where time is taken into account. Due to G-map definition, only darts and attributes of incident (sub-)objects are parameters of operations. Scripts may be parameterized, for instance by the clock, or by attributes associated with (sub-)objects : for instance, the operations described by the script can be applied for a (set of) value(s) of the clock (if time is not explicitly taken into account, the operations are applied at each step). Topological and embedding attributes are usually employed (filiation, order, etc.), for instance in order to define context-dependent evolutions (cf. section 2.3). A script associated with a (sub-)object may partially or completely control the evolution of an other (sub-)object: the script associated with an axis can control evolutions of its volumes; when a (sub-)object is growing by generating new volumes, its associated script controls also the initial attributes of the created volumes (a classical mechanism consists in associating attributes which values are equal to or deduced from that of the father-volume).

Topological operations are intrinsically discrete ones, but embedding modifications may be continuous ones. For instance, continuous or discontinuous functions are used for the control of embedding evolutions. More precisely, an embedding attribute associated with a volume is usually a reference to an interpolation function. It is thus possible to define embedding evolutions according to the clock, orders, topological or geometric distances, etc. More generally, interpolation functions may be used for defining any attribute (integer or real), for instance for defining the order of a volume when it is created, for defining photometric attributes, etc. Moreover, for our experiments, we define these functions in such a way that a (discrete) topological operation does not imply an apparent shape modification (for instance, a topological volume appears with a null geometric volume, which increases during time by controlling its associated shape attributes using an interpolation function). So, continuous-like animations have been realized. In practice, linear interpolation functions have been used, providing satisfying results for our experiments, but other ones can be used.

Controlling an animation mainly consists in incrementally defining the structure of objects, scripts, an initial object and values of its attributes. At each step, scripts control the evolutions of their associated (sub-)objects according to their parameters, generating new (sub-)objects and their associated attributes, removing (sub-)objects, etc.

• Application to the "internal" growth of wood

Topological structure. A vegetal tree can be seen as a subdivided 3-dimensional object, structured into axes composed by internodes ; the increasing of their thickness is due to the development of new age-rings (cf. section 2.1). An age-ring can be modeled by a single volume (cylinder or torus). Nevertheless, an age-ring is here represented by a set of elementary volumes (cf. figure 9.b). This (arbitrary) subdivision of age-rings simplifies the simulation, since the amount of wood produced during the tree growth is not uniform around the circumference of the tree. We think that it is easier to simulate this phenomenon by controling the shapes of elementary volumes which compose an age-ring. Moreover, the subdivision of age-rings into elementary volumes simplifies the control of junctions between trunk and branches, when simulating their simultaneous growings.

Here, a part of a tree is modeled by a 3-G-map, each volume of which corresponding to a part of an age-ring. The 3-G-map is structured using a filiation tree, structured itself into axes, in the following way. Axes of order i (for i > 0) correspond to the most internal part of vegetal axes : each volume of order i corresponds to the central age-ring (cylindrical age-ring) of an internode. Axes of order 0 are inserted on these axes of order i. Each volume of order 0 corresponds to an elementary part of a non-central age-ring (torus). The simulation principle consists in simulating the activity of principal and secondary meristems. Meristems correspond to faces. For instance, a new part of a tree (central part of internode or part of non-central age-ring) appears when the operation for creating a volume on a face is applied. The filiation relation, which defines the filiation tree (oriented by distinguishing the first created volume) corresponds here to growth directions in the vegetal tree. Orientations of axes of order i (i > 0) correspond to main growth directions of the corresponding vegetal axes. Orientations of axes of order 0, which are inserted on an axis of order i, correspond to secondary growth directions of the corresponding vegetal axis of order i. A vegetal axis of order i is thus modeled by an axis of order i and by the set of axes of order 0 which are inserted on it. The central part of a vegetal axis of order i corresponds to the corresponding axis of order i. An internode is modeled by a volume of order i and the set of axes of order 0 which are inserted on it (the representation of an internode is called a *layer*). A central age-ring is modeled by a volume of order i. A non-central age-ring is modeled by the set of volumes of order 0 which belong to an internode and such that all distances between the volumes and the central volume of the internode are equal (i.e. the topological distances, according to the filiation tree). A scenario is described in the following section, which defines a simple evolution of the topology of a part of a tree. Only basic operations (defined above) are used in this scenario, and the operations are parameterized by attributes associated with volumes (order, etc.).

Embedding control. We have described in section 2.2.2 the method we employ for computing the embedding of a G-map structured using a filiation tree. It is necessary to control :
  • The size of each volume of order 0, and its evolution during time, which locally defines (the evolution of) the thickness of an age-ring ;
  • The size of each volume of order i (i > 0), and its evolution during time, which mainly defines (the evolution of) the length of the corresponding internode ;
  • The bending of each axis of order i (if necessary) ;
  • The aspect of all volumes.

Scaling ratios associated with volumes are used in order to control the size of elementary volumes which compose age-rings. More precisely, in order to get variations of the thickness of age-rings, the value of scaling ratio h randomly varies between two extreme values. The user has only to define these two extreme values (we have also experimented extreme values which vary during time, or according to other parameters, using interpolation functions ; in a classical manner, it is then necessary to specify bounding values for each extreme value, and the intervals of definition of parameters). Extreme values are here "arbitrary" ones ; nevertheless, extreme values associated with elements produced during summer are less than that associated with elements produced during spring, wood production being maximal during this season. It is obvious that these values could be defined according to stochastic laws, obtained by measures on vegetal trees, as for AMAP method [REFJP88].

Growing of internodes is controlled by a function which interpolates scaling ratio h, according to space and time. Interpolation is a spatial one, since h depends on the topological distance between the volume and the origin of the axis to which it belongs. Two bounding values have to be specified, one of them corresponding to the scaling ratio associated with the origin of the axis, the other one corresponding to the scaling ratio associated with the extremity of the axis, when its growth is complete. Simultaneously, interpolation is a temporal one, since bounding values are reached after x steps (x is the age at which an element has its maximal size). This other value has to be specified as a parameter of the interpolation. The interpolation function is completely specified by these three values.

The bending of an axis is controlled by specifying variations for rotation angles associated with volumes of order i (i > 0), as for scaling ratios.

Aspect is controlled in a very simple way. Wood being produced in spring and summer, two colors are predefined ; the first one (resp. the second one) is associated with faces and edges incident to volumes created during a season (resp. the other season). Other examples are being realized, where a bark texture is associated with "external" faces of the tree, and where color of internal faces is interpolated in order to produce more realistic metamorphoses.

2.3.- Experiments and results

In practice, when defining a metamorphosis, we try to distinguish between topological and embedding aspects, for the definition of scripts and parameters : this seems to simplify definitions and adjustings. We describe a simple scenario among those which have been realized, which control the topological part of the growing of an axis. As seen above, controlling embedding evolution mainly consists in controlling the embedding of a tree in a hierarchical way, this problem being a very classical one (cf. for instance [AK84], [REFJP88], [Lien88]). Here, each step corresponds to one year, during which we distinguish two parts for the growing of the trunk : wood production during spring and during summer.

Scenario1 : trunk growth

• clock = 1 (first year)
  /* Spring */
  0.- Creation of the initial volume (order 1) having extremity faces of degree DK: figure 9.a. /* The filiation tree is composed by a single axis of order 1*/.
  /* Summer */
  1.- creation of a volume of order 0 on each lateral face of the initial volume: figure 9.b. /*New axes of order 0 are thus created*/.
• Next steps (next years)
  /* Spring */
  3.- Creation of a new volume of order 1 on the extremity face of the axis of order 1. Splitting of lateral faces of this volume (fig. 9.c, and 9.k,l,m); identification of new faces with faces of the underlying layer (fig. 9.d). /*Corresponding faces are determined in a way similar to that described below for other identifications*/.
  4.- Creation of a volume of order 0 on each extremity of axes of order 0 (figure 9.e). Identification of lateral faces of new volumes with that of adjacent volumes belonging to the same age-ring. /*In fact, for each *free* lateral face of an axis of order 0 (i.e. incident to a single volume), a free adjacent lateral face is computed, such that it does not belong to the same axis, but it belongs to the same age-ring (this search only uses adjacency relations). If a face is found, the two faces are identified. */
  5.- Splitting of lateral faces of the extremity volume of the axis of order 1 (figure 9.f); identification of new faces with faces of the underlying layer (figure 9.g).
  /* Summer */
  6.- Creation of a volume of order 0 on each extremity of axes of order 0 (figure 9.h). Identification of faces of this new age-ring as described above.
  7.- Creation of a volume of order 0 on each free lateral face of the axis of order 1; /*so, new axes of order 0 are created (figure 9.i). Now, we distinguish two steps for identifying the free lateral faces of axes of order 0*/ Identification of faces which belong to a same age-ring, as above; Identification of faces which belong to adjacent age-rings (figure 9.i). /*In fact, for each free lateral face of order 0, a free adjacent lateral face is computed, such that they do not belong to the same age-ring. If a face is found, the faces are identified*/.

• the value of the clock is increased ;

<u>end</u> scenario1

Remark. Degree DK of the extremity faces of volumes of the axis of order 1 is a parameter of the scenario. For objects represented on figure A (see appendix), DK = 32 ; for objects represented on figures 9 and 10, DK = 8, for clarity.

118

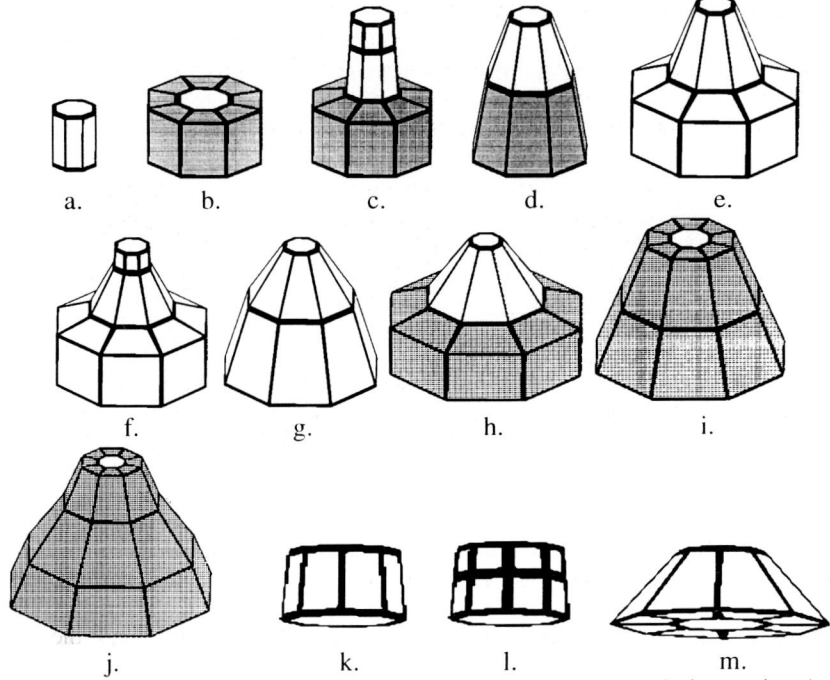

Figure 9.- Internal growth of a trunk. Color of volumes created during spring (resp. summer) is light (resp. dark). a. and b.– First year. c. to i.– second year (c. to g.– spring ; h. to i.– summer). j.– Third year. k. to m.– An extremity volume of the axis of order 1, and the split of lateral faces (k.– the volume ; l.– split of lateral faces ; m.– Embedding : in fact, embedding is controlled by faces incident to the underlying layer: cf. figure 8.c and 8.d).

Figures A.1–A.4 have been produced by this simulation.
Figure A.1 shows 6 steps of the trunk growth, between the second and the fourth year. Object 1 : trunk at year 2. Object 2 : growing in length and thickness of the volumes which compose the trunk (embedding evolution only). Object 3 : trunk at year 3. New volumes appears (topological modification), and, simultaneously, the length and thickness of previously created volumes increase. Object 4 : embedding evolution. Object 5 : trunk at year 4, showing evolutions of topology (new internode and new age-rings) and of embedding. Object 6. embedding evolution.
Figures A.2 and A.3 show a 5 years old trunk, composed by five internodes. Figure A.4 shows the wood production (age-rings) of the first internode during the fifth year (down) and a cutting of the trunk, near the third internode (top).

Simultaneous growth of a trunk and a branch
Simulation principle is similar. But, during the trunk growth, an axis of order 2 appears on the extremity of an axis of order 0, corresponding to the origin of the branch (figure 10.a,b). This creation can be easily parameterized by the value of the clock. Since the degree of extremity faces of axes of order 0 is 4 and the degree of the extremity of an axis of order 2 is DK, faces are split in order to join elements belonging to the branch with elements belonging to the trunk, when their thickness is increased (due to the creation of new age-rings, or to embedding evolutions). This

is mainly realized by a search of faces which are adjacent by several edges to other faces of an other age-ring (figure 10.c). This process can be obviously generalized for simulating the growth of a bigger part of a tree, including several branches. We are still experimenting such simulations, in order to take into account the fact that different branches can meet during their growths, and that parts of such branches are glued together.

 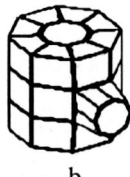 

a.   b.   c.

Figure 10. a.- The grey face is the extremity of an axis of order 0. An axis of order 2 (representing the origin of the branch) will appear on this face. b.– The first volume of the branch appears on the grey face. c.– Adjacent faces are split ; parts of the branch and of the trunk will be glued together when their thickness will increase.

Figures A.5–A.8 have been produced by this simulation, and they show a little part of a trunk on which a branch is inserted; Figure A.5 : a side-cutting through the central part of the branch. The angle according to which the branch is inserted is $\pi/2$, in order to clearly show the internal structure; Figure A.6: an other side-cutting of the same part; Figures A.7 and A.8: other cuttings, which clearly show the wood knots.

Remarks.
Sequential or parallel. When he defines scripts, the user explicitly defines the order according to which (sub-)objects and their associated scripts will be taken into account during a step. A sequential order can be explicitly specified (cf. scenario1 in section 2.3). We have also experimented parallel applications (cf. [Terr94]).

Context-dependence. A script can take into account relations between (sub-)objects (cf. scenario1). For instance, the script which control face identifications uses adjacency relations between faces in order to select faces, according to some conditions. Scripts of this type are context-dependent, or adaptative ones [Zelt85]. Within an object, the script associated with one of its parts can take into account the "state" of an other part (relations between darts can be handled in order to traverse the object and check the state of an other part).

3.- Higher-level control mechanisms: an application to the simulation of the growing of fishes.

We discuss in this section a first experiment about the simulation of the growing of fishes, in which new control mechanisms, based on basic tools similar to that presented before, are employed. We made strong simplifications *a priori*, though more complex transformations are taken into account:
  • We only deal with metamorphoses of the external surfaces of fishes;
  • We don't take scales and gills into account ;

• The first step of a metamorphosis is a macroscopic one (larva).

3.1.– Analysis of (the growing of) fishes

We discuss here some characteristic steps of the growing of a "standard" fish (cf. Figure 11), in order to explain the hierarchy of parts and associated scripts we use for simulations.

If we analyse apparent common points and differences between growing steps (from larva to young fish), we see :
• some persistency in the structure : head (eyes, lower and upper jaws, nostrils, etc.), body (at each step, it is quite symmetrical according to a longitudinal plane, but not for the other standard planes), fins, composed by two types of parts : parts of the first type are usually not divided nor ramified, parts of the second type are often divided and ramified, and all or some parts of a fin are sometimes joined by a membrane.
• transformations : evolution of the shape of the body (from larva to young fish, when the fish is swimming), evolution of the structure of fins (new parts can appear in a fin, extending the insertion area of the fin onto the body), growing of parts of fins, new fins can appear (from alevin to young fish), etc.

So, there are "deformations" of the fish and transformations of the fish structure (i.e. general metamorphoses).

    a.   b.   c.   d.
Figure 11.- Growing of a "standard" fish. a.- spawn (1-2 days). b.- Larva (several days). c.- Alevin (several weeks). d.- Young.

3.2– Simulation

Basic tools employed here have been described in section 2 for 3D subdivisions. For simulating metamorphoses of subdivided surfaces, 2-dimensional generalized maps are employed, and their definition is quite similar to that of 3-dimensional generalized maps (a set of darts and 3 bijections). Since our basic mechanisms have been defined in order to handle embedded generalized maps (which definition does not specify the number of applications defined on darts), they are employed without modifications for embedded 2D generalized maps. But the definitions of basic (sub-)objects have to be changed. For instance, filiation trees of 2D generalized maps are "trees" of faces. Basic topological operations are face creation, edge identification, edge and face splitting. Embedding is controlled through reference systems and shapes associated with faces.

As before, the basic idea consists here in simplifying control by mainly exerting it through a skeleton of the object, which is a topologically 1-dimensional object (the shape of a fish is related to that of its skeleton).

Since we simulate metamorphoses of external surfaces of fishes, a skeleton is not a (connected) part of the corresponding fish. Mainly due to symmetry, a very poor approximation of the real skeleton is used here (cf. Figure 12). The front part of the skeleton corresponds to jaws, the bottom part corresponds to the bottom of the head and to the body. This skeleton is a surface, in order to only have to handle surface subdivisions; in fact, it is assimilated to an oriented tree, i.e. an origin face is distinguished. We can thus compute topological distances in the tree (topological distance between a face and the origin face), in order to control metamorphoses (cf. below).

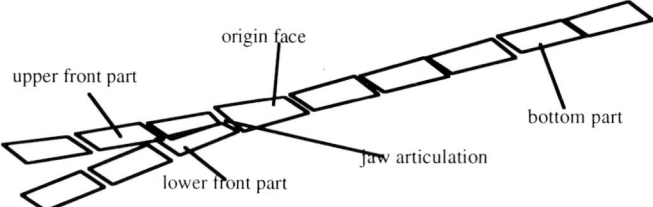

Figure 12. Skeleton of a "fish".

Control of deformations of the body according to the skeleton (cf. Figure 13). We distinguish in the body an upper part (corresponding to the back of the fish) and a lower part (corresponding to its belly). Each of them looks like a half generalized cylinder, i.e. with variations of the radius (similar for the upper and lower jaws). In fact, the body (upper jaw, lower jaw) is composed by "sections", each one corresponding to a basic element of the skeleton (so each section can be identified by the distance between the corresponding face of the skeleton and the origin face). Each section is in fact a thin subdivided cylinder composed by an upper part and a lower part, each part having the shape of an half ellipse. By using a classical hierarchized control of the embedding (cf section 2.2.2), we can control the motions of the skeleton : the shape of the skeleton at one step is controlled by an interpolation of angles and lengths according to distances, and motions of the skeleton by a double interpolation where time is taken into account. Similarly, using a hierarchal embedding of the body according to that of the skeleton, we control the relative shape at one step, or relative deformations as distention by similar interpolations of the values which characterize half-ellipses. These controls are thus easy, and a little number of parameters is needed. Similar techniques are used for controlling the two parts of the front of the head according to the two front part of the skeleton.

Different shapes of fishes are shown on figure B (see appendix), and also evolutions of shapes : global or local distensions and inverse phenomena, swimming (motions of the mouth, different profiles and their evolutions are shown in [Terr94]). A similar hierarchical control of embedding is used for the fins, so motions of fins are also easily controlled.

Values of parameters and interpolating functions are deduced from measures on pictures representing real fishes.

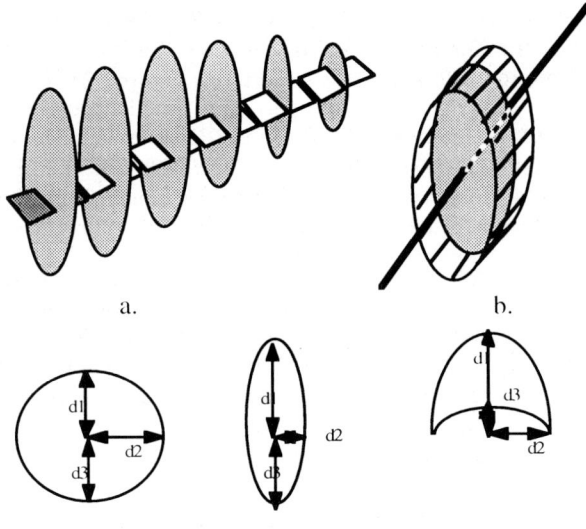

a.   b.

c.

Figure 13. a.– Shapes of sections (two half-ellipses) and evolutions along the skeleton. b.– A section and the underlying half-ellipses. c.– Control of the shapes of half-ellipses using 3 values.

We have seen how to control deformations by quite classical methods. The constitution of a fish is often modified during its growing. For instance, new fins sometimes appear, and the structure itself of a fin can be transformed very strongly. Controlling the growing of a fin mainly consists in controlling the evolution of its insertion area, the evolution of its constitution (relative importance and location of the two types of parts of the fin), the growing itself of these parts, and the development (or not) of a membrane joining these parts (obviously, time can be taken into account in order to control these aspects).

As before, the main mechanism we use for this control is the notion of oriented filiation tree. The idea is here similar. Relations between faces are established during the growth, making a "tree of faces" : cf. Figure 14 ; the control of the evolution of the tree is detailed below. Trees of faces are also structured into axes : the underlying tree of the body is very simple : it is composed by a main axis on which secondary axes are inserted. Any face of the surface can be identified according to this tree, using notions of distances between the face and the origin face of the tree, between the face and the origin of the axis, etc. (the mechanism is similar to that described above for the skeleton). Controlling the fact that a fin appears is easily exerted by using these distances as parameters in order to control the location of the insertion area, its length, the locations of the different parts of the fin, etc. Ramified parts are structured into trees using the same principle, and the control of their growings is very close to that used in methods for simulating the growing of vegetal trees (control of the degree of ramification, of the growing of axes, ...).

For instance, when a part of the fin is growing by the generation of a new sub-part, the last and the new extremities of the part are joined by filiation relation. In practice, a fin appears by "tearing" the surface of the body (i.e. inverse operation of identification), and by growing on the resulting boundary. The development of a membrane is controlled by using similar parameters. In practice, a membrane results from the "fusion" of the boundaries of parts of the fins (cf. Figure 15).

A similar type of control is used for the development and growth of spines on the body itself of a fish (this phenomenon does not really exist ; sometimes, existing spines are located along the body, and they can rise on the body). Similar control is employed for generating eyes, and also for some modifications of the constitution of the body in order to produce an evolution of its aspect. In fact, the initial fish (here the larva) is generated in the same way : this is true for the generation of the skeleton, and for the generation of the larva according to the skeleton ; this explains why the initial fish is directly structured ; simply, the larva is generated during one step, though other evolutions between successive steps seem to quite imperceptible ; thus, a metamorphosis seems to be continuous (only some representative steps are shown in figure B !).
It is clear that such metamorphoses and deformations can be simultaneously controlled.

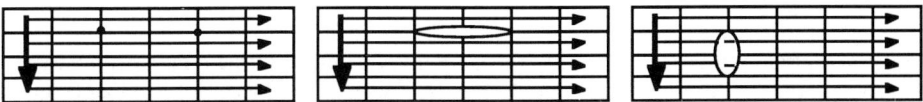

Figure 14. A new fin appears during the growing of an alevin. Its location is mainly controlled through the filiation tree. Here, a part of the body is shown, where the thick arrow corresponds to the main axis, thin arrows correspond to secondary axes.

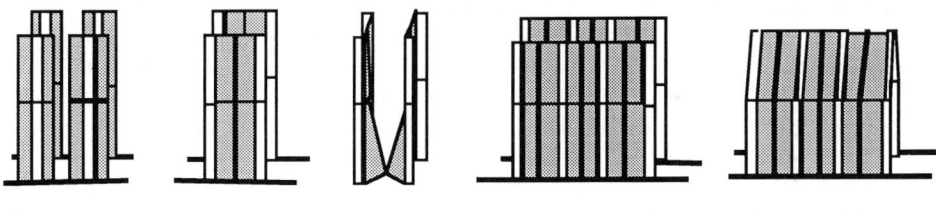

a.   b.

Figure 15. a.- Two types of junctions of boundaries of parts of fins, used in order to control the development of a joining membrane. b.- A fin has two sides, and their upper parts are joined (right). If the fin still growths, this is achieved in the same way used for controlling its appearance ("tearing", local growing and identification).

Figure 16. Different structures (and shapes) of fins, obtained by controlling their growings.

Figure B.1 (see appendix): different steps extracted from an animation showing the growing of a fish (from larva to young fish). Figure B.2 : same steps, with an other point of view. Figure B.3: larva.

Control of deformations : on the length of the skeleton, for the growing of the body ; using interpolations of parameters controlling the size of sections (i.e. the underlying half-ellipses), for removing the prominence of the belly ; on the lengths of parts of fins, in order to extend them.

Transformations of constitution : new fins appear and grow (two pectoral fins, two ventral fins, between alevin and young fish steps) ; transformation of the structure of existing fins during their growing (increasing of the insertion area of the dorsal and anal fins onto the body, between larva and alevin steps) ; development of membranes.

Figure B.4–B.5 : Distention of the body, and simultaneously, spines appear and grow (this is not a simulation of the real reaction of *Diodon holocanthus* !). Figure B.6 : control of aspect, through filiation tree. Figure B.7: : simulating swim (easy control through the skeleton).

4.- Conclusion

The procedural method described in this paper allows one to define metamorphoses of subdivided two- and three-dimensional objects. This method is a topology-based one, and thus presents the following characteristics :
- double discretization :
  - temporal discretization : time is a discrete one, an animation (i.e. a metamorphosis) is a sequence of objects, each object corresponding to one step of the animation ;
  - spatial discretization : each object of a metamorphosis is a structured subdivision.
- animation system at an animator level : a metamorphosis is here defined by a scenario, i.e. a program which controls the animation.

As basic L-systems, this method is not devoted to a particular application. Its main characteristic is the fact that it is a topology-based animation method for simulating metamorphoses of subdivided two and three-dimensional objects. Few methods deal with this type of objects, due to the complexity of the objects and of their metamorphoses. In fact, we have studied one way for applying principles of topology-based methods for simulating metamorphoses of this type of objects. Tools have been conceived and experimented for the simulation of the internal growing of a tree (topologically 3D) and the simulation of the growing of fishes (topologically 2D).

Basically, an object is a subdivision of a 2- or a 3-dimensional manifold represented by a 2- or 3-dimensional generalized map, linearly embedded into E^3. A general mechanism has been defined, in order to allow one to define a structure of the object into sub-objects, providing thus high-level mechanisms for controlling animations. Due to the definition itself of generalized maps, it is a simple generalization of the notion of orbit. Since the formalism is unique, its implementation and the definition and implementation of related operations are not difficult. For most examples (here, the simulation of the internal growth of trees and the simulation of the growing of fishes ; cf. also [TL93] and [Terr94]), objects are structured using filiation trees. Schematically, this tree describes the "history" of the object evolution ; it corresponds to a skeleton of the object, oriented according its growth directions. Control of metamorphoses is mainly exerted through filiation trees, i.e. the control of 2- and 3- dimensional object metamorphoses mainly consists in controlling metamorphoses of 1-dimensional objects, reducing thus the complexity of control.

The filiation tree is also used in order to control the evolution of embedding during time. Embedding is a hierarchical one, defined in a classical way. A reference system and a default shape are computed for each face or volume, according to embedding attributes associated with the cell (angles, translation and scaling ratios ; in fact, these values are the results of functions. So, it is possible to simulate embedding evolutions according to time, or to other parameters : for instance, interpolations of embedding during time or along an axis). These mechanisms generalize, for topologically 2- and 3-dimensional objects, classical mechanisms defined for lower-dimensional objects.

As for other topology-based methods, describing a metamorphosis consists here in describing evolutions of objects and sub-objects, i.e. their associated scripts, mainly by composing basic operations. Scripts can control parameterized and context-dependent evolutions. Main parameters are time, creation date, life time, attributes which define the structure of objects as the order of a cellule, computed parameters. Using these parameters, one can define "families" of metamorphoses or families of objects.

The tools described above have been implemented and experimented. Due to the complexity of topologically 3-dimensional objects itself, defining metamorphoses of such objects is more difficult than for lower-dimensional objects. As presented before, the global control is exerted through the filiation tree. Local control is more critical, since it can be necessary to precisely control geometric relations (embedding and topological relations) between low-level sub-objects (e.g. volumes). It seems that it is necessary to define a structure of these low-level sub-objects in order to simplify the control of metamorphoses. For this low-level control, we use mechanisms similar to that which were employed for controlling metamorphoses of any subdivisions of any surfaces [TL93] : for instance, the boundary of a volume is structured by distinguishing origin, extremity and lateral faces.

Interpreted object-oriented language Smalltalk is used for implementing our approach. Implementation of G-maps and sub-objects is achieved by progressive enrichment of the basic model. Mechanisms of inheritance and polymorphism are widely used in order to simplify the implementation, by progressive definitions (for instance, the topological kernel is distinct of the embedding kernel).

• Developments
We think that the basic tools presented in this paper (cf. also [Terr94]) simplify the control of metamorphoses of 2D and 3D subdivided objects, but it is necessary to widely experiment and develop them for more specialized applications. We have studied different metamorphoses, but the knowledges which are taken into account are rudimentary ones, and it is necessary to improve these aspects. Such studies are also

important for the conception of higher-level tools which could simplify the conception of scripts. Moreover, we think it is necessary to check if it is possible to build a system based on this approach and other ones, for instance physically-based ones, in order to simulate other types of phenomena. For these reasons :

○ we are studying more deeply agronomical and botanical knowledges about the (internal) growth of vegetal trees. For instance, in collaboration with agronomists, we study the simulation of tree growth in order to take into account knowledges in bio-climatology ;

○ we study the use of our approach in order to simulate deformations of (homogeneous or non homogeneous) objects. Incidence and adjacency relations can be used in order to propagate the effects of deformations. Such mechanisms could be used in order to simulate compressions and collisions on fruits [WDR91], including consequences as lacerations.

○ Metamorphoses of 2D fishes could be improved (adding scales and gills, using textures). In fact, we are now working on the simulation of the growing of topologically 3D fishes, in order to gradually get metamorphoses more faithful to real growings. The structure employed for 2D is well-adapted for its extension for 3D (but the skeleton will be a part of the fish !). It will be necessary to simulate the growth of a more elaborated skeleton. Some controls will be more "natural" (e.g. it will be unnecessary to "tear" the body for simulating the growing of fins). We intend to add more realism by using more knowledge about real fish growing, but also to study some phenomena as the relative influence of fins in the motions of fishes (stabilization vs propulsion). Very interesting works are described in [TTG94] and in [TT94].

We think that it is also interesting to compare our approach with :

○ morphing (cf. [LV94] and [DG94], for instance). Schematically, morphing is the study of the automatic transformation of a shape into an other shape. Since our approach is a topology-based one, the first question is : given two shapes, what criterions have to be taken into account in order to deduce topological structures from these shapes, such that we can "easily" transfom one into the other using our approach ?

○ mechanisms which have been studied in order to transform a polyhedron into an other one, using Minkowski sums [KR92], [KR94].

○ L-systems. L-systems have been widely used and developed in order to simulate metamorphoses of subdivisions of 1-, 2- and 3-dimensional objects, and applied for simulating the growth of trees and vegetal organs, cellular divisions, etc. [DL83], [FPB90], [PHM93], [PL90]. We think that L-systems and our approach mainly differ from a technical point of view, but not in their "principles". L-systems handle mechanisms which allow one to take time, context, attributes into account (timed L-systems" [PL90], "parametric L-systems" [PL90], "differential L-systems" [PHM93]). Both methods are topology-based ones. For instance, "map L-systems" are used in [FPB90] in order to simulate cellular divisions. Scripts correspond to production rules, and a map is computed (in the meaning of topological maps as G-maps). It would be interesting to carefully compare advantages, drawbacks and fundamental mechanisms of both methods.

Tools we have studied are basic ones. It is thus also necessary to conceive higher-level mechanisms, which could simplify the conception of scripts. We are studying this problem for specialized applications (agronomical ones).

References

[AK84] M. Aono, T. Kunii. *Botanical Tree Image Generation.* Computer Graphics and Applications, 4, 5, 1984, pp. 10-34.

[BB88] R. Barzel, A. Barr. *A modelling system based on dynamic constraints.* Computer Graphics, 22, 4, 1988, pp. 179-188.

[BDFL93] Y. Bertrand, J.F. Dufourd, J. Françon, P. Lienhardt. *3-Dimensional Manifold Modeling using 3-Dimensional Generalized Maps.* Research report 93-03, Centre de Recherche en Informatique, Université Louis Pasteur, Strasbourg, France, 1993.

[Bech94] D. Bechmann. *Space Deformation Models Survey.* Computer & Graphics, 18, 4, 1994.

[BJL93] P. Borianne, M. Jaeger, J.M. Leban. *Prototype pour la représentation réaliste des noeuds du bois.* Conference INRA-CIRAD "Modélisation et simulation de l'architecture des arbres fruitiers et forestiers", Montpellier, France, november 1993.

[Bloo85] J. Bloomenthal. *Modeling the mighty maple.* Computer Graphics , 19, 3, 1985, pp. 305-311.

[Bori91] P. Borianne. *Conception d'un modeleur de subdivisions de surfaces orientables ou non orientables, avec ou sans bord.* PhD thesis, Université Louis Pasteur, 1069, Strasbourg, France, 1991.

[Bris89] E. Brisson. *Representing Geometric Structures in d Dimensions : Topology and Order.* Proc. of 5th A.C.M. Symposium on Computational Geometry, Saarbrücken, F.R.G., 1989, pp. 218–227..

[CL92] X. Chen, P. Lienhardt. *Modeling and Programming Evolutions of Surfaces.* Computer Graphics Forum, 2, 5, 1992, pp. 323-341.

[Coq90] S. Coquillart. *Extended Free-Form Deformation: A Sculpturing Tool for 3D Geometric Modeling.* Computer Graphics , 24, 4, 1990, pp. 187-196.

[DG94] P. Decaudin, A. Gagalowicz. *Fusion of 3D Shapes.* 5th Eurographics Workshop on Animation and Simulation, Oslo, Norway, 1994.

[DL83] M. De Does, A. Lindenmayer. *Algorithms for the Generation and Drawing of Maps Representing Cells Clones.* Lecture Notes in Computer Science, 153, 1983, pp. 301-316.

[Dufo91] J.F. Dufourd. *An OBJ3 Functional Specification for the Boundary Representation.* Proc. of 1st ACM Symposium on Solid Modeling Foundations and CAD/CAM Applications, Austin, Texas, 1991, pp. 61–72.

[EVJA89] G. Eyrolles, X. Viennot, N. Janney, D. Arquès. *Combinatorial Analysis of Ramified Patterns and Computer Imagery of Trees.* Computer Graphics, 23, 3, 1989, pp. 31-40.

[FL94] J. Françon, P. Lienhardt. *Basic principles of topology-based methods for simulating metamorphoses of natural objects.* in Artificial Life and Virtual Reality, Thalmann eds, Wiley, 1994.

[FPB90] F. Fracchia, P. Prusinkiewicz, M. de Boer. *Animation of the Development of Multicellular Structures.* Proc. of Computer Animation'90, Genève, Suisse, 1990.

[Fran91] J. Françon. *Sur la modélisation informatique de l'architecture et du développement des végétaux.* Colloque "L'arbre. Biologie et développement", Naturalia Monspeliensa, C. Edelin ed., Montpellier, 1991.

[GA92] J.P. Gouret, P. Afflord. *Three-Dimensional Texture Generator Supervised by a Small Number of Parameters.* The Journal of Visualization and Computer Animation, 3, 2, 1992, pp. 105–127.

[HA92] G. Hegron, B. Arnaldi. *Computer Animation: motion and deformation control.* Course of Eurographics'92, Cambrige, Great Britain, september 1992.

[Jaeg87] M. Jaeger. *Représentation et simulation de croissance des végétaux.* PhD thesis, Université Louis Pasteur, 328, Strasbourg, december 1987.

[KR92] A. Kaul, J. Rossignac. *Solid Interpolating Deformations : Construction and Animation of PIPS.* Computer Graphics, 16, 1, 1992, pp. 107–115.

[KR94] A. Kaul, J. Rossignac. *AGRELs and BIPs: Metamorphosis as a Bezier Curve in the Space of Polyhedra.* Computer Graphics Forum, 13, 3, 1994, pp. 179–184.

[LCJ93] F. Lazarus, S. Coquillart, P. Jancène. *Interactive Axial Deformations.* Proc. of IFIP TC 5/ WG 5.10 Working Conference on Geometric Modeling, Genova, Italy, 1993, in Modeling in Computer Graphics, B. Falcidieno and T.L. Kunii eds, Springer, 1993, pp. 241–254.

[LF87] P. Lienhardt, J. Françon. *Vegetal leaves image synthesis.* Proc. of MARI87, 3° semaine de l'Image Electronique, Paris, may 1987.

[Lien88] P. Lienhardt. *Free-form surfaces modeling by evolution simulation.* Proc. of Eurographics'88, Nice, 1988, pp. 327-341.

[Lien91] P. Lienhardt. *Topological Models for Boundary Representation : a Comparison with N-Dimensional Generalized Maps.* Computer-Aided Design 23,1, 1991, pp. 59–82.

[Lien94] P. Lienhardt. *N-Dimensional Generalized Combinatorial Maps and Cellular Quasi-Manifolds.* Int. Journal of Computational Geometry and Applications, 4, 3, 1994, pp. 275–324.

[Luci91] A. Luciani. *Les catégories de modèles en animation et simulation du mouvement.* Working group "Animation et simulation", Grenoble, october 1991.

[LV94] F. Lazarus, A. Verroust. *Feature-Based Shape Transformations for Polyhedral Objects.* 5th Eurographics Workshop on Animation and Simulation, Oslo, Norway, 1994.

[MT83] N. Magnenat-Thalmann, D. Thalmann. *The Use of 3D High-Level Graphical Types in Mira Animation System.* Computer Graphics and Animation, 9-16, december 1983.

[PHM93] P. Prusinkiewicz, M. Hammel, E. Mjolsness. *Animation of Plant Development.* Computer Graphics, Annual Conference Series, 1993, pp. 351-360.

[PL90] P. Prusinkiewicz, A. Lindenmayer. *The Algorithmic Beauty of Plants.* Springer-Verlag, New York, 1990.

[RDB90] P. de Reffye, P. Dinouart, D. Barthélémy. *Architecture et modélisation de l'orme du japon, Zelkova Serrata (Thmb.) Makino (Ulmacae): la notion d'axe de référence.* Colloque "L'arbre. Biologie et développement", Naturalia Monspeliensa, C. Edelin ed., Montpellier, 1990.

[Reev83]   W. Reeves. *Particle systems : a technique for modeling a class of fuzzy objects.* Transactions on Graphics, 2 , 2, 1983, pp. 91-108.

[REFJP88]   P. de Reffye, C. Edelin, J. Françon, M. Jaeger, C. Puech. *Plant Models Faithful to Botanical Structure and Development .* Computer Graphics , 22, 4, 1988, pp. 141-150.

[Reyn82]   C.W. Reynolds. *Computer Animation with Scripts and Actors.* Computer Graphics , 16, 3, 1982, pp. 289-296.

[Reyn87]   C.W. Reynolds. *Flocks, Herbs and Schools: a Distributed Behavioral Model.* Computer Graphics, 21, 4, 1987, pp. 25-34.

[TL93]   O. Terraz, P. Lienhardt. *Some aspects of a method for programming metamorphoses of any subdivisions of any surfaces.* Proc. of Compugraphics'93, Alvor, Portugal, 1993.

[Terr94]   O. Terraz. *Programmation de métamorphoses d'objets surfaciques et volumiques.* PhD Thesis, Université Louis Pasteur, 1874, Strasbourg, France, 1994.

[TPBF87]   D. Terzopoulos, J. Platt, A. Barr, K. Fleischer. *Elastically deformable models.* Computer Graphics , 21, 4, 1987, pp. 205-214.

[TTG94]   D. Terzopoulos, X. Tu, R. Grzeszczuk. *Artificial fishes: Autonomous locomotion, perception, behavior, and learning in a simulated physical world.* Artificial Life, 1, 4, 1994, pp. 327-351.

[TT94]   X. Tu, D. Terzopoulos. *Artificial fishes: Physics, locomotion, perception, behavior.* Computer Graphics (Proc. Siggraph'94), pp. 43-50.

[WDR91]   C.Wenian, F.Duprat, A.-C Roudot. *Evaluation de l'importance de la géométrie du tissu cellulaire dans les déformations observées sur les pommes après une compression ou un choc.* Sciences des aliments, 11, 1991, pp. 105-116.

[Zelt85]   D. Zeltzer. *Toward an integrated view of 3-D computer animation.* IEEE CG&A, 1985, pp. 87-101.

Basic notions about (the growing of) fishes were found in :

[DKPT75]   V. Val Desco, W. Klausewitz, B. Peyronel, E. Tortonese. *La vie de l'aquarium.* Fernand Nathan, 1975.

[LMG89]   P. Louisy, T. Maitre-Allain, G. Gourdon. *Les poissons d'aquarium.* Collection Nature, Edition du Rocher, 1989.

[HMS82]   P. Hunnam, A. Milne, P. Stebbing. *Tout l'aquarium.* Bordas, 1982.

Editors' Note: see Appendix, p. 229 f. for coloured figures of this paper

Position Control of the Center of Mass for Articulated Figures in Multiple Support

Ronan Boulic[1], Ramon Mas[2],
Daniel Thalmann[1]

(1) Computer Graphics Laboratory, Swiss Federal Institute of Technology, DI-LIG, CH1015 Lausanne, Switzerland

(2) Department of Mathematics and Computer Science, Balearic Islands University, 07071-Palma de Mallorca, Spain

Abstract. We extend a recent approach for the position control of the center of mass for any tree-structured articulated figure in a multiple support context. Our approach fits into existing high level interfaces of behavioral control of human figures; it brings the necessary realism for static positioning according to the mass distribution of the figure. The single support case is first recalled prior to the presentation of the mass distribution partitioning and the general case of multiple support. Simulations of 3D reaching behaviors are presented in single and multiple support.

1   Introduction

Static positioning of an articulated body is a very important problem in Robotics, Computer Animation and Ergonomics. For calculating such static postures in an efficient way, the most popular technique is inverse kinematics. However, as inverse kinematics does not take into account the mass distribution of the figure it is a poor approach for the design of balanced postures. This requires the ability to control the position of the center of mass. We proposed a general solution exploiting the mass distribution of any tree-structured articulated figure in single support [1-4] and the present article extends it to the multiple support case. The proposed technique fits into existing high level interfaces of behavioral control for human figures. It allows interactive control as its computation cost is comparable with inverse kinematics. Furthermore, it can be combined with this latter thus permitting simultaneous balance control of any articulated figure together with other goal-oriented behaviors (e.g., reach). After a brief review, we recall the single support solution. we generalize it for multiple support by evaluating the fraction of the articulated structure which is supported by each supporting site (their so-called *influence tree*).We present several 3D examples oriented towards reach analysis.

2   Background

From the various kinematic approaches addressing the problem of controlling the balance of articulated figures [5-8], the one described in [5-6] is the most effective because it allows some control over the position of the center of mass. It considers the center of mass of a human figure as an end effector attached to the lower torso region. Its position is controlled with an iterative process based on inverse kinematics. The constraint variables are the ankle, knee, and hip joints of the dominant leg (i.e. the one supporting most of the weight). However, its insufficient theoretical grounding prevents its generalization as we have demonstrated in [4].

In the studies dedicated to multiple-legs robots the position of the center of mass is a constraint rather than an explicit variable of the motion control problem. For the statically stable case (i.e. at least three supporting feet on the ground and a slow forward motion) the constraint is to maintain the balance by always keeping the center of mass within the support polygon (convex hull of the supporting feet). So the problem addressed in that field is to optimize the sequence of support polygons so that the center of mass always remains inside them while achieving a desired motion trace for the body [9].

Dynamics [10-11] and optimal control [12-13] can produce physically-based postures and animations. Nevertheless they usually do not provide direct manipulation of the center of mass position, and they face high computation cost for large dimension systems (i.e., more than fifty). Moreover, as stated in [10], the associated parameter space added by the control approach are not intuitive or easy to handle for an animation designer.

We have recently proposed a new approach to solve the center of mass position control in a way consistent with the mass distribution of the articulated figure [1-4]. It is called *Inverse Kinetics* because it combines the information of the articulated structure kinematics together with its mass distribution. Moreover, our control technique can be combined with standard inverse kinematics in a hierarchical fashion [3]. A first validation was achieved in 2D owing to radiographs of living animals [1]. More recently complex 3D case studies were presented on a human model [3] and the second order approach was evaluated for motion design [4].

3   Direct and Inverse Kinetics

The key point of our algorithm is to evaluate the *kinetic influence* of any joint (i.e. the center of mass instantaneous velocity induced by the joint instantaneous velocity). For that purpose we use the joint associated *augmented body* : this is the imaginary rigid body supported by the joint in the current state of the system [14-15]. Figure 1 shows the center of mass of all the augmented bodies of an arbitrary articulated chain and more particularly the one associated with joint j (with its own center of mass G_{aj}). *Direct kinetics* explicitly relates the instantaneous joint rotations to the corresponding instantaneous translation of the total center of mass G. The instantaneous velocity V_{Gaj} on the partial center of mass G_{aj} due to a unit variation of joint j is given by (Figure 1) :

$$V_{G_{aj}} = \omega_j \times O_j G_{aj}$$

(1)

where x is for the cross product of the unit instantaneous rotation vector ω_j with the lever arm vector O_jGa_j . For direct kinetics we need to evaluate the contribution of joint j to the velocity of the center of mass of the whole body (noted V_{Gj}). It is given by applying the principle of the conservation of the momentum to the augmented body of mass m_{aj} and velocity V_{Gaj} and to the whole body of mass m and velocity V_{Gj}.

$$mV_{G_j} = m_{aj}V_{G_{aj}}$$

(2)

$$V_{G_j} = (\frac{m_{aj}}{m})V_{G_{aj}}$$

(3)

Equation (3) corresponds with one column of the jacobian matrix J_G (see [2] or [4] for an alternate demonstration of direct kinetics). Once the jacobian is established for all the joints, we can evaluate the instantaneous velocity on the total center of mass V_G corresponding to any instantaneous variation of the joints (noted $\dot{\theta}$):

$$V_G = J_G\dot{\theta}$$

(4)

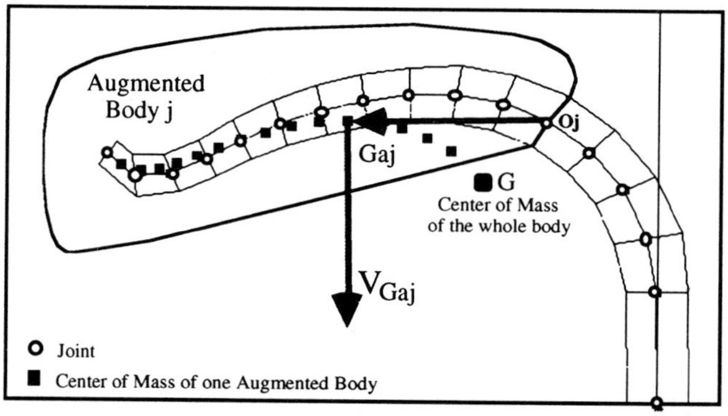

Augmented
Body j

Gaj

O_j

G
Center of Mass
of the whole body

V_{Gaj}

O Joint
■ Center of Mass of one Augmented Body

Fig. 1. one joint 's augmented body with its center of mass and instantaneous velocity

Conversely, *inverse kinetics* provides the instantaneous joints rotation realizing a desired instantaneous translation of the total center of mass. This property is used in its variational formulation as an approximation to solve the position control of the center of mass (under the hypothesis of small movements[14]). In a parallel fashion to inverse kinematics, we can invert the direct kinetic jacobian by evaluating its pseudo-inverse. In a redundant context (i.e. more joints than dimensions to control) we can use the classic decomposition of the solution into a pseudo-inverse solution and a homogeneous solution [16]. The general expression of discrete inverse kinetics is then (see Figure 2):

$$\Delta\theta = J_G^+ \Delta x_G + (I - J_G^+ J_G)\Delta z_o \qquad (5)$$

where :

$\Delta\theta$ is the unknown vector in the joint variation space (dimension n),

Δx_G expresses the so-called *main behavior*, see below (dimension m)

J_G is the kinetic jacobian (mxn) and J_G^+ is its unique pseudo-inverse (nxm),

I is the identity matrix of the joint variation space (nxn),

$(I - J_G^+ J_G)$ is the projection operator on the *null space* of the linear transformation J_G (i.e. any joint variation belonging to this sub-space is mapped by J_G into the null position variation of the center of mass),

Δz_o is a so-called *secondary behavior*, see below (dimension n)

The first component of the solution is the *main behavior* realizing the variation Δx_G of the center of mass position in Cartesian space. Its dimension *m* can be smaller than 3 as for the balance control of a multi-legged robot where only the two coordinates of the center of mass projection on the ground are to remain within the support polygon [6,9].

The second component of the solution is the user-defined *secondary behavior* Δz_o expressed in the joint variation space (dimension *n*). It is partially achieved due to its projection on the null space which dimension is in the best case *n-m* (Figure 2). This dimension clearly translates the potential of the secondary task. As inverse kinetics and inverse kinematics share the same joint variation space, we can take advantage of the already existing optimization behaviors in this space [1-4,16,17].

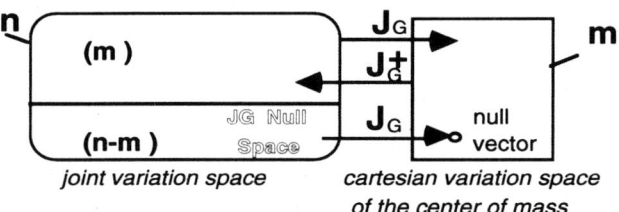

joint variation space   *cartesian variation space of the center of mass*

Fig. 2. Illustration of the joint variation space partitioning with inverse kinetics

Let us conclude this section by recalling two characteristics of such a variational approach. First, this method provides a local solution. It is more suited for static posture optimization rather than pure motion control, as already stated for inverse kinematics in [5]. Second, the configuration may become singular. This well-know problem can be solved with the damped least square [18] without modifying the validity of our method.

4   Mass Distribution in Multiple Support

In the multiple support context the articulated figure relies on more than one supporting site to achieve balance. This environment deeply changes the way a joint

134

variation alters the position of the center of mass as the support may continuously shift from one supporting site to another. In this section, we first introduce the concept of Influence Tree which generalizes the concept of augmented body to the multiple support context.

4.1 The Influence Propagation Algorithm (IPA)

To begin with let us define the *supporting influence* of each *supporting site* as the fraction of the total body mass it supports (we note it m_i). The whole set of supporting influences realizes a partition of the total mass :

$$\sum m_i = 1. \tag{6}$$

We evaluate the diffusion of this supporting influence beginning from each supporting site and propagating within the body. The body is modeled as a tree-structured graph of *mass nodes* each holding a fraction of the total body mass. The purpose of the Influence Propagation Algorithm (IPA in short) is to extract of the body graph as many *influence trees* as there are supporting sites. As the algorithm is very general we use the words *influence, site, node* and *tree-structured graph* without mentioning their specific nature.

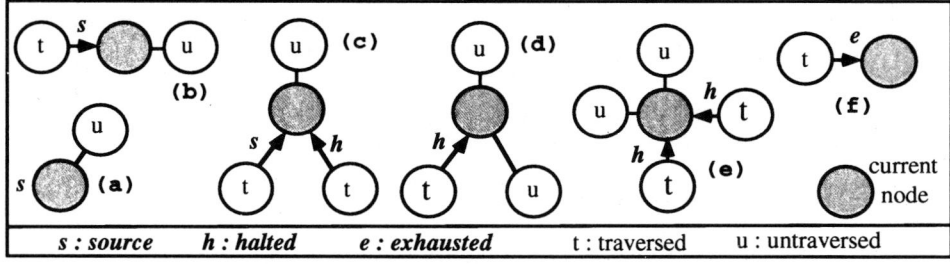

Fig. 3. various cases illustrating the three different group status

The algorithm evaluates for each node the percentage of influence coming from each site. For that purpose, we consume the influences while propagating within the body structure. Initially, a site can be associated with any node, either terminal or internal, of the tree-structured graph. Moreover, during the propagation, the influences of different sites can jointly propagate along the same sub-graph. Fore these reasons the propagating entity is called a *group* because it maintains the current state of the influence propagation of either isolated (Figure 3a,b) or jointly propagating (Figure 3c) sites. A node can have one of the two following status : either *untraversed* as long as it is not consumed or *traversed* once it is consumed. While propagating, each group maintains the information of a *current node* which is the node to be consumed. The current node may hold some neighbor nodes in the graph. The node from which the group has reached the current node is called its ancestor node while the other ones are called its *successor*(s). Due to the tree structure of the graph a group may have three different status:

- **_source_** : the group can consume the current node because it points to a unique untraversed successor (Figure 3 a,b,c). The propagation continues after consumption.

- **_halted_** : *a)* the group can not consume the current node because it points at least to two untraversed successors (Figure 3 d,e). The propagation stops temporarily.
       b) the group can not fully consume the current node because its influence is insufficient. The propagation stops temporarily.

- **_exhausted_** : the group can consume the current node because it points to zero or one untraversed successor. Moreover, the group influence exactly matches the one associated with the node, thus ending the propagation (Figure 3f).

The general outline of the Influence Propagation Algorithm (IPA) is detailed in Figure 4 and is immediatly followed by the description of its major functions.

```
Initialize each group with one site and its status with source
Do until all groups' status becomes exhausted
{
    For each source group "Propagate Loop"
    {
        Propagate() until status becomes halted or exhausted
    }

    For each current node "Fuse Loop"
    {
        Fuse() the groups halted at that node
    }

    For each halted group "Solve Loop"
    {
        For each untraversed successor (their number is noted nbus)
        {
            Integrate() the influence of the sub-graph rooted at that node

            If (all sub-graph influences are negative)
            {
                Consume() the current node
                Split() the group into nbus new source groups
            }
        }
    }
}
```

Fig. 4. The Influence Propagation Algorithm

The Propagate() function is applied whenever the current source group encounters a node to consume with zero or one untraversed successor (Figure 3a,b,c). If eventual halted groups were stopped at that node, the Fuse() function is applied to merge them with the current source group in a larger source group (Figure 3c). The resulting source group applies the Consume() function to the current the node. If its remaining influence is null the group status becomes *exhausted* and its propagation stops. Otherwise the unique successor becomes the new current node and the group status is updated to *source* or *halted* according to this new context. The propagation can continue only if the group's status is *source*.

The Consume() function is applied on the current node of a group. It consists in :
- reducing the group influence by the amount associated to the node
- reducing the sites influence according to their current site ratio (Cf. Fuse())
- marking the node as traversed.

The Integrate() function is applied whenever a *halted* group needs to evaluate the influence flow (positive or negative?) of the sub-graph rooted at an untraversed successor (Figure 3d,e). So this function propagates in the untraversed nodes of the sub-graph to cumulate the positive influence of other halted groups and the negative influence of the nodes. A resulting negative value indicates a deficit of sites influence in the sub-graph. This function is not applied if the group is halted due to insufficient influence to consume the current node.

The Fuse() function gathers multiple group entities into one group. It calculates the current group influence by summing all the current individual influences. It also updates the site ratio vector of the resulting group as :
    site ratio = [current site influence] / [current group influence]

The Split() function divides a group into a set of groups propagating in independent sub-graphs. Each new group influence is given by multiplying the former group influence with its split ratio :
    split ratio = [sub-graph influence] / [sum of sub-graph influences]
In order to retain all the sites which were composing the former group and also to keep unchanged the site ratio vector in every new group, the current site influences also split according to the split ratio vector.

4.2   An Example of Influence Trees Construction

We now show the IPA execution on a simple toy-like articulated structure (Figure 5).

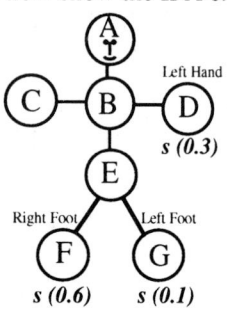

Each mass segment of this structure is given a name (from A to G) and hold a fraction of the total body mass (see first column of Table 1). We want to evaluate the propagation of the supporting influence of three supporting sites (with their supporting influence): right foot (60%), left foot (10%) and left hand (30%). They are noted in short RF, LF and LH respectively. The successive steps of the IPA are summarized in Figure 6. Three iterations of the main loop were necessary to propagate within the whole graph. In the first Propagate loop nodes F and D are consumed respectively by RF and LH while LF is immediately halted due to insufficient influence to consume node G (Fig 6a).

Fig. 5. Toy-like structure

There is no fusion prior to the Integrate loop (Fig. 6b) which detects that RF can consume E and further split into two source groups. In the second Propagate loop (Fig. 6c) node G is consumed by (RF+LF). LF status becomes exhausted. A fusion occurs between RF and LH prior to the Integrate loop which triggers node B consumption and the splitting of (RF+LH) group into two new source groups. The third Propagate loop sees the consumption of the nodes C and D by the two independent (RF+LH) groups (Fig. 6e).

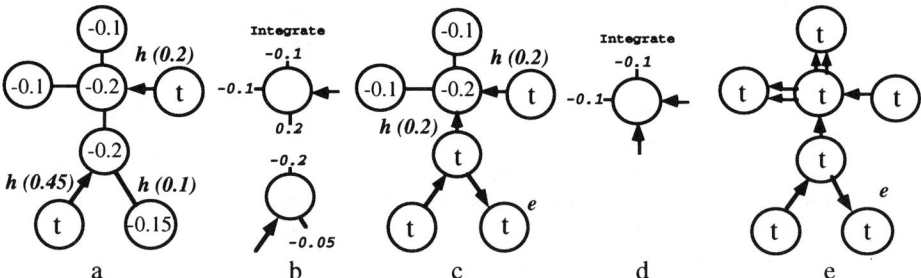

a   b   c   d   e

Fig. 6. Propagate (a,c,e) and Integrate (b,d) steps of a simple Influence Propagation

Table 1 summarizes the final influence distribution. For each node, we can see the respective influence coming from each supporting sites (the left value indicates sites proportions while the right one indicates the corresponding fraction of body mass). Figure 7 visualizes the equivalent influence trees rooted at the different supporting sites

Table 1 Mass distribution resulting from the support configuration

nodes	Supporting sites -> fraction of total mass	Right Foot		Left Foot		Left Hand	
A	0.1	0.5	0.05	0.	0.	0.5	0.05
B	0.2	0.5	0.1	0.	0.	0.5	0.1
C	0.1	0.5	0.05	0.	0.	0.5	0.05
D	0.1	0.	0.	0.	0.	1.	0.1
E	0.2	1.	0.2	0.	0.	0.	0.
F	0.15	1.	0.15	0.	0.	0.	0.
G	0.15	0.33	0.05	0.66	0.1	0.	0.
Total	1.		0.6		0.1		0.3

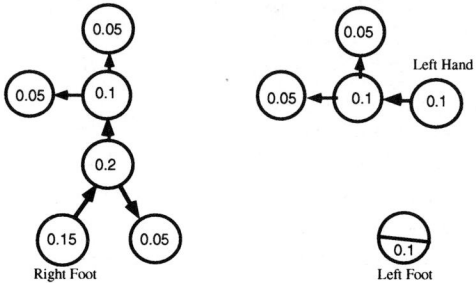

Fig. 7. Resulting Influence Trees associated with the three supporting sites

5 Position Control of the Center of Mass

We now show how this information is used to build the direct kinetics jacobian and what are the specific constraints added by the multiple support context for inverse kinetics. Then, we recall the equilibrium condition for posture in multiple support which becomes the operational formula linking the mass distribution to the center of mass position.

5.1 Computing the Multiple Support Jacobian

Direct Kinetics in multiple support becomes transparent once the influence tree concept is adopted to model the influence of a distributed support. Moreover this representation provides a continuous solution for variations of the mass distribution in multiple support. Section 3 has explained how the direct kinetics jacobian was computed in single support. Now, we have the same approach for each supporting site for which we compute a partial direct kinetics jacobian. We use the associated influence tree to delimit its influence :
- the motion is rooted at the supporting site
- only joints belonging to the influence tree are involved in the jacobian
- only the mass belonging to the influence tree is used to compute the augmented bodies.

As the law of conservation of the momentum is still applied on the whole body center of mass, all the partial direct kinetics jacobians can be summed in order to get the direct kinetics jacobian in multiple support.

5.2 Specific Constraints for Inverse Kinetics

Using directly expression (5) for inverse kinetics in this new context is insufficient. Only one supporting site, usually the more important, can be the root of the graph traversal for the update of the global transformations. So we have to provide a means ensuring that the position constraints of other supporting sites are also met.

This is done with the so-called *cascaded control* introduced in [1-4] (section 6 recalls one example in single support). With this technique the main behavior of an inverse kinematic control scheme ensures the position constraints of the supporting sites considered as end effectors (as in [5-6]) while the secondary behavior is then the result of the inverse kinetics control as defined by expression (5). With such an architecture we can easily evaluate the reachable space of the center of mass for a given set of supporting sites because the support constraints always have the highest priority among behaviors.

One important point to stress is that any other behavior-oriented end effector(s) can be integrated in this evaluation. For example a hand performing a reach behavior can also be integrated in the main behavior as an additional end effector of the inverse kinematic process.

5.3   Mass Distribution and Posture

With the control scheme presented before we are able to control the position of the center of mass for a given set of supporting sites with an associated mass distribution. The problem now is to enhance the design of realistic postures for articulated figures in multiple support. The user specification of the mass distribution on the supporting sites can be viewed as a powerful degree of freedom to play with in the posture design process. However, our basic approach is to reduce ,whenever possible, the number of variables to specify . In the present context we use the condition of static equilibrium to automatically relate the mass distribution to the posture and vice-versa.

As stated by the fundamental law of Statics, whenever a posture is in static equilibrium, both the sum of external forces and the sum of their moments, expressed at the global center of mass, have to vanish . We now consider only the vertical component of the reaction forces due to the supporting sites (a discussion on the horizontal component is beyond the scope of this paper).

The vertical component of the reaction forces directly reflects the mass distribution on the supporting sites in order to counterbalance the total weight acting at the center of mass (Cf. expression (6)). Regarding the vanishing of the sum of their moment a sufficient condition is to position the center of mass on the vertical line Δ_e passing through the barycenter G_e build (in the horizontal plane) from the supporting site locations S_i weighted by their supporting influence m_i :

$$\sum m_i . G_e S_i = 0. \tag{7}$$

So we can now deduce the following methodology :

- for a desired mass distribution to produce a balanced posture, inverse kinetics has to be applied so that the center of mass lies on Δe (regarding the principle, we extend an approach which was applied to two feet with inverse kinematics in [6]).

- given an initial balanced posture in multiple support (see previous point), if one desire to obtain a new location of the center of mass while maintaining the equilibrium constraint, then the two following operations have to be performed for each position variation of the center of mass (under the hypothesis of small movement) :

    - apply inverse kinetics to realize the position variation for
       the current mass distribution.

    - update the mass distribution according to the new position
       of the center of mass.

6   Simulation Results

6.1   Balance Control in Single Support

In the example presented here the cascaded control (see [1-4]) is used with inverse kinetics as the main behavior (maintaining the balance) while inverse kinematics is the secondary behavior to control two end effectors (right hand, left foot). The end effectors have to reach each other, say, to remove a thorn from the foot. The balanced posture achieving all these constraints (figure 8a) can be compared with a real posture (figure 8b).

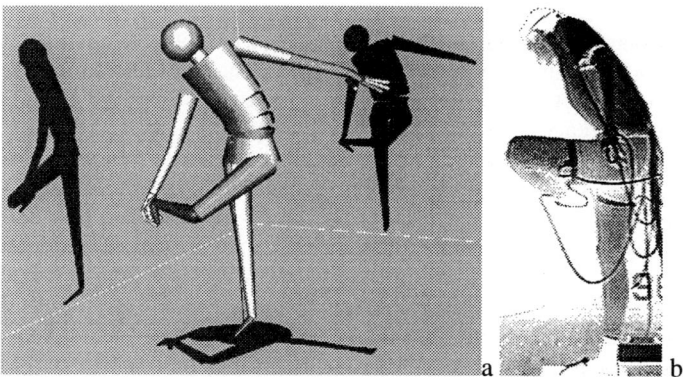

Fig. 8. Removing a thorn from one's foot with right hand and left leg as end effectors

6.2   Building the Influence Trees

Two examples illustrate the propagation of the supporting influence (without considering the equilibrium condition).

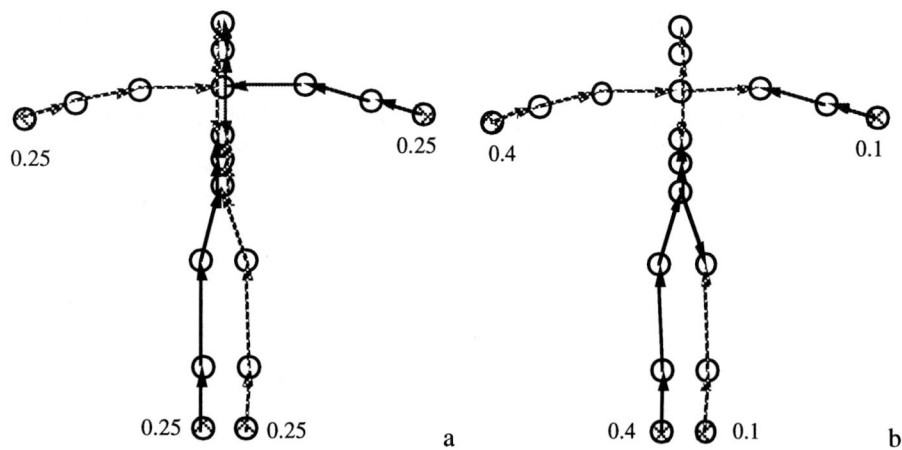

Fig. 9. Propagating the influence

The interactive display of influence propagation is made with color coding, one basic color per supporting site (red for right hand, blue for right foot, green for left hand, cyan for left foot). The colors also mix when the supports propagate in groups . The color plate from the appendix correspond to Figure 9a,b where we only show a graph representing the influence propagation of the following mass distributions :

- Equal support for each site ; the influence trees meet in the abdomen (figure 9a)

- larger support on the right side ; notice the extension of the right side trees (figure 9b)

6.3 Balance control in multiple support

In the climbing posture simulation (Figure 10a,b) the support distribution is the following : 0.75 for the right foot, 0.1 for the right hand and 0.15 for the left hand. The resulting posture has been obtained by assigning a goal-oriented behavior to the left foot in order to raise it to a higher position. The center of mass is represented as the small square which is projecting over the right foot.

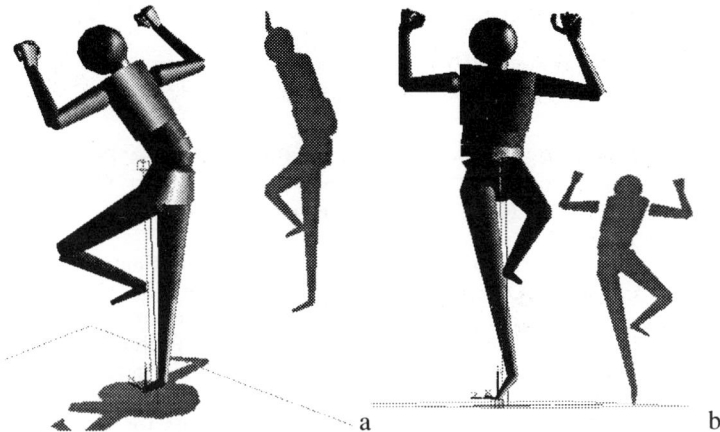

a   b

Fig. 10. a climbing posture with support distributed on the right foot and the hands while the left leg is brought to a higher position

7 Conclusion

In this paper we have presented a general and efficient approach for the control of the position of the center of mass in single and multiple support. Its purpose is to help the design of realistic postures in the sense of static analysis according to the mass distribution of the figure. Three major arguments advocate the use of our approach. First, the mass distribution is a very intuitive set of parameters; it does not add the cognitive burden of the additional parameter space appearing in sophisticated control methods. We can even automatically deduce it from the center of mass position under the static equilibrium constraint. Second, the calculation cost is comparable with

142

Inverse Kinematics for the same amount of degrees of freedom. Interactive design of complex postures is therefore possible in many cases (up to 20 dof) on middle range graphics workstation (e.g. SGI Indigo II Extreme). Third, our approach fits into existing high level interface of behavioral control of human figure; it significantly improves the realism for static postures.

Many questions remain open to discussion especially about the support distribution on the supporting sites. Some support distributions are clearly unrealistic and should be automatically discarded ; this is especially true when the arms are used as they are much weaker than the legs either under traction or under compression. A strength-based approach, as the one developed in [19], can efficiently complete the optimization carried out in the previous section. Moreover, we plan to extend our recent evaluation of the second order inverse kinetics solution for motion control from 2D cases [4] to complete 3D context.

8 Acknowledgments

The authors wish to thank the reviewers for their numerous comments. The research was partly supported by the Swiss National Foundation for Scientific Research and l'Office Fédéral de l'Education et de la Science.

References

1. Boulic R. and Mas R. "Inverse Kinetics for Center of Mass Position Control and Posture Optimization", Technical Report 94/68, 40 pp, Computer Sciences Department, EPFL, DI-LIG, Switzerland, September 1994

2. Boulic R., Mas R., Thalmann, D. "Inverse Kinetics for Center of Mass Position Control and Posture Optimization", Race Workshop on "Combined real and synthetic image processing for broadcast and video production (Monalisa Project)", Hamburg, 23-24 November 1994, Y. Parker & S. Wilbur Edt, Workshop in Computing Series, Springer-Verlag, ISBN 3-540-19947-0, April 95

3. Boulic R. and Mas R. "Hierarchical Kinematic Behaviors for Complex Articulated Figures", in "Advanced Computer Animation" Thalmann & Magnenat-Thalmann (Eds.) , Prentice Hall, 30 pp, to appear in August 1995

4. Boulic R., Mas R., Thalmann, D. "A Robust Approach for the Control of the Center of Mass with Inverse Kinetics", Proc. of CEIG'95 *Congreso Espanyol de Informatica Grafica*, Palma de Mallorca, June 1995

5. Phillips C.B., Badler N. " Interactive Behaviors for Bipedal Articulated Figures" Computer Graphics 25 (4), pp 359-362, July 1991

6. Badler N.I., Phillips C.B., Webber B.L "Simulating Human, Computer Graphics Animation and Control", Oxford University Press 1993.

7. Zeltzer D., Sims K. "A Figure Editor and Gait Controller to Task Level Animation", SIGGRAPH 88 Tutorial Notes on Synthetic Actors : The impact of A.I. and Robotics on Animation, (1988).

8. Maiocchi R "A Knowledge based approach to the Synthesis of human motion", IFIP TC5/WG5.10 "Modeling in Computer Graphics", Tokyo April 1991.

9. Choi B.S., Song S.M. "Fully Automated Obstacle-Crossing Gaits for Walking Machines", IEEE Trans. SMC, 18(6), pp 952-964, Nov. /Dec. 1988

10. Raibert M.H., Hodgins J.K., "Animation of Dynamic Legged Locomotion", Computer Graphics 25 (4), pp 349-358, 1992

11. McKenna M., Zeltzer D., "Dynamic Simulation of Autonomous Legged Locomotion", Computer Graphics 24 (4), pp 29-38, 1990

12. Witkin Kass "Spacetime constraints", Computer Graphics 22 (4),1988, pp159-168

13. Girard M "Constrained optimization of Articulated Animal Movement in Computer Animation" in "Making Them Move: Mechanics, Control, and Animation of Articulated Figures", Badler, Barsky & Zeltzer Editor, Morgan Kaufmann, 1991, pp209-232

14. Leborgne M. "Modélisation des Robots Manipulateurs Rigides", Publication Interne n°248 IRISA, 75 pp, Campus de Beaulieu, F-35042 Rennes, France

15. Orin D. and Schrader W. "Efficient Jacobian determination for robot manipulators" sixth IFTOMM Congress, New-Delhi, India, 1983

16. Liégeois A. "Automatic Supervisory Control of the Configuration and Behavior of Multibody Mechanisms" IEEE Trans. SMC, 7(12), pp 868-871, 1977

17. Maciejewski A.A. . "Kinetic Limitations on the Use of Redundancy in Robotics Manipulators", Proc. of IEEE Conf. on Robotics and Automation, pp 113-118,1989.

18. Maciejewski A.A. "Dealing with Ill-Conditioned Equations of Motion for Articulated Figures", IEEE CGA 10,3, pp 63-71 (1990)

19. Lee P.L.Y. "Modeling Articulated Figure Motion with Physically- and Physiologically-based Constraints", PhD Dissertation in Mechanical Engineering and Applied Mechanics, University of Pennsylvania, 1993.

Editors' Note: see Appendix, p. 231 for coloured figure of this paper

Keyframe Motion Optimization By Relaxing Speed and Timing

Zicheng Liu

Department of Computer Science

Princeton University

Princeton, NJ 08544

zl@cs.princeton.edu

Michael F. Cohen

Microsoft Research

Redmond, WA 98052

mcohen@microsoft.com

Abstract. While physically based approaches have been shown to be effective for creating graceful and realistic motions, keyframing systems are still the predominant tool for animation. This is due primarily to the control provided to the animator, as well as to the simple fast computation of in-between frames. In contrast, physical simulation systems automate the creation of realistic motion sequences, but remove most of the control from the animator. Recent work with spacetime constraints and optimal control has focused on balancing control and automation. However, either the algorithmic and computational complexity or the continuing lack of control have made it difficult to integrate these developments into real animation systems.

The goal of the research reported here is to avoid disturbing the basic framework of keyframe systems while still offering many of the advantages of optimization based systems. We present an animation paradigm in which, as in keyframe systems, the user specifies a small number of keyframes for the figure to pass through. As in spacetime constraint systems, the animator may also indicate constraints such as the height of a jump. In constrast to both systems, the time at which the figure reaches the keyframes and the velocity with which it passes each keyframe can be left open and are then determined automatically through an energy minimization. This heavily constrained optimization problem is much smaller than a full spacetime constraints problem and thus converges very quickly. In addition, the familiar keyframe paradigm offers a high level of control to the animator, while freeing the inexperienced animator from the less intuitive timing and velocity specifications. Including time itself as a variable within the optimization framework is an important change from previously reported systems. Our experiments show that this method is able to create smooth and realistic motions efficiently for complex 3D figures.

1   Introduction

There have been two major categories of systems for animating linked figures. The first is *keyframe* based, while the other is *physically* based. In keyframe based systems, the animator specifies poses, or keyframes, that the figure must pass through at predetermined times. The motion is then obtained by simply interpolating these keyframes, typically with cubic splines [10]. Commercial systems such as those from SoftImage, Alias, and Wavefront rely primarily on this paradigm. Although these systems give a high level of control to the animator, and can be very useful when coupled with good interactive tools, they do not offer any means to make the motion appear physically plausible beyond the skills of the animator. This is particularly apparent when the character needs to perform athletic motion in which inertial forces play a significant role.

In contrast, physically based systems begin from a description (or approximation) of the physical world, and derive the motion through simulation [1, 4, 5]. This implicitly guarantees (approximately) physically realizable motion, but these systems tend to be computationally expensive and offer very little control to the animator over the final motion sequence.

1.1   Constrained Optimization Systems

More recently, constrained optimization methods have been developed to try to return some control to the animator, and/or to provide the figures being animated with some internally motivated motion, while still maintaining aspects of physical simulation. One of these approaches, dubbed "spacetime constraints" tries to find optimal *trajectories* of a figure's degrees of freedom (DOF) based on a set of user-specified constraints and an objective to maximize (minimize) [13, 3, 8]. A related set of "optimal control" approaches optimizes over the space of possible *control* functions (essentially the internal forces exerted) and uses a simulation system both to create the final animation and to evaluate possible solutions [12, 9].

The spacetime constraint formulation leads to a non-linear constrained variational problem that typically has no closed form solution. In practice, the solution is found by reducing the space of possible trajectories to those representable by a linear combination of basis functions, for example cubic B-splines or wavelets. Finding the finite number of coefficients for the choice of basis involves solving the related constrained optimization problem, (i.e, finding the coefficients to create motion curves for the DOF that minimize the objective while satisfying the constraints). Unfortunately, there are no efficient numerical methods available to apply to such nonlinear constrained optimization problems although some advances have been reported with the use of wavelets [8].

A similar set of choices is made in the optimal control systems. A basis is chosen for the control functions which may take the form of weights in a neural net [12], or coefficients in a stimulus-response network [9], and some form of search is undertaken to find the unknowns. These control based systems suffer a similar complexity problem, as they rely on a full simulation to test each possible

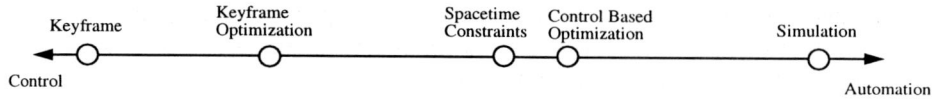

Figure 1: Control vs. Automation

solution. In addition, the lack of explicit control in these systems makes them unsuitable when the animator wants to maintain a high degree of specification.

1.2 The Idea

Figure 1 lists the choices of animation paradigms outlined above by their extent of control versus automation (The portion of the work which the computer does to generate a motion). The approach presented in this paper (labeled "keyframe optimization") fills a gap between simple keyframe systems and other optimization based systems. The central idea in the work presented here is to maintain as much of the semantics and control offered by keyframe systems as possible, while still providing some of the benefits of optimization based systems.

We also wish to provide results at interactive speeds (i.e., a few seconds) to encourage the iterative modification and evaluation of the animation design process. Reducing the complexity of the numerical process is achieved in a number of ways: by reducing the dimensionality of the space of possible solutions, by creating a more linear problem, by constraining the problem more tightly (implicitly reducing the space as well), and by providing a better starting guess for solutions.

The observation we make in reformulating the problem to achieve these goals is that the animator may have a good sense of specific key positions a character should pass through (the keyframes). But in general, the inexperienced animator may have less intuition about the precise timing of the keyframes and the velocity of the individual DOF as they pass these unknown points in time. Beyond the implicit constraints of the keyframes, the animator may also know specific instances of higher level constraints on the motion. For example, given a desire to have the figure jump to a certain height, the vertical velocity of the center of gravity (COG) at the beginning of a jump can be specified.

Based on these observations, the solution we propose is to

1. fix the user specified keyframed positions as constraints, as well as a few key time points selected by the animator,

2. allow specification of other higher level constraints, for example the velocity of the center of gravity for a jump, or the velocity of an end effector to achieve a physically realistic throw, and

3. select a piecewise cubic Hermite interpolation between keyframes as the underlying representation of the trajectories, but

4. leave the time of most keyframes and the first derivative of each DOF needed to fully specify the Hermite segments as unknowns to be solved for by a simplified optimization process.

These choices satisfy the criteria set out above in that they "trust" the animator to position the character at keyframes. This leaves intact any user interface for positioning the keyframes themselves. The animator is also implicitly fixing the amount of freedom in each DOF function through the number of keyframes chosen (i.e., additional keyframes inserted automatically increase the freedom in the resulting trajectory).

The optimization problem is greatly simplified as there are only time marks and velocity unknowns per DOF per keyframe. This contrasts with previous systems which solve for an unknown number of position values for each DOF. In addition, in our approach, the velocity terms appear as linear terms in an energy functional as opposed to the quadratic position terms. The choice of piecewise Hermite cubic curves for the trajectories matches the mix of known and unknown quantities in the system (i.e., known position, unknown velocities and timing).

1.3 Comparison to Standard Keyframing and Constrained Optimization

Compared to a pure keyframe system, the method outlined here uses optimization only to decide velocities and those time marks not explicitly specified by the animator. These constitute arguably the most difficult part of a keyframe system to produce a graceful and natural looking motion. In essence, these ideas primarily replace the interpolation step (and the parameter-to-time, i.e. "ease-in, ease-out" function) in traditional keyframe systems. Since the optimization is fast, the method is well suited to be implemented in any keyframe system.

This method differs from the optimal control interpolation method of [2] which solves the complete animation from a sequential solution of a series of two-point boundary value problems. In contrast, we perform a unified solution over as many time intervals as desired.

Another feature which is different from previous work is that the timing between keyframes is relaxed. In the spacetime constraint setting [13, 3, 8], the user had to specify when each constraint was to hold [1]. Our experiments suggest that leaving the timing to the optimization process results in significantly better results at a minimal cost. It is inexpensive since there is only one time value per keyframe, that is, it is not tied to the figure's complexity.

There are, of course, disadvantages in the proposed system. The reduction in the space of possible solutions requires more specification from the animator (i.e., this is not a system for creating autonomous creatures). The results are also not guaranteed to be physically accurate, as the space of solutions is highly constrained by the choice of keyframes. Furthermore, beyond what is provided

---

[1] It appears that a similar concept may have been employed in one of the examples in [13], however, it is not reported as such.

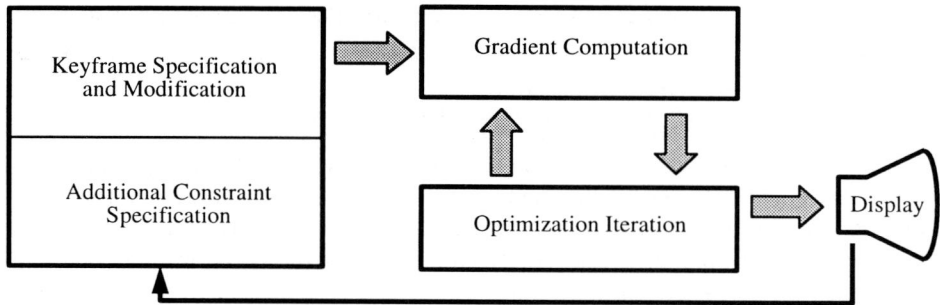

Figure 2: System Overview

in standard keyframe systems, objective functions such as energy minimization of energy, or other physically based objectives such as maintaining balance must be specified, and be able to be evaluated and differentiated. Finally, it can also be argued that the system being proposed really does very little for the animator, since the keyframes provide the backbone of the animation sequence. However, we will show that the subtleties of timing and velocity add significantly to the lifelike feeling of an animation. Although a highly skilled animator may have the ability to directly specify this also, many animators cannot.

2 System Overview

The animation system can be thought of either as a keyframe system relying on a spacetime constraint paradigm for interpolation between keyframes, or as a spacetime constraint system taking keyframes as constraints (see Figure 2).

The user interactively defines figures and manipulates them by changing the rotation angles of individual joints or through the use of any inverse kinematics method[2] The time points for a few keyframes may also be fixed in time, as may be velocities, if so desired. Higher level constraints can be specified as well[3]. For example, the COG of the figure or an end effector can be constrained to have a specific velocity at some keyframe.

Given the user specified keyframes, and an objective function (currently a minimum energy objective), the optimization process is run, and the resulting motion is displayed. At this point, the user may go back and modify or add keyframes and other constraints, and rerun the optimization procedure.

The optimization process involves iterative gradient computation and an optimization step. The optimization step is made either with a line search along the negative gradient or along a gradient modified by the pseudo-inverse Hessian constructed with the Broyden-Fletcher-Goldfarb-Shanno (BFGS) nonlinear op-

---

[2] The interactive system used to test the ideas in this work is quite rudimentary compared to commercial systems and is not discussed here.

[3] There is no high level interface developed for the experiments reported in this paper, but the symbolic method as developped in [7] should provide a good interface for such animation system.

timization algorithm [11, 8]. Typically 3 to 10 iterations of from 1 to 5 seconds are required.

2.1 Hermite Interpolation as DOF Representation

Piecewise cubic Hermite splines were selected as the underlying representation for the DOF trajectories due to their good match between the animator specification and optimization parameters, and the Hermite basis. Each Hermite segment is defined by endpoint positions (the keyframes), endpoint velocities (unknowns to be determined through optimization), and endpoint parameter values (in this case time, also to be determined). Thus, for m time segments, there are $2n(m+1)+m$ parameters in total (the position and velocity of each DOF at each of $m+1$ keyframes plus the m time values.

Since the animator's keyframes are taken as explicit solutions for the positions, there are only half of these $n(m+1)+m$ remaining as unknowns. Some of the remaining velocities are also prescribed by the animator, such as perhaps starting and ending at rest, as are some time points, further reducing the problem size. The problem, then is to find these $n(m+1)+m$ (or fewer) parameters so that the objective is minimized.

2.2 Relaxing Speed and Timing

A soccer player serves as an example to demonstrate how this idea works. Suppose the soccer player, starting from an initial standing position, is to kick a ball into the goal, and return to a standing position (see the middle of Color Plate). The animator has some intuitive notion about how to kick a ball, for example, the player swings his leg backward to prepare for the kick, then swings it forward to kick to ball. Thus, four keyframes are defined with the leg swung backward, with the leg about to kick the ball (in this keyframe, we make sure that the toe is at the ball's position), plus one keyframe each for the beginning and final standing positions. The timing of and velocities through the middle two keyframes is left unspecified. The first and last keyframes are fixed both in time and with zero velocity. One additional constraint requires the foot to have sufficient velocity to kick the ball at the time of the third keyframe. With the figure constrained to start and stop at rest, we are left with a very small optimization problem with only the second and third velocities, and the three time intervals as unknowns. These $(2 * n + 3)$ unknowns represent a much smaller, albeit more restrictive, problem than those that arise in general spacetime constraint problems. Although the solution space is quite restrictive, it is generally still big enough to contain good solutions (given reasonable keyframes of course). In experiments below, a smooth and realistic kicking motion of a 3D figure with 15 degree of freedoms was found in 3 seconds on an R4000 processor.

3 Keyframe Optimization

The optimization used in this work is a standard BFGS quasi-Newton solver [11]. BFGS defaults to a simple gradient descent for the first iteration. In fact, for small problems, we have found a pure gradient descent is all that is required. Each iteration consists of a local gradient determination followed by a bisection line search (see, for example, [11]) along the negative gradient. The ability to use such a simple system is due in part to the fact that a simplistic interpolation of the keyframes already places the solution near a local minimum, and thus in a well behaved region of the solution space. In addition, the unknown velocities of the DOF appear as linear terms in the goal constraint(see the next paragraph for the reason) as opposed to the positions that appear as nonlinear terms in a general system. The time values and higher level constraints are nonlinear, however, the initial values implied by the animators keyframes provide a sufficient starting point for a local downhill search.

The reason that the unknown velociteis of the DOF appear as linear terms in the goal constraint is the following. After the configuration is fixed, the goal constraint is a constraint on the velocity of the end effector or the center of gravit with the form $\dot{P}(t) = V$. Notice that $\dot{P}(t) = J(t)\dot{\Theta}(t)$ where J is the well-known Jacobi matrix, the constraint becomes $J(t)\dot{\Theta}(t) = V$. Since $J(t)$ is a constant matrix due to the fixed configuration, the left hand side is a linear function of $\dot{\Theta}(t)$.

3.1 Linked Figure Construction

The figure structure is represented as a rooted tree structure with links as vertices and joints as edges. Each joint can have up to 3 degrees of freedom (the Euler angles). Each link is attached to a coordinate system which rotates with the link.

A completely general optimization system requires a symbolic differentiation and compilation scheme as described by Kass [6]. The generalities of these systems come, however, at the cost of implementing the symbolic system, and the fact that symbolic expressions explode exponentially with the depth of the tree representing the figure. In the work presented here, the limited number of constraint types and the fixed objective lend themselves to an analytic gradient determination. The fast recursive algorithm for the derivations of the analytic gradients for the constraints and objective in the paper has been extended by the authors to develop a general and efficient symbolic interface to constraint based animation systems[7]. The user is refered to [7] for details about the derivations of the analytic gradients.

3.2 The Objective Function

The objective function is a weighted sum of the integral of the square of the change in energy of the figure, and any violations of the user specified constraints. Unfortunately, there is no closed form solution for this, thus a numerical quadrature is made by sampling the energy state and by squaring the differences between sampled states:

$$\sum_{i=0}^{r}(E(x_i) - E(x_{i-1}))^2 \tag{1}$$

where $t_0 = x_0 \leq x_1 \leq ... \leq x_r = t_f$, r is an input parameter.

For each link, $E(t)$ is equal to the sum of the kinetic energy at the center of mass, the rotational energy of the link around the center of mass, and the potential energy due to gravity.

4 Results

A series of experiments were conducted on two figures[4]. The first is a truncated 3D human-like figure with 2 legs (jointed at the knees), a pelvis and a body, with a total of 15 rotational degrees of freedom plus translation and rotation within the environment. The second figure is a more complete humanlike creature with 29 internal DOF. There is a ground plane and a ball with which the figures interact. The experiments involved jumping, landing from a jump, walking, running, and motion throwing and kicking a ball. In each case, short animation segments were explored. Transitions between segments were also explored with the same techniques, for example transitioning from walking to running to kicking a ball.

A first guess interpolation can be found by fixing the times of the keyframes at evenly spaced intervals. The velocities for this interpolation are taken from the central finite differences between previous and future keyframes (or forward or backward differences at end frames). This simple interpolation is also shown in the video, as a point for comparison although one would expect a skilled animator to do better than this on a first pass.

In general, each optimization iteration took approximately 1 to 2 seconds for the simple figure and 4 to 5 seconds for the more complete figure on an R4000 SGI machine. The dominant portion of the time was taken by gradient computation and objective evaluation during the line search. Solutions for short segments were often found in only two iterations, however, some continued to improve for 10 iterations.

The first example is a jumper. There are four keyframes: the initial relaxed position, swing backward, swing forward, takeoff. The center of gravity is constrained to have a desired upward velocity at take-off. The position of the COG is based on free flight dynamics after leaving the ground. The optimization process determines the velocities at the second, third, and fourth frames and the three time segment lengths are relaxed (48 unknowns). Six iterations (about 10 seconds), result in a realistic jumping motion with desired takeoff velocity results (see top of Color Plate).

A similar landing sequence was also determined (seen in the accompanying video). Given the landing velocity, the figure is required to land, absorb the

---

[4]A video is provided with the draft of the paper, as it is difficult to demonstrate animation results on paper.

energy of the fall, and then stand up. There are three frames: landing, follow through, and standing up. Four iterations result in a natural looking motion.

The second experiment looks at a soccer player. Initially in a standing at rest position, the player kicks the ball (hopefully) into the goal and comes back to his rest position. The ball's motion is computed from simple Newtonian physics assuming it simply takes on the velocity of the foot at impact. There are four keyframes: the first and fourth are trivial rest configuration. The second one is the prekicking configuration with the foot drawn back, and the third one represents when the foot strikes the ball. A constraint is set for the velocity of the foot at the third keyframe so as to kick the ball into the goal.

The total of 33 variables are determined in two iterations resulting in a kick with an anticipatory bend of the knee and a follow through that projects the ball with desired velocity (see Color Plate).

Further experiments were run on a throwing motion with the larger figure (see bottom of Color Plate). As in the kicking motion there are 4 keyframes, and a constraint for the velocity of the hand. Experiments were run both holding the time points constant and with the full model. The ability to relax the time values shows a marked improvement in finding a lower energy (and more natural looking) solution. The roughly doubled number of DOF led to approximately 5 second iterations, with the solution taking 20 iterations. The gradient determination is at worst quadratic in the size of the tree describing the figure.

A multisegment motion was constructed starting from a standing position, the soccer player walks, then runs and finally kicks the ball into the goal to score. The run, walk and kick motions are created first. Then the three transition motions are created: from initial standing to a periodic walk, from walking to running, and from running to the kick. Transition phases may take their first and last keyframes from other segments and may at the animator's discretion have intermediate keyframes specified. Each piece of the motion including transitions is individually optimized, and the results are spliced together. Each individual part took from 2 to 6 iterations, or about 3 to 10 seconds of CPU time.

5 Conclusions

The goal of combining intuitive user control with automated solutions for animation sequences is a delicate balancing act. This paper has presented an animation paradigm to try to achieve a good balance in this continuum. The animator is required to specify keyframes for which he intends the figure to pass through, as well as any additional key constraints on the figure's motion. The velocities and timing are then computed by an optimization process. The inclusion of the time points within the optimization is distinct from other systems and has proven to be an important addition. The DOF functions are represented by piecewise hermite splines. Initial results of the use of such a system were reported.

This paradigm effectively unburdens the optimization process so that it runs fast enough for use in an interactive setting. It has been shown to be able to effectively create graceful and realistic 3D complex figure animations. In addition, since the Hermite representation and the gradient computation are easy to implement, this method can be integrated in any keyframe system.

The objective function and the constrains in the experiments reported here are hard coded, because the known general symbolic method[8] suffers from exponential growth as the size of the figure increases. Currelty we are developping a more efficient symbolic interface as reported in [7].

How to incorporate contact and collision into such animation system is an interesting problem which we are planning to investigate in the future. And we hope to further explore the use of the paradigm developed here in more complex animations by integrating this work into commercial animation systems.

References

1. Bill Armstrong and Mark Green. The dynamics of articulated rigid bodies for purposes of animation. In *Proceedings of Graphics Interface*, pages 407–415. Computer Graphics Society, May 1986.

2. Lynn Shapiro Brotman and Arun N. Netravali. Motion interpolation by optimal control. In *Proceedings of SIGGRAPH'88 (Atlanta, Georgia, August 1–5, 1988)*, volume 22, pages 309–315. ACM, August 1988.

3. Michael F. Cohen. Interactive spacetime control for animation. *Computer Graphics*, 26(2):293–302, July 1992.

4. James Hahn. Realistic animation of rigid bodies. In *Proceedings of SIGGRAPH'88 (Atlanta, Georgia, August 1–5, 1988)*, pages 299–308. ACM, August 1988.

5. Paul M. Isaacs and Michael F. Cohen. Controlling dynamic simulation with kinematic constraints, behavior functions, and inverse dynamics. In *Proceedings of SIGGRAPH'87 (Anaheim, California, July 27–31, 1987)*, pages 215–224. ACM, July 1987.

6. Michael Kass. Condor: Constraint-based dataflow. In *Proceedings of SIGGRAPH'92 (Chicago, July 26–31, 1992)*, pages 321–330. ACM, July 1992.

7. Zicheng Liu and Michael F. Cohen. An efficient symbolic interface to constraint based animation systems. In *Proceedings of 6th EuroGraphics Workshop on Animation and Simulation*, (Maastricht, The Netherlands, September2-3 1995).

8. Zicheng Liu, Steven Gortler, and Michael F. Cohen. Hierarchical spacetime control. *Computer Graphics*, pages 35–42, July 1994.

9. J. Thomas Ngo and Joe Marks. Spacetime constraints revisited. In *Proceedings of SIGGRAPH'93 (Anaheim, August 1–6, 1993)*, pages 343–350. ACM, July 1993.

10. Cary B. Phillips, Jianmin Zhao, and Norman I. Badler. Interactive real-time articulated figure manipulation using multiple kinematic constraints. In *Proceedings of Symposium on Interactive 3D Graphics (Snowbird, Utah, March, 1990)*, volume 24, pages 245–250. ACM, March 1990.

11. Willaim Press, S. Teukolski, W Vetterling, and B Flannery. *Numerical Recipies in C, The Art of Scientific Computing*. Cambridge University Press, 2 edition, 1992.

12. M. van de Panne and E. Fiume. Sensor-actuator networks. In *Proceedings of SIGGRAPH'93 (Anaheim, August 1–6, 1993)*, pages 335–342. ACM, July 1993.

13. Andrew Witkin and Michael Kass. Spacetime constraints. *Computer Graphics*, 22(4):159–168, August 1988.

Editors' Note: see Appendix, p. 232 for coloured figure of this paper

Pulse-Modulated Locomotion for Computer Animation

Jean-Luc Nougaret and Bruno Arnaldi

SIAMES team, IRISA

Campus Universitaire de Beaulieu, 35042 Rennes cedex, France

nougaret@irisa.fr   arnaldi@irisa.fr

Abstract. In this paper, we address the problem of animating and controlling the locomotion of bodies which are propelled by pulse-like and periodic muscle activation. This kind of locomotion mode is encountered in a variety of real animals and an even larger variety of imaginary creatures could be propelled in this way. We propose a step-by-step methodology for the design of feedback controllers that can propel a dynamic model with an "intelligent" pulse-train of muscle efforts. The idea is to proceed in three steps: *(i)* a feedback controller is designed just as if muscles could deliver continuously regulated efforts. *(ii)* a pulse-modulator is inserted into the feedback controlled system, so as to take the muscle activation pattern into account. *(iii)* Synchronised kinematic cosmetics are added to the motion. The technique is illustrated by applying it to dynamic models of increasing complexity.

1   Introduction

Realistic animation of locomoting animals certainly implies a significant part of dynamic simulation, which is a necessary condition for providing a feeling of weight and power. Dynamic locomotion is a tough and interesting challenge for researchers in computer animation [13, 3, 4, 16, 9, 12].

Several recent approaches to dynamic locomotion control consist in hardwiring the periodicity property into the controller. For instance, Terzopoulos et al. [15] work with Fourier series decomposition of the muscle efforts. On the other hand, Van de Panne et al. use finite-state controllers with timed transitions in Pose Control Graphs [4] as well as in Sensor-Actuator Networks [3] (in this case, sensors operated as triggers).

In spite of its relevance, the periodicity assumption is not sufficient and misses an important point: though animal gaits are roughly stationary, direction changes and velocity variations are associated with some intelligent and real-time adaptation of the gait. For instance, during bird flight or fish swim, the wings, or the fins, seemingly beat periodically but these are slightly tuned, or modulated in real-time, in order to steer the animal towards its goal. To overcome the periodicity limitation, we suggested that the gait pattern be generated by expanding the gait trajectories on a wavelet basis instead of Fourier series [10, 11]. The idea was that the gait pattern could be fine-tuned by optimizing the wavelet coefficients. Such flexibility could be used for steering the synthetic animal towards a desired target. A similar idea of real-time adaptation of the gait was also expressed in [1, 2].

Apart from its quasi-periodic, modulated nature, there is another interesting feature in animal locomotion: this is the pulse-like activation of the propelling muscles. Indeed, for a variety of locomotion modes, such as a bird's rowed flight [14, 5], muscles are activated rather momentarily and periodically whereas they are almost inactive the rest of the time (see figure 1).

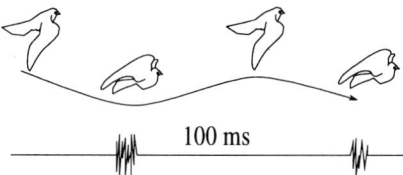

Figure 1: Pectoral muscle activation during a bird's rowed flight, from Dial et al 1988., modified

Thus, one may view the muscle output as a quasi-periodic and pulse-like train. The name of the game then consists in modulating this pulse-train in order to ensure that on a time-average, the animal is propelled towards its goal.

In this paper we present a comprehensive approach to the design of embedded models for animating the kind of locomoting creatures, which are propelled by periodic pulse-like muscle activation. The method is three-step and is illustrated in figure 2:

(i) In order to ease the design of the motion controller, the periodic pulse-like nature of the actual muscle activation pattern is first neglected, and it is supposed that muscles can deliver fictitious and continuous efforts. For instance if a bird were to be animated, we can think of temporarily replacing its wings by a pair of continuously regulated rockets. By doing so, we can design a feedback controller to be fitted to the model.

(ii) In the second step, the muscle activation pattern is taken into account by inserting a pulse-modulator into the system. Its role is to deliver pulse-like modulated muscle efforts, in such a way that when averaging their effects over time, they are roughly equivalent to the fictitious efforts. This means that the feedback controller does not need to be redesigned. In other words, the pulse-like periodic nature of the muscles can be treated *a posteriori*, once the controller has already been designed. For the bird example, the rockets are activated in pulse-like manner, so as to emulate the actual wing beat. By doing so, one ensures that motion of the bird exhibits realistic undulations.

(iii) In the final step, synchronised cosmetic kinematics are added for improving visual realism. For the bird example, wings are restored at this stage, and their motion is time-synchronised with the propelling pulses.

The paper is organized as follows. In the next section, we describe the pulse-modulator, which acts as a tunable pacemaker for locomotion. Not only does this pacemaker generate the gait pattern (by sequencing the actuators' successive activity), it also generates a pulse-train the features of which (amplitude, pulse duration and

156

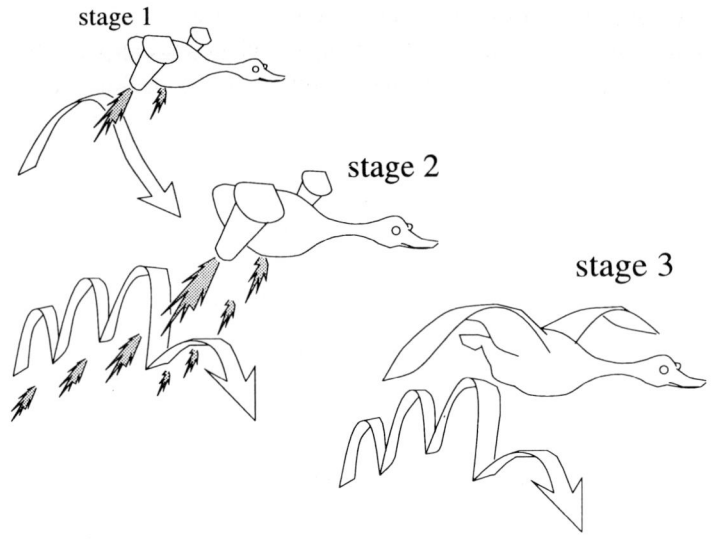

stage 1

stage 2

stage 3

Figure 2: A three-step approach for the design of embedded models of locomoting animals

frequency) can be regulated in realtime for efficient tuning of the generated gait pattern. In section 3, we illustrate the step-by-step approach by on the problem of controlling the rowing pattern of a kayakist. In section 4 we also assess the validity of our approach by applying it to the locomotion of a simplified 3D fish. These two experiments result in ready-to-use embedded models, the motion of which can be specified in realtime by high-level parameters, such as the required velocity (direction and magnitude).

2 Pulse-Modulated Locomotion

Problem Statement: Discontinuous Propulsion

For simplicity and clarity, let us first suppose that we consider the locomotion of a 1D imaginary type of jellyfish, shown in figure 3. The jellyfish moves in a constant direction and is propelled by successive contractions of its contractile body. The contraction pattern is considered to be roughly periodic with period T. Considering that the water friction coefficient is λ, the motion equation along the jellyfish direction is simply expressed by:

$$m\dot{V} = F - \lambda V \tag{1}$$

where: V is the velocity, and F represents the T-periodic force pulse-train generated by the contractile body. When the mechanical system time-response $\tau = m/\lambda$ is significantly longer than T, the velocity exhibits some variations around its average equivalent value V_{eq} (time-averaged over a duration Δt, corresponding to a few τ). Let ΔV be the measure of $V(t)$ variations around its short-time averaged equivalent value V_{eq}: $\Delta V = max_{\Delta t}|V(t) - V_{eq}|$. It can be easily verified that as the ratio τ/T tends towards $0, \Delta V$ tends towards 0, in which case motion seems to be continuous despite the discontinuous nature of muscle activation. In such conditions, motion is smoothed by the mechanical system which operates as a time-integrator.

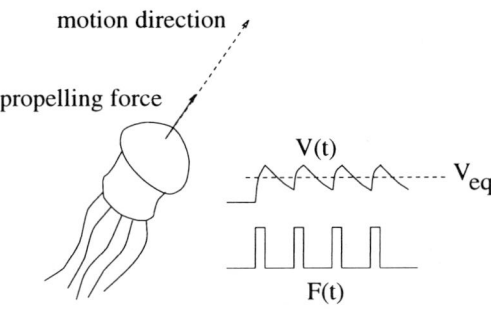

Figure 3: 1D motion of the jellyfish

Now, when considering slower systems (with ratios τ/T tending towards 1 or more), the effects of force pulses become even more visible as ΔV increases.

Principle: Pulse-Modulation

Considering the jellyfish, let us suppose we wish to control its motion, by controlling its velocity V over time. For this purpose, we need to gain control over the force pulse-train $F(t)$ which is delivered by the contractile body. We assume that such a pulse-train can be approximated by a succession of square pulses, where each pulse p_i is characterised by three features: its amplitude F_i, its duration δ_i and period T_i. When averaging the effect of the square pulse over T_i, it is equivalent to an average force F_{eq} the value of which is:

$$F_{eq} = \frac{1}{T_i} \int_{t_0}^{t_0+T_i} F(t)dt \tag{2}$$

which can be computed as:

$$F_{eq} = \frac{F_i \delta_i}{T_i} \tag{3}$$

From equation 3, it can be seen that the pulse-train can be modulated in three distinctive ways, by adjusting one of the three parameters of the pulse while keeping the two others constant. The corresponding modulation schemes are listed below and these are well-known to power electrical engineers and communications engineers.

modulation scheme	modulated variable	constant parameters
amplitude PAM	$F_i(F_{eq})$	T, δ
pulse-width PWM	$\delta_i(F_{eq})$	F, T
frequency PFM	$T_i(F_{eq})$	F, δ
hybrid	$F_i, \delta_i, T_i(F_{eq})$	none

Although all modulation schemes are rather similar in terms of controller performance, they have very different effects on the qualitative aspect of motion: The PAM-modulated jellyfish would accelerate by expelling larger quantities of water, whereas the PFM-modulated jellyfish would increase the frequency of its body contractions. Thus, it may be of great interest to be able to choose between these different modulation schemes. Moreover, a hybrid modulation scheme would consist of regulating simultaneously $F_i(F_{eq})$, $\delta_i(F_{eq})$ and $T_i(F_{eq})$. For this purpose, a weighted-sum strategy may be designed in order to provide additionnal flexibility to the modulation schemes.

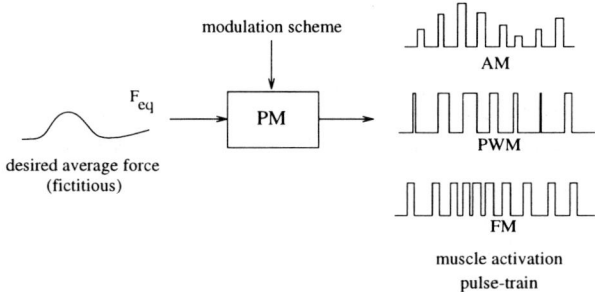

Figure 4: Pulse-modulator functionning

It is also interesting to note that the physical limitations of the muscles can be taken into account by setting saturation limits on the pulse amplitude, on the pulse frequency, on the pulse width, or on the average equivalent torque F_{eq} that can be delivered by the pulse-modulator.

3 Illustration: paddling a kayak

In order to illustrate the proposed approach, we addressed the problem of controlling the dynamically simulated kayak shown in figure 5. The model takes into account the river flow velocity as well as water friction. When moving the paddle through the water, the rower exerts a discontinuous piecewise constant force F_{right} or F_{left}, which is considered to be roughly collinear to the kayak. In the same time, F_{right} and F_{left} generate an alternating torque which causes the kayak to rotate around its vertical axis. We suppose that the paddling pattern is periodical. However, the rower can decide to paddle more energetically by increasing the duration of his effort over the paddling period.

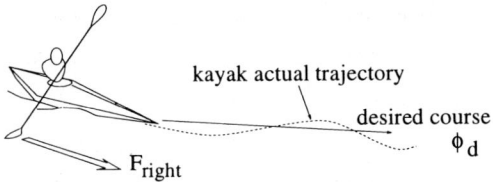

Figure 5: In our example, the periodic paddling pattern is modulated, in real-time, in order to steer the kayak's course for the desired direction, at the desired speed.

(i) Problem simplification

As stated above, the problem of controlling the kayak's motion may look difficult. This is the reason why we first act as if the kayak could be propelled continuously, by fitting it with two motors as shown in figure 6.

The fictitious propeller engines may deliver a torque T_{eq} and a force F_{eq}, that can be simply deduced by:

$$\begin{cases} F_{eq} = F_{right} + F_{left} \\ T_{eq} = L \times (F_{right} - F_{left}) \end{cases} \tag{4}$$

where: L is roughly equal to half the paddle length.

Or in matrix form, $[F_{eq}, T_{eq}] = K^{-1} [F_{right}, F_{left}]$. The invertible matrix K is interesting because introducing F_{eq} and T_{eq} enables complete decoupling of the effects of F_{right} and F_{left}.

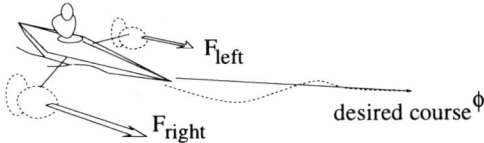

Figure 6: Feedback control is designed just as if the paddle was replaced by two motors, the efforts of which can be continuously regulated

Designing a controller for this simplified system, is a classic job for people with a background in control theory: as the kayak equation relative to ϕ is linear ($J_z \ddot{\phi} = T_{eq} - \lambda \dot{\phi}$ where λ is a water friction coefficient), it is convenient to control the input torque with a PD control law, such as in [7], whose feedback gains can be computed automatically, using standard design methods [8] :

$$T_{eq} = K_\phi(\phi_d - \phi) - K_{\dot{\phi}}\dot{\phi} \tag{5}$$

For speed control, a simple proportional feedback gain K_v was chosen and it could be adjusted by hand.

(ii) Muscle activation pattern

At this stage, the feedback controller ensures that the kayak can be steered in real-time towards a specified direction ϕ_d and at a specified velocity V_d, with a time response directly associated with the feedback gains. However if nothing else were to be done, motion would be unrealistic in the sense that the pulse-like and periodic nature of the paddle activation has been neglected. In order to take this effect into account, a model for the rower is inserted into the system, as shown in figure 7.

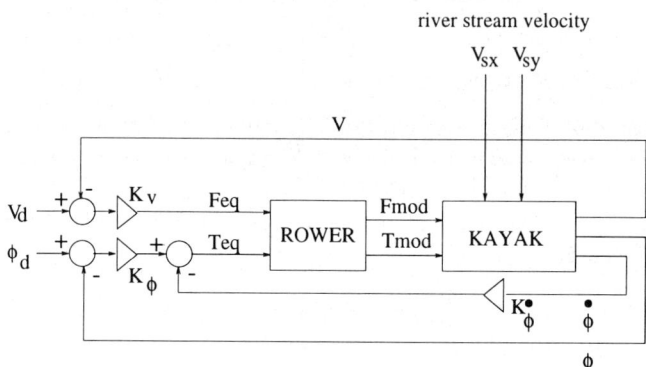

Figure 7: Motion controller for the kayak

The rower model shown in figure 8 activates the paddle periodically and modulates the duration of the delivered effort. In other words, this propulsion model produces a periodic, pulse-like alternating train of forces F_{right} and F_{left} in such a way that their alternating sequence, is equivalent to T_{eq} and F_{eq}, on a time-average.

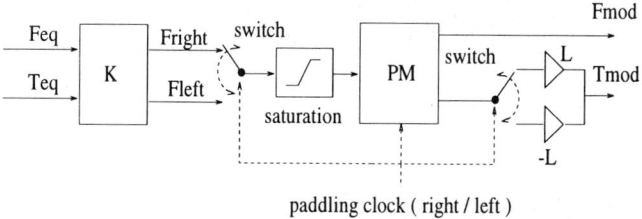

Figure 8: The rower model generates pulse-modulated forces associated to the paddle activation

At the heart of the rower model is the paddling pattern generator that we described earlier on. Each time the paddle is activated, the "intensity" of rowing is regulated in such a way that the paddle delivers the same amount of energy as if the kayak was propelled by the fictitious motors (associated to F_{eq} and T_{eq}). The good thing is that when the rower model is added, there is no need to modify the values of the feedback gains $K_{\dot{\phi}}, K_{\phi}\ K_v$ which were computed earlier on. As explained in pulse modulation theory [6], the time-averaged behaviour of the kayak is not modified by the rower model, although its effects are visible locally.

(iii) Synchronised kinematic cosmetics

The pulse-modulator generates parameters F, δ or T that are used for synchronising the kinematic trajectories of the paddle. An inverse-kinematic algorithm automatically derives the posture of the kayakist.

Figure 9: Arm's movement is time-synchronised with the kayak motion

4 Third example: fish locomotion

In this section, we consider a 3D synthetic fish which propells itself by generating impulsions on its caudal fin, as a real fish does. On the other hand, the fish pectoral fins operate as the aerofoils of an airplane, by controlling the fish pitch angle and thus allowing depth control as shown in figure 10.

As explained by Renous in [14] low-speed locomotion of a fish is characterised by a very low Reynolds number (< 1), in which case the drag is proportionnal to velocity. Hence the first-order equation set 6.

162

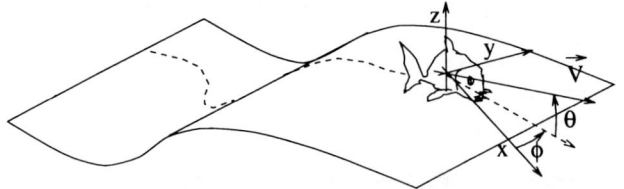

Figure 10: Fish servo-controlled parameters

$$\begin{cases} \dot{V} &= F_{mod} - \lambda' V \\ \ddot{\phi} &= T_{mod} - \lambda'' \dot{\phi} \\ \ddot{\theta} &= T_{depth} - \lambda''' \dot{\theta} \end{cases} \qquad (6)$$

where: F_{mod} represents the longitudinal hydrodynamic force engendered by the caudal fin, T_{mod} is the hydrodynamic torque and T_{depth} is the pitch torque generated by the pectoral fins.

This mechanical model is more simple than those used by Terzopoulos et al. in [15, 16] but it still captures the essentials of fish locomotion dynamics. Indeed, the focus of this paper is the propulsion model, not the dynamic equations of motion.

The caudal fin is activated in a quasi-periodic pulse-like manner. The fish is propelled forward while the tail expels water backward. Accordingly, the fish's motion can be considered to be generated by a pulse-train of forces as shown in figure 11.

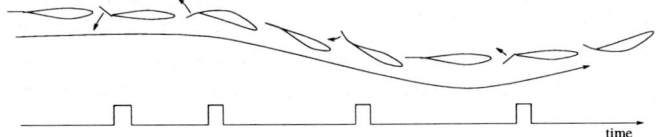

Figure 11: Propelling pulse-train generated by the periodic activation of the tail during the fish swim

Using the technique we described above, designing a feedback controller for the fish is straigthforward. Indeed, equations relative to V and ϕ are rather similar to those observed for the kayak model. Thus, the controller for the tail can be designed in almost the same way as for the paddling generator described earlier on. For depth control, a regulation feedback is added for servo-controlling the pectoral fin.

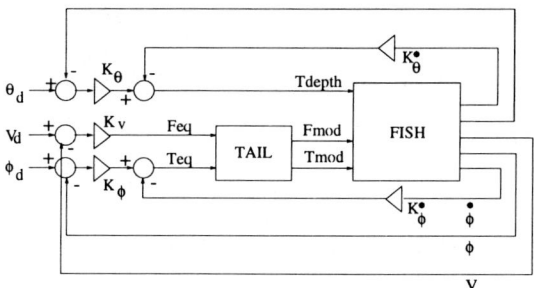

Figure 12: Motion controller for the 3D fish: a pulse-modulator controls the tail whereas the pectoral fins are continuously regulated by a depth PD-controller

5 Conclusion and future works

This paper has focused on a new propulsion model for computer-animated locomoting animals. Simple dynamic models with saturation nonlinearities were considered for validating the propulsion model. As the complexity of the mechanical model increases, two issues will need specific care: nonlinearity and coupling between the degrees of freedom. For both these issues, control theory provides workable solutions and there should be no trouble in inserting the pulse-modulator for generating the muscle activation pattern. The scope of this technique should thus encompass aquatic and aerial locomotion with no major difficulty as future works will try to demonstrate. Legged locomotion may be more difficult because sensory information for terrain adaptation may be needed, as in [3, 1, 2].

Pulse-modulation can be an efficient tool for controlling the locomotion of a variety of computer animated animals. The three above-mentionned examples are interesting because there is probably no other efficient way to control them than the method we propose here: locomotion is controlled from a higher level of abstraction, by regulating the activation of muscles through time-averaged effects.

References

1. R. Boulic and D. Thalmann. Combined direct and inverse kinematic control for articulated figure motion editing. *Computer Graphics Forum*, 11(4):189–202, October 1992.

2. R. Boulic and D. Thalmann. Track a kinematic goal-oriented animation system for coordinated editing of joint-space based motions". In *Proceedings of the Third EUROGRAPHICS workshop on animation and simulation, Cambridge, UK*, Sept. 1992.

3. M. Van de Panne and E. Fiume. Sensor-actuator networks. *Proceedings of SIGGRAPH '93, ACM Computer Graphics*, pages 335–342, August 1993.

4. M. Van de Panne, R. Kim, and E. Fiume. Virtual wind-up toys for animation. *Graphics Interface '94. Banff, Alberta, Canada, May 16-17*, May 1994.

5. K.P.Jr Dial, S.R Kaplan, G.E.Jr Goslow, and F.A. Jenkins. Functional analysis of the primary upstroke and downstroke muscles in the domestic pigeon (*columbia livia*) during flight. *Journal of Experimental Biology*, 134:1–16, 1988.

6. J.P. Ferrieux and F. Forest. *Alimentations a decoupage. Les convertisseurs de l'electronique de puissance.* Masson, Paris, 1976.

7. A. Lamouret, MP. Gascuel, and JD. Gascuel. Combining physically-based simulation of colliding objects with trajectory control. *The journal of Vizualisation and Computer Animation*, 5:1–20, 1995.

8. P. De Larminat. *Automatique Commande des systèmes linéaires.* Hermes, 14, rue Lantiez, Paris 17, 1993.

9. J.T. Ngo and J. Marks. Spacetime constraints revisited. *Proceedings of SIGGRAPH '93*, pages 343–350, August 1993.

10. JL. Nougaret, B. Arnaldi, and R. Cozot. Optimal motion control using a wavelet network as a tunable deformation controller. In *Proceedings of the Fifth EUROGRAPHICS workshop on animation and simulation, Oslo, Norway*, Sept 1994.

11. JL. Nougaret, B. Arnaldi, G. Hegron, and A. Razavi. Quick tuning of a reference locomotion gait. In *IEEE Proceedings of Computer Animation '95, Geneva*, April 1995.

12. C.W.A.M. Van Overveld. Small steps for mankind: Towards a kinematically driven dynamic simulation of curved path walking. *The Journal of Visualization and Computer Animation*, 4:143–123, 1994.

13. M. Raibert and J. Hodgins. Animation of dynamic legged locomotion. *Computer Graphics*, 25(4):349–358, July 1991.

14. S. Renous. *Locomotion.* Dunod, Paris, 1994.

15. D. Terzopoulos, X. Tu, and Radek Grzeszczuk. Artificial fishes with autonomous locomotion, perception, behavior, and learning in a simulated physical world. In MIT Press, editor, *Artificial Life IV Workshop*, July 1994.

16. X. Tu and D. Terzopoulos. Artificial fishes: Physics, locomotion, perception, behavior. *Computer Graphics*, pages 43–50, August 1994. In proceedings of SIGGRAPH'94.

Editors' Note: see Appendix, p. 233 for coloured figure of this paper

Guided Optimization for Balanced Locomotion

Michiel van de Panne
Department of Computer Science
University of Toronto

Alexis Lamouret
iMAGIS/IMAG-INRIA
Grenoble

Abstract. Teaching simulated creatures how to walk and run is a challenging problem. As with a baby learning to walk, however, the task of synthesizing the necessary muscle control is simplified if an external hand to assist in maintaining balance is provided. A method of using guiding forces to allow progressive learning of control actions for balanced locomotion is presented. The process has three stages. Stage one involves using a "hand of God" to facilitate balance while the basic actions of a desired motion are learned. Stage two reduces the dependence on external guidance, yielding a more balanced motion. Where possible, a third stage removes the external guidance completely to produce a free, balanced motion. The method is applied to obtain walking motions for a simple biped and a bird-like mechanical creature, as well as walking, running, and skipping motions for a human model of realistic proportions.

1 Introduction

The synthesis of realistic walking and running gaits is a difficult problem that has been the focus of a large body of research in computer animation, biomechanics, and robotics. Solutions to the low-level control of walking and running are key elements in the construction of "high-level" locomotion behaviours that deal with direction and speed as opposed to actual joint motion. Unfortunately, existing solutions to the low-level control problem for the physics-based animation of walking and running are few and have many limitations. This impedes the construction of high-level behaviours, which must know the capabilities and limitations of the constituent low-level control primitives. In an attempt to remedy this deficit, we present a new computational method for making synthetic actors of arbitrary design progressively acquire the necessary control for balanced locomotion.

The logical sources of inspiration to draw upon when designing a sensory-motor control mechanism for synthetic actors (both human, animal, and imaginary) are the solutions evolved by nature. Unfortunately, present efforts in this direction often lead to an immense respect for the finely-tuned design of these systems rather than a complete understanding of the complex mechanisms involved. At the same time, it is reasonable to suspect that biological sensory-motor systems are highly tuned to the bodies they live in, the external environment, and the required motions. As such, they may provide hints towards designing similar control systems for synthetic actors, but they will in no case yield a complete solution[1].

We propose a multi-step process for the automated synthesis of balanced gaits. This process draws upon our everyday experience by making use of *motion guidance* to simplify the learning problem. Consider a parent helping a child learn how to walk or skate by providing a helping hand. Just as this hand serves to stabilize the motion being learned, we shall introduce a similar 'hand of God' to the aid of learning synthetic actors. Another good example is that of the traning wheels of a bicycle, which offer external support to simplify the learning problem. Rehabilitation techniques for pathological human gaits also employ guiding mechanisms[8].

The guided optimization technique we present uses an external torque to enforce a balanced upright posture during walking or running. We hereafter refer to this guiding external torque as the "hand of God", or HOG for short. With the HOG in effect, the problem of balance is temporarily (and artificially) resolved, simplifying the process of finding the appropriate control actions to produce a desired motion. Once a basic control strategy for a gait has been synthesized, the external support can subsequently be reduced or eliminated through further optimization. First, the initial control strategy is refined so that the HOG performs less work in helping to maintain balance. This typically produces a motion with a small residual external guiding torque. Second, any remaining HOG work can be removed in sequential pieces.

It is worthwhile elaborating that while the synthesis of motion control for synthetic actors is difficult, it is to some extent a side issue in computer animation, where only the final motion and not its underlying complexity is an issue. It is necessary to hide the underlying complexity in order to produce simple-to-use animation tools. This was a strong consideration for our choice of a synthesis tool whose effects on the final motion are obvious and direct.

The remainder of this paper is divided into four sections. In section 2 we present related work. Section 3 discusses the HOG and its use in the automated optimization process. Section 4 presents results for newly-invented synthetic animals as well as a human model. Lastly, section 5 concludes.

2 Previous Work

The study of walking and running motions has long been a subject of fascination. The easiest way to animate such motions for humans is to capture and store the motion of a real human being. The data can be gathered from film or video (rotoscoping) or by pasting electronically-trackable sensors directly on live actors (motion capture). While no technique can hope to do better than the direct capture of the real phenomena, motion capture has several limitations. Besides requiring special hardware, it is best suited towards animating humans, given the difficulty of finding the extremely rare live Robo-bird and Simpleton creatures discussed later in this paper. Furthermore, once a motion is captured it is difficult to change or reuse in multiple situations. In contrast to relying on instances of existing acted motion, we shall rely on existing tools for motor learning, namely the principle of guiding a motion.

The specific challenge of creating tools for human animation has been taken on by few. The work of Badler et al.[2], Magnenat-Thalmann and Thalmann[17], and Boulic et al.[4] illustrate the present state of the art in modeling humans using predominantly kinematic methods. The method presented in [3] includes the use of kinematically-guided corrections to motions. A method of generalizing existing rotoscope data while preserving original motion characteristics is presented in [14].

Beyond kinematic methods, there have been several proposals to produce animated walking motions using physics-based models. Girard[9] uses a mix of kinematic and dynamic methods to achieve a variety of biped and quadruped motions. Bruderlin and Calvert[5] use a similar mix of techniques to generate realistic parameterized walking motions for a kinematically complex human model, and later show that parameterized walks can also be achieved using a purely kinematic model[6]. The gaits are constructed using important features extracted from experimental gait data.

The work of Raibert[23] and Raibert and Hodgins[24] demonstrates an elegant and robust control solution for balanced hopping and running creatures having 1, 2, or 4 legs. Hodgins[10] uses a similar solution to control a running motion for a realistic planar human model. As well, Hodgins et al.[11] have developed a variety of control algorithms for other tasks. Stewart and Cremer[26] use changing sets of desired constraints to control the walking motion of a human-like model. McGeer[18] shows that stable passive walks can be achieved down modest inclines. McKenna and Zeltzer[19] show how to synthesize a variety of gaits for a fully-dynamic hexapodal model. There is a significant body of robotics research concerning the control of bipedal walking motions, as well as in biomechanics for simulating human motion. While specific control solutions abound, there has been relatively little work on the learning of gaits in a general setting, i.e., for creatures of arbitrary design.

The challenge of *learning* motor-control functions must thus be addressed if we hope to use physics-based simulations as a tool for creating animations. The space-time constraints technique of Witkin and Kass[29] and the subsequent work of Cohen[7] and Liu et al[16] show that optimization can be used as an effective tool for this purpose. Van de Panne et al.[27] propose a general method for the synthesis of closed-loop control, but this method is restricted to simple systems. The work of Pandy et al.[22] represents a significant advance, showing how to optimize parameterized control histories to obtain desired jumping motions for a human model. The work of van de Panne and Fiume[28], Ngo and Marks[21], and Sims[25] further shows how parameter optimization techniques can be applied with the goal of animation in mind, using a variety of different control representations and optimization techniques. The guided optimization technique presented here proceeds onwards from these optimization techniques by giving additional thought to the optimization process and drawing upon some tricks humans use to help themselves learn. We note that the notion of adding external forces to help achieve a desired motion exists implicitly in the work on space-time constraints, and has also been previously proposed by Lamouret and Gascuel[15].

168

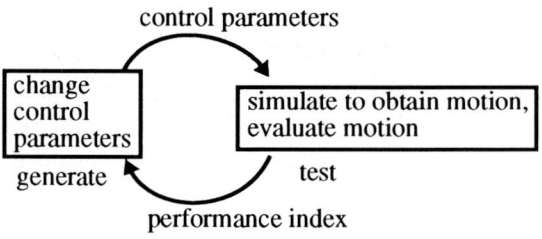

Fig. 1. Nonlinear parameter optimization.

3 Guided Optimization

The HOG exists as a tool to simplify the kind of optimization problems encountered in animation. This need arises from the large search spaces that must be explored by methods based on parameter optimization. While the synthesis procedure we propose relies on parameter optimization, the use of the HOG leads to a simplified optimization problem that can be solved in several stages. Following a brief review of parameter-optimization methods, the implementation of the HOG and its use in learning is described.

3.1 Parameter Optimization for Animation

The general structure of parameter optimization techniques is shown in Figure 1. Typically the control parameters are desired positions for the joints or muscles of the animated figure, which we shall collectively refer to as Ω_d. For articulated figures, these are translated into torques using proportional-derivative servomechanisms defined by $\tau = k_p(\theta_d - \theta) - k_d\dot{\theta}$, where τ is the torque computed for the joint, k_p is a proportional gain constant, θ_d is the desired joint angle, θ is the joint position, k_d is a damping constant, and $\dot{\theta}$ is the joint velocity. These internal torques are subsequently translated into an actual movement by carrying out a mechanical (physical) simulation. The goal is thus to determine how to manipulate the control functions $\Omega_d(t)$ in order to achieve a desired motion.

The first step in solving this problem is to choose a finite-dimensional representation for $\Omega_d(t)$. This can be done using any number of basis functions, ranging from simple discrete samples to more continuous basis functions such as splines, sinusoids, or wavelets. Using a finite set of basis functions to express $\Omega_d(t)$ over a finite time T yields a finite set of numbers which serve to define the applied control. If motions can be evaluated with a scalar performance index that measures their 'desireability', then the problem of generating a desired motion is converted into one of parameter optimization, as expressed in Figure 1. An alternative to making Ω_d a function of time is to allow it to be a function of sensory information[21][25][28]. This can also easily be posed as a parameter optimization problem. Regardless of the choice of representation, there are many numerical techniques that can be applied to the resulting parameter-optimization problems. However, they must all take into account that the parameter space is high-dimensional and possibly replete with local minima. In this work, we choose to make Ω_d a piece-wise constant function of time, although the same representation also allows for a piece-wise linear representation, as illustrated later in Figure 5. The controlling torques are calculated at every time step of the simulation.

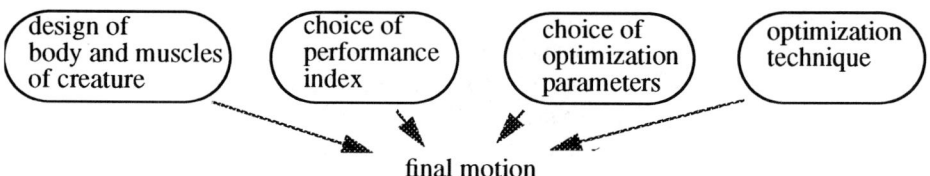

Fig. 2. Using optimization to generate animation.

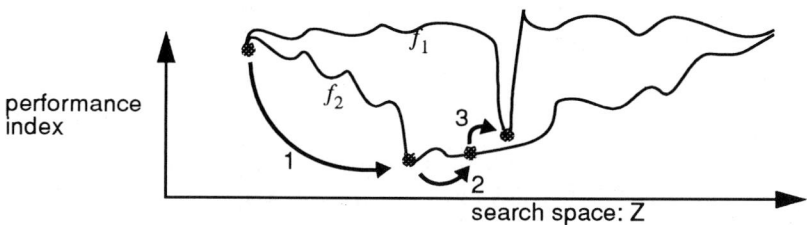

Fig. 3. The effect of shaping an optimization problem. The desired balanced motion is represented by the global minimum of f_1. Guiding forces change the equations of motion and allow for partial success to be rewarded, thus yielding a simpler optimization problem, as shown by f_2. The effect of the three stages of the optimization process is shown schematically. Stage 1 finds a good solution for the simpler problem, stage 2 finds a point on f_2 which minimizes the guiding forces, and stage 3 returns to the original equations of motion.

There are ultimately several factors that influence the motion produced using parameter optimization techniques. These are summarized in Figure 2. Two important characteristics can make a parameter optimization problem difficult. The first is dealing with the size or dimensionality of the search space. Methods such as genetic algorithms and simulated annealing are typically used in an attempt to cope with this. A second often-overlooked factor is the fraction of the search space occupied by useful solutions and similarly, the ability of the performance index to guide the parameter search towards this subset of parameter space. It is this factor which makes balanced locomotion a challenge to synthesize. The situation is illustrated in Figure 3.

For a biped, balanced motions exist for a small part of the parameter search space, making it a difficult problem to solve. This difficulty can be overcome in two ways. The first is to change the performance index to reward partial progress. This redesign of the performance index unfortunately has the animator learning how to construct appropriate performance metrics instead of keeping to our original goal of having the virtual actor do the 'learning'. The second method is to modify the system being controlled in order to work with a simpler projection of the problem, and then revert back to the original projection when a solution to the simpler projection has been obtained. One example of this method might be that of a baby learning to walk with large, stable feet and then gradually having the feet shrink in size. The technique we propose avoids altering the body design, instead using an external HOG to take care of the balance requirements, which can then progressively be reduced or removed.

Fig. 4. The hand of God (HOG). The HOG operates by applying an external torque vector τ to ensure that the up-vector b, fixed to the torso, never deviates significantly from its ideal direction given by u.

3.2 The Hand of God

The hand of God (HOG) is an externally-applied torque vector which serves to keep the body or torso of an animated figure in an upright posture, as illustrated in Figure 4.

It is up to the animator to specify the desired 'upright' posture using the vector b, which is defined in the coordinate frame of the torso. This allows walks where the torso is leaning forward or to the side, for example. The HOG ensures that the upright posture is maintained by applying a torque $\tau = k_p (b \times u) - k_d \omega_b$, where k_p and k_d are spring and damper constants, u defines the desired up direction, and the vector ω_b is the angular velocity of the torso. Note that although the HOG causes an upright orientation to be maintained, it is the legs that must at all times bear the weight of the torso.

3.3 Stages of Optimization

The optimization process using the HOG is divided into three stages, as shown in Figure 5. The goal is to first learn the basics of the motion with external assistance, and then to reduce or remove this assistance as learning proceeds. Our particular application of locomotion benefits from being a cyclic motion, so we can use a cyclic representation of the control function $\Omega_d(t)$ for the first two stages of the learning process. Our choice of control representation consists of sampling the cycle period T at n uniform intervals, and constructing an interpolant of order k, $k \leq n$ through the control samples. The resulting parameter set Z has nq elements, where q is the number of actuators to be controlled. As part of the design of the animated figure, the animator is responsible for defining Z_{min} and Z_{max}, which serve to bound the parameter space to be searched. These correspond to joint-limits when animating articulated figures. Our choice of optimization technique is a greedy gradient-descent algorithm, although a variety of other parameter-optimization algorithms can equally well be substituted. In practice, a gradient-descent algorithm seems to work well with the projections of the optimization problem obtained with the HOG.

As a result of the HOG, an automated parameter search to produce a basic stepping motion is a simple task. Performance indices useful for this stage of the optimization are typically related to the distance travelled over several periods of the cyclic motion. In the case of human motion, it can also be convenient to construct a performance index which measures the similarity to existing human gait data. A simple index we propose for this is given by $J = \int \Sigma w_i (\theta_i - \hat{\theta}_i)^2 dt$, where $\hat{\theta}_i$ is the experimental data

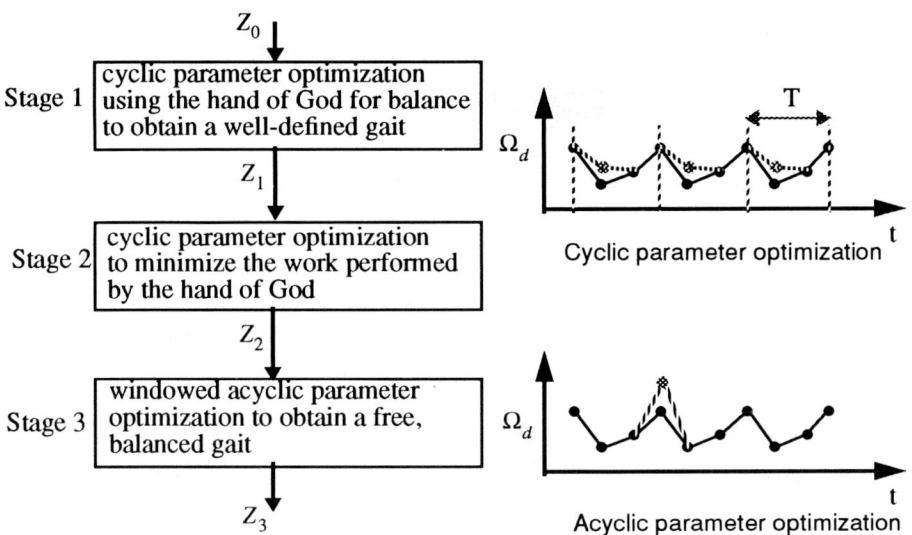

Z_0

Stage 1 | cyclic parameter optimization using the hand of God for balance to obtain a well-defined gait

Z_1

Stage 2 | cyclic parameter optimization to minimize the work performed by the hand of God

Z_2

Stage 3 | windowed acyclic parameter optimization to obtain a free, balanced gait

Z_3

Ω_d ... T ... t

Cyclic parameter optimization

Ω_d ... t

Acyclic parameter optimization

Fig. 5. Stages for a guided optimization. Each stage ensures that the next stage has a suitable starting point for parameter optimization.

for joint i, and w_i defines the relative importance of each joint in the performance index. If a periodic swaying of the torso is desired, the definition of the desired upright vector u can be changed cyclically to accomodate this.

The second stage of the optimization continues to use the HOG, but minimizes the reliance of the motion upon it. Beginning with the parameter set produced by the first phase, Z_1, the motion is optimized to minimize the work performed by the HOG, defined here as $J = \int (\tau \cdot \tau)\, dt$, where τ is the moment applied by the HOG as previously defined. The resulting parameter set Z_2 yields a motion with the HOG playing a greatly reduced role, but not completely eliminated. This is typically the result of the synthetic actor being unable to sustain the desired torso position using muscle action alone, which manifests itself as a torso motion which is excessively rigid.

The last stage of optimization is first described in terms of its real-life analogy. Consider a baby taking a first free step into his parents arms. If this step is successful, the parent will have to perform little or no work in helping to restore the child's balance. After it has been determined how to take a successful first step, the parent retreats another step, allowing for two free steps before helping out. The third stage of the optimization algorithm operates according to this description until a true free walk has been generated.

The process is illustrated in Figure 6. A first point to note is that the cyclic constraint on the parameter set is released, thus allowing for small perturbations to the predominantly cyclic control in order to take the corrective actions necessary to maintain balance. Two adjacent windows of fixed size serve to define the duration of the simulation trials: the *optimization window* and the *evaluation window*. The optimization window defines the parameter subset Z_w to undergo optimization. These are the control param-

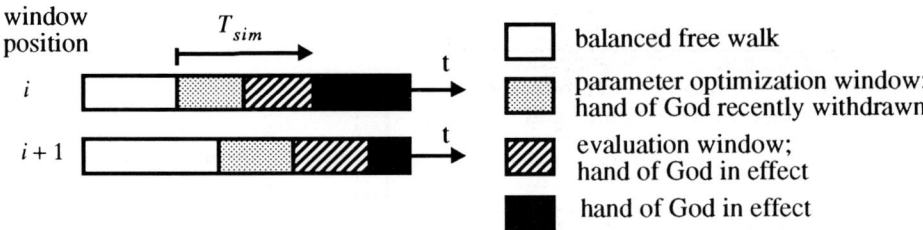

Fig. 6. Stage 3: progressive removal of the hand of God

eters affecting the motion immediately before the restoring action of the HOG is applied. The evaluation window measures the amount of work, J, necessary to restore a balanced position at the end of the free-portion of the motion. The optimization itself consists of minimizing J over the parameter subset Z_w. The windows are moved forward in time when J has been appropriately minimized for the current window position.

4 Results

Our synthetic actors are articulated figures having 5, 12, and 15 links, having 6, 11, and 16 actuators respectively.The equations of motion are obtained using the mechanical simulation package described in [12]. Ground contact is modelled using a stiff spring-damper system which is modified to allow for the simulation of friction and slippage. The simulations require from 3 to 10 seconds of compute time for each second of simulation time. Four second simulation trials were used for most of the motions. Although the optimization process has been defined as having three stages, we have noted that in many cases visually-satisfactory motion is obtained after the application of only stages one and two.

4.1 Simpleton

One of the goals of this work is to show that difficult problems can be tackled effectively using this technique. Figure 7 shows Simpleton, a run-of-the-mill biped. Because the biped has point feet, it is non-trivial to arrive at a balanced walking motion.

For our experiments we used a cycle discretization of $n = 4$ in our control representation. Given six actuated joints, this produces a parameter set of size 24. The initial conditions for the parameter set can be chosen at random if it is desired that Simpleton learn how to walk without the use of a priori information. We often found it useful to specify the initial conditions for the parameter set Z_0 directly because an initial parameter set that already crudely represents the motion is a simply way to save on some otherwise random searching. For the case of a walking gait, this is equivalent to specifying two keyframes: one having the right leg straight and the left leg bent, and the other vice-versa. Distance-travelled over the simulation interval remains the most useful optimization metric we have found. The intermediate results of the optimization

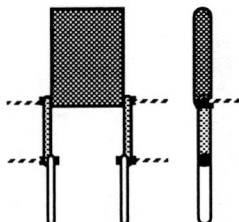

Fig. 7. Simpleton. This three-dimensional figure has pin hinges at the knees and two degree-of-freedom hinges at the hips.

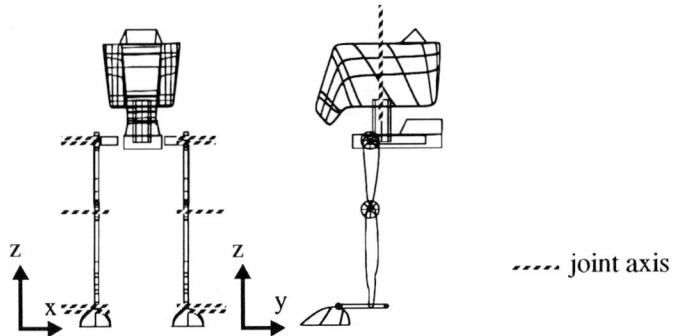

$\cdots\cdots$ joint axis

Fig. 8. Robo-bird. Each leg has 5 actuated, aligned pin-hinges. The 'neck' has an additional pin-hinge allowing it to turn from side to side.

can be saved in order to be able to retrieve gaits of any desired speed, ranging from a slow trundle to a loping run.

The effect of the HOG can sometimes be easily recognized after stage 1 due to a clearly off-balance movement that nevertheless remains upright. In an experiment where 'upright' was defined as leaning forward, this had the effect of looking like it was pulling something heavy. The stage 2 optimization removes such artifacts, resulting in changed foot placements to yield an improved balanced motions. Stages 1 and 2 typically require 50 to 200 trials to achieve reasonable results. Stage 3 is more expensive to apply, requiring approximately 500 trials to produce 5 seconds of free, balanced walking. An optimization window size of one-half stride with an evaluation window of one stride works well in practice. Plate A shows the result of a stage-two walking motion over variable terrain.

4.2 Robo-bird
The imaginary robotic bird shown in Figure 8 provides a good example of a more realistic figure one might choose to animate. In order to deal with the large number of degrees of freedom on each leg (five), a set of left-right symmetry constraints were imposed on the parameter set, in addition to the cycle constraint. The image in Plate B shows the creature walking using the control automatically synthesized after stages 1 and 2. A cycle discretization of $n = 4$ was used. Interestingly enough, the animated walk rotates from side to side, even though all the joints in the leg are coaxial. This is a

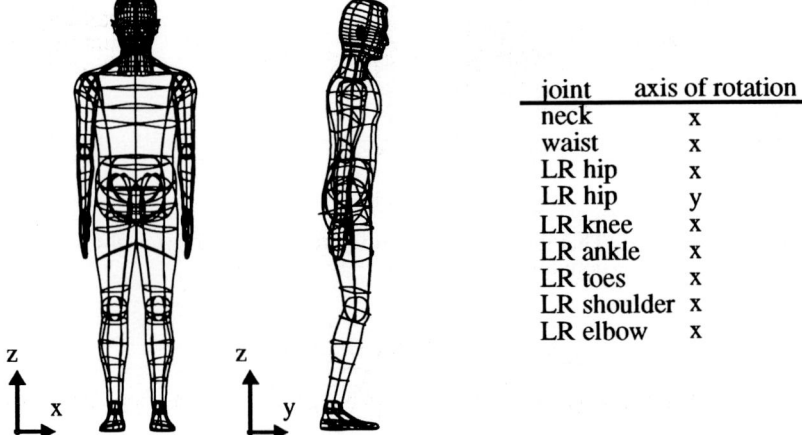

joint	axis of rotation
neck	x
waist	x
LR hip	x
LR hip	y
LR knee	x
LR ankle	x
LR toes	x
LR shoulder	x
LR elbow	x

Fig. 9. A human model with 16 actuated internal degrees of freedom. The model can walk, run, and skip.

good example of the type of secondary motion we can expect to emerge from physics-based animations.

Another point of interest is that stage 3 for Robo-bird cannot find an entirely HOG-free balancing gait. This makes us aware of the common possibility that an animator can easily design a creature which is simply not capable of performing the desired motion, although we cannot guarantee that this was the case here. Using the technique of guided optimization, desired motions can be approximated, even though the actual desired motion might be physically unfeasible.

4.3 Human Model
Last, we present a three-dimensional human model of realistic dimensions and physical parameters[20]. In keeping with our goal of having synthetic actors learn balanced locomotion, we present the human model as a challenging test case. The model we use is shown in Figure 9. While the physical model and the controllers we synthesize have 16 actuated degrees of freedom, 8 of these can be treated in a largely passive fashion, thus leaving 8 significant joints to be controlled. Symmetry conditions are employed along with the cyclic representation of the parameter set is used in order to halve the effective size of the parameter set. A cyclic discretization of $n = 8$ is used.

Using stages 1 and 2, walking, running, and skipping gaits were synthesized for the model. The motions were distinguished by using different initial parameter sets during stage 1, as well as being given different performance indices. The initial parameter set for the walking motion consisted of four keyframes defining a crude alternating stepping motion for the legs. These initial keyframes make the model walk in place when the HOG is first applied. The running motion was initiated with a more energetic set of keyframes, using the ankles to push the body into the air, making for an alternating-leg, in-place hopping motion. The initial parameter set for the skipping motion is chosen to allow for an in-place skipping motion. For all three motions, the motions were then

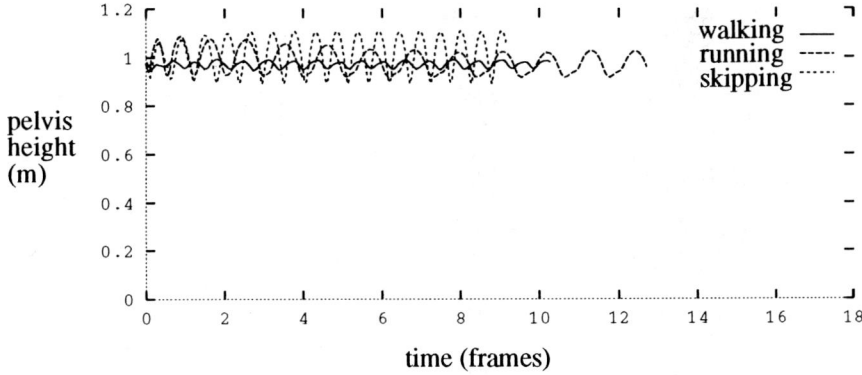

Fig. 10. Average hieght of pelvis during walking, running, and skipping motions.

optimized for speed (stage 1), similarity to known human motions[13] (stage 1), and for balance (stage 2). The trajectory of the midpoint on the pelvis is shown for the various motions in Figure 10.

The resulting human motions are convincing when a simple line-based visual representation is used, but the motion still retains unconvincing qualities when detailed geometrical models are used to animate the result. The image in Plate C illustrates our 'dressed' geometric model in a running pose. One of the general advantages of parameter-optimization based techniques over manually-designed control systems for the various gaits is that they offer a uniform framework for treating different gaits, such as walking, running, and skipping.As well, the technique proposed here is intended to be general in order to be applicable to the animation of arbitrary types of articulated figures.

5 Conclusions

It is difficult to imagine that we could do better at teaching virtual actors how to walk and run than we would do at teaching real human beings. As such, it is worthwhile looking at the techniques that are employed for teaching motor-control skills to children, patients with pathological walks, or athletes learning a new manoevre for the first time. The guidance techniques commonly employed in these situations can be used effectively in the context of physics-based animation as well. The hand-of-God concept is the first step in trying to borrow from human motor-learning techniques and applying them in a virtual setting.

Guided optimization seeks to address the problem of motions which are difficult to synthesize directly using parameter optimization techniques. In these cases, the desired motion typically corresponds to an infinitesimal region of the parameter space to be searched. While it might be possible to construct modified performance indices which reward partial progress, just how to accomplish this is not clear. Using the hand of God has a predictable effect and solves the same problem in a more straightforward fashion. Guided optimization also provides a means of synthesizing an acceptably-close result

176

to a desired motion even though the desired motion might prove to be impossible, a situation which easily arises when the physical design of a creature is left to a non-expert.

While the use of *sensor-based* motor control has not been directly addressed, we believe that the use of guiding is perhaps even more important for motions to be controlled using sensory information. An initial guided version of the motion serves to determine which sensory inputs are meaningful and which are not. This is likely an important step in the construction of a sensory-motor control system. We feel that the learning of other types of motion can also benefit from guiding techniques. Because the use of harnesses can aid in the learning of many athletic manoevres, we foresee virtual guiding harnesses as being a flexible and powerful tool.

References

[1]   N. I. Badler, B. Barsky, and D. Zeltzer. *Making Them Move.* Morgan Kaufmann Publishers Inc., 1991.

[2]   N. I. Badler, C. B. Phillips, and B. L. Webber. *Simulating Humans.* Oxford University Press, 1993.

[3]   R. Boulic, D. Thalmann. Combined Direct and Inverse Kinematic Control for Articulated Figures Motion Editing. *Computer Graphics Forum*, 2 (4), 1992, 189-202.

[4]   R. Boulic, N. M. Thalmann, D. Thalmann. A global human walking model with real-time kinematic personification. *The Visual Computer*, 1990, 6, 344-358.

[5]   A. Bruderlin and T. W. Calvert. Goal-Directed Dynamic Animation of Human Walking. *Proceedings of SIGGRAPH '89*, In *ACM Computer Graphics*, vol. 23, July 1989, 233-242.

[6]   A. Bruderlin and T. W. Calvert. Interactive Animation of Personalized Human Locomotion. In *Proceedings of Graphics Interface '93*, 1993, 17-23.

[7]   M. F. Cohen. Interactive Spacetime Control for Animation. *Proceedings of SIGGRAPH '92.* In *ACM Computer Graphics*, 26, 2 (July 1992), 293-302.

[8]   R. Dickstein, Z. Smolinski, and T. Pillar. Self-propelled weight-relieving walker for gait rehabilitation. *Journal of Biomedical Engineering*, 1992, vol. 14, July, 351-355.

[9]   M. Girard. Interactive design of 3-D computer-animated legged animal motion. *IEEE Computer Graphics and Applications*, June 1987, 39-51.

[10]   J. K. Hodgins. Simulation of Human Running. IEEE Conference on Robotics and Automation, 1994, 1320-1325.

[11]   J. K. Hodgins, P. K. Sweeney, and D. G. Lawrence. Generating Natural-looking Motion for Computer Animation. *Proceedings of Graphics Interface '92*, 265-272, May 1992.

[12]   M. G. Hollars, D. E. Rosenthal, and M. A. Sherman. *SD/FAST User's Manual.* Symbolic Dynamics Inc., 1991.

[13]   V. T. Inman. *Human Walking.* Williams and Wilkins, 1981.

[14]   H. Ko and N. I. Badler. Straight Line Walking Animation Based on Kinematic Generalization that Preserves Original Characteristics. *Proceedings of Graphics Interface '93*, May 1993, 9-16.

[15]   A. Lamouret, M.-P. Gascuel. An approach for guiding colliding physically-based models. *4th Eurographics Workshop on Animation and Simulation*, Barcelona, 1993.

[16]   Z. Liu, S. J. Gortler, M. Cohen. *Hierarchical Spacetime Control, Proceedings of SIGGRAPH '94*. In ACM *Computer Graphics* Proceedings, 1994, 35-42.

[17]   N. Magnenat-Thalmann and D. Thalmann. *Computer Animation: Theory and Practice*. Springer-Verlag, New York, 1990.

[18]   T. McGeer. Passive Dynamic Walking. *The International Journal of Robotics Research*, 9, 2, 1990, 62-82.

[19]   M. McKenna and D. Zeltzer. Dynamic Simulation of Autonomous Legged Locomotion. *Proceedings of SIGGRAPH '90*. In *ACM Computer Graphics*, 22, 4 (August 1990), 29-38.

[20]   NASA. *The Anthropometry Source Book*. NASA reference publication 1024, Johnson Space Center, Houston, 1978.

[21]   J. T. Ngo and J. Marks. Spacetime Constraints Revisitied. *Proceedings of SIGGRAPH '93*. In *ACM Computer Graphics*, 27 (August 1993).

[22]   M. G. Pandy, F. C. Anderson, and D. G. Hull. A Parameter Optimization Approach for the Optimal Control of Large-Scale Musculoskeletal Systems. *Journal of Biomechanical Engineering*, 114 (November 1992), 450-460.

[23]   M. H. Raibert. *Legged Robots that Balance*. MIT Press, Cambridge, 1985.

[24]   M. H. Raibert and J. K. Hodgins. Animation of dynamic legged locomotion. *Proceedings of SIGGRAPH '91*, In *ACM Computer Graphics*, 25, 4 (July 1991), 349-358.

[25]   K. Sims. Evolving Virtual Creatures. Proceedings of SIGGRAPH '94, In *ACM Computer Graphics* proceedings, 1994, 15-22.

[26]   A. J. Stewart and J. F. Cremer. Beyond Keyframing: An Algorithmic Approach to Animation. In *Proceedings of Graphics Interface '92*, 1992, 273-281.

[27]   M. van de Panne, E. Fiume, and Z. Vranesic. Reusable Motion Synthesis Using State-Space Controllers. *Proceedings of SIGGRAPH '90*, In *ACM Computer Graphics*, 1990, 24, 4, 225-234.

[28]   M. van de Panne and E. Fiume. Sensor-Actuator Networks. *Proceedings of SIGGRAPH '93*, In *ACM Computer Graphics*, August 1993, 335-342.

[29]   A. Witkin and M. Kass. Spacetime Constraints. *Proceedings of SIGGRAPH '88*. In *ACM Computer Graphics*, 22, 4 (August 1988), 159-168

Editors' Note: see Appendix, p. 234 for coloured figures of this paper

Part III:
Simulation Based Animation Systems

Parallel Spacetime Animation

Martin Preston
Computer Graphics Unit, Manchester Computing,
University of Manchester, M13 9PL, U.K.
Email: *preston@mcc.ac.uk*

Abstract. The application of parallelism to the rendering of frames for animation is a well established target for research effort. However, with the advent of more complicated motion synthesis tools, the creation of *movement*, rather than images, requires the most computation. Such techniques, whilst likely to widen the popularity of animation as a visualisation tool, are often regarded as too expensive for use in commercial motion production. This paper addresses the problem by describing a distributed algorithm for the generation of motion from high level spacetime controls, which employs parallelism to improve the ease and speed by which realistic animation can be created. Such an approach permits the use of novel architectures in animation, and widens the scope for the application of intuitive interfaces to high quality motion synthesis.
Keywords: *Parallelism, Spacetime Control, Computer Animation.*

1 Introduction

Animation has, during its widely publicised history, provided a hugely powerful tool which enables scientists and entertainers to present large quantities of information in a pleasant manner. The expense of producing a stream of images, from which a human viewer perceives motion, however, originally restricted the techniques use to the extent that the creation of high quality animation was confined to a few world-renowned centres of expertise.

Consequently, when the first graphics computers were applied to the production of animation, the focus of development was increasing the speed at which images could be generated [14]. Since the early sixties the quality and speed at which acceptable pictures may be synthesised have improved rapidly, thanks to the efforts of the computer graphics research community, many of whom have advocated the application of parallelism to frame production [12].

However, as the image production techniques advanced, the methods used by animators to create and model *motion* had remained largely similar to the techniques used by traditional cel animators. In recognition of this animation researchers have, for many years, concentrated on the development of higher level motion control techniques, which enable realistic movement to be produced *easily*, by animators who do not necessarily possess 'cel-animation' skills.

A variety of techniques have been generated for these purposes, all of which share a common theme, that of increased computational load in comparison to more traditional techniques. The perceived sluggishness of such tools has hampered their adoption by many animation houses, and so the state of the commercial art in animation lags considerably behind current research.

The speed of rendering individual images for animations, then, whilst still very important, no longer restricts the widespread use of animation. Instead the most significant hindrance is the speed and ease of motion control, both for animation and interactive motion production.

This paper advocates the use of parallelism in the synthesis of *movement*, rather than purely images, as a way of addressing this problem. It describes a motion generation algorithm, employing spacetime control abstractions[16], and its efficient implementation on both tightly coupled parallel machines, and networks of connected workstations (a resource more likely to be available to a contemporary animation facility).

The adoption of a parallel approach to motion synthesis allows animators to achieve acceptable performance by increasing the number of processors available for generating the movement, which may be replayed using more conventional methods. Previously the use of parallelism in achieving such results, for general (non-particle [13]) animation, has not been widely investigated [11], and the only published attempts have achieved poor performance [5][9].

Following a discussion of the relevant spacetime control algorithms, and the limited use of parallelism in animation synthesis (in Section 2), we outline the pertinent features of the new motion generator in Section 3. In order to parallelise this approach Section 4 identifies the features of this tool which contribute to its computational expense, and from these the areas for parallel exploitation.

This technique has been used on a KSR-1/64 multicomputer, and section 5 describes the relevant details of an initial parallel design and implementation in this environment. Optimization of this basic algorithm for a variety of purposes, on both the KSR and workstations, is described in section 6. The performance of this algorithm is the topic of section 7. Finally the applicability of both this technique, and general animation synthesis tools, in a parallel setting, are discussed in section 8.

2 Related Work

Most high level motion synthesis tools rely on the application of physical properties to the virtual world. Given this information, the animator may cause motion by application of forces, the results of which are determined through the use of Newtonian simulation processes. Unfortunately, for all but the most trivial cases, such simulations are too expensive to perform interactively, and must be executed in batch runs.

In recognition of this Armstrong,Green & Lake [1], as part of their development of an efficient method of simulating the behaviour of chains of linked bodies, proposed the adoption of some parallel computation. Unfortunately this promising idea was never pursued. Friedmann & Pentland [5] describe a similar distributed implementation of a simulation process, and some parallelism was found, but the implementation used an unsuitable platform, which produced poor results. However, whatever the success of improving an implementation of dynamics simulation, most animators find force control of any animation other than simple reactive motion counter-intuitive, and so higher level interfaces to the simulation process have been developed.

The most general, and therefore promising, techniques rely on animators describing the properties of the motion most desired in statespace terms, commonly called spacetime constraints, which the motion generator uses to produce an optimal solution to the problem. If the motion is incorrect, the animator alters the hints and re-synthesises the motion.

Witkin & Kass' [16] spacetime tool operated by being supplied an initial animation path, and a collection of minimisation functions, which were used to iteratively perturb the initial trajectory in the pursuit of a 'better' path. Creation of more suitable methods of control has attracted some effort, notably from Cohen [3] and Liu *et. al.* [8], who have proposed the animator should steer the refinement process, which can be made more efficient by using advanced spline representations.

Possibly the most serious problem with spacetime control methods, though, is the computational expense of statespace minimisation. The principal strength of the space-time approach is its intuitiveness in comparison to conventional dynamics control, but it is difficult for an animator to control a technique which requires hours of computation.

The expense of this minimisation could be ameliorated by reducing the number of times it must be performed, and Van de Panne, Fiume and Vranesic [15] have proposed creating *reusable* controllers using spacetime control. However, the creation of sufficient numbers of these controllers is often more expensive than refining a new path each time for realistic motion, and so does not provide a general solution.

In recognition of this Ngo and Marks [9] advocated the use of genetic algorithms to *evolve* animation controllers in parallel on a Connection Machine 2. This motion generator takes simple indications of the forms of motion, e.g., move left to right, and creates a controller by examining a large set of possible solutions, the desirable elements of which are combined using genetic programming techniques. The authors describe synthesis times of between 30 minutes and an hour for quite simple abstracted problems on > 4000 (1 bit) processors. Though, unfortunately, this control mechanism exhibits limitations which prevent its widespread use, and is extremely slow, it does indicate the susceptibility of this area to parallelism.

Spacetime control, then, is recognised as a promising control methodology for general animation production. Unfortunately, due both to limitations of interfaces and the large amounts of computation required, it has yet to be accepted as a commercially viable procedure. However, an implementation of this technique which can operate promptly is likely to attract widespread use. The application of parallelism to the synthesis of movement, for general problems, has not been adequately explored [11], yet seems to provide a productive solution to the problems exhibited by spacetime techniques.

3 Discretised Spacetime Control

Existing spacetime motion synthesis tools are geared towards relatively efficient implementation on a serial platform. In order to produce an algorithm which may operate in a parallel environment, and take full advantage of large numbers of processors (i.e., be scalable), it is necessary to substantially modify these approaches. This section presents a spacetime motion creation technique which is better suited to distributed computation, and supports control by a higher level interface. For the purposes of this paper only the characteristics of the algorithm which influence its parallelism are presented. The full algorithm is discussed elsewhere [10].

Section 3.1 outlines the principal features of the new approach, and sections 3.2 to 3.5 discuss the key elements of its implementation.

3.1 Parallel Motion Synthesis

We can describe the behaviour of any actor during an animation as a path through an n-dimensional space, where each dimension corresponds to some pertinent value we use to represent the actor. For example, the statespace of a single non-deformable body could be minimally described in six dimensions, 3 Cartesian and 3 Euler:

$$(x, y, z, rx, ry, rz) \tag{1}$$

Consequently the production of animation can be thought of as the creation of a path through this statespace. Such a path can be modelled as a trajectory in this space if we include time, t, as an extra dimension. Although all animation tools can be described in such terms, most hide the statespace nature of the trajectory. Spacetime motion generators, though, use the statespace as the control medium.

Most spacetime techniques operate by finding an 'optimal' path through statespace. The belief that optimised motion is inherently more realistic has its roots in the thinking that most animal motion is motivated by reducing energy expenditure. Logically, if we express terms which describe the energy expended by a particular movement, then finding movement which achieves its goals, but requires less effort, is likely to lead to better animation.

Spacetime techniques commonly require an initial trajectory as a way of providing a starting point for minimisation [16][3], the control of which is provided by animator created functions.

However another approach is to discretise the statespace itself, and refine the extents of this volume. The new statespace this algorithm produces is, then, the area in which an optimal path lies. As the volume of the statespace is reduced we get closer to the actual optimal. Indications of exactly what must be minimised are still required, but an initial, possibly misleading, trajectory is no longer always needed.

Rather than expending effort to produce an accurate path which is difficult to control, then, we concentrate our efforts on being able to interactively produce approximations, which can easily be refined to create the finished animation. This refinement process is therefore an iterative one, where the algorithm is used to reduce the subset of statespace within which the optimal path must lie. How this volume is determined is the focus of the rest of this section.

We can think of the new volume of statespace as a collection of sub-volumes, through which the optimal path passes. As we know the start position of the animation, we can view the motion synthesis process as repeatedly determining approximations to the best *exit* from each sub-volume, because this will tell us which sub-volume we need to examine next.

For an approximation to the optimal path to be useful it must provide an indication of the form of motion it contains (in order to let the animator decide whether further refinement is advantageous). This chosen best exit will provide us with enough information to construct a sample animation, i.e., a path which traverses the list of best exits we generate. To illustrate this Figure 1 shows the set of volumes, V_i, which enclose the approximate optimal path, together with a sample path.

The most important part of this process is its technique for discretising statespace into sub-volumes, as a poor tactic will hamper the generation of a plausible animation. In order to understand the factors which influence the choice of discretisation we will

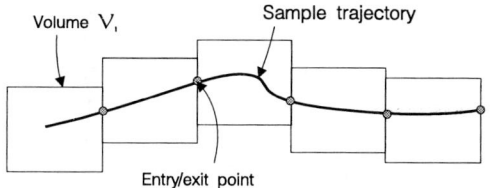

Figure 1 The path passes through a series of sub-volumes.

first discuss how an approximate best exit from each sub-volume is produced. Then, in section 3.3, we describe the discretisation algorithm used. How this technique is applied to multi-body animation is the topic of section 3.4, and finally in section 3.5 we review the strengths of the process.

3.2 Finding an exit from a sub-volume

Most spacetime techniques use energy as the focus of minimisation. However, to help the animator, we would like to hide the physical properties of the underlying world model, and so 'cost' is a more useful representation.

Given a sub-volume, centred around our current position in statespace, we wish to find the approximate best exit in a particular time. This is achieved by examining a large variety of routes, one of which is shown in Figure 2, the component costs of which can be split into

$$C(V, S_1, S_2, D) = M(V, S_2) + CP(S_2) + CR(D) \qquad (2)$$

If we increase the number of routes sampled we have a greater chance of finding a more accurate exit, but obviously there is a computational overhead.

The first term of (2) accounts for the cost assigned to the movement. This is determined by a line integral over the trajectory, to which a cost may be assigned, with higher costs representing larger forces. The second term allows us to control the motion using a higher level mechanism. This works by assigning a cost to each portion of statespace, which represents the desirability of the animation traversing that point. Such control is normally achieved by allowing the user to interactively place *cost-areas* in statespace, which are regions for which a particular cost/point function allows us to find the cost influence. For example, the animator may wish to define a function with a high cost at the centre of the region, dropping to no cost at the perimeter, as a way of discouraging the trajectory from traversing this region.

The final term, $CR(D)$, represents the cost accrued by the *route*, and allows us to account for effects such as collisions, or the cost of traversing cost-areas.

3.3 Discretising the statespace

Given the algorithm for finding the best exit from a sub-volume, we must consider how we determine the collection of sub-volumes which contain plausible animations. For the motion to be acceptable it must reach the destination in the given time. Therefore the discretisation uses two techniques to ensure acceptable routes are examined:

• A large cost-area is created which ensures that routes which approach the destination are cheaper than those which don't.

• Volumes are considered which guide the route towards the destination, though some freedom is allowed.

This second factor influences how we discretise space. We must consider volumes, whose exits we evaluate, which guide the motion towards the destination, and we must

186

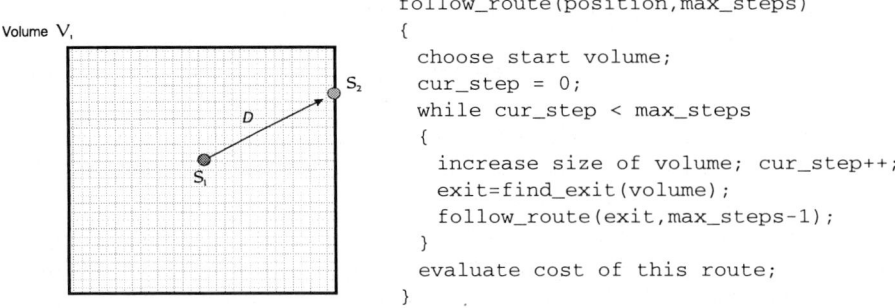

Volume V,

S₂

D

S₁

```
follow_route(position,max_steps)
{
  choose start volume;
  cur_step = 0;
  while cur_step < max_steps
  {
    increase size of volume; cur_step++;
    exit=find_exit(volume);
    follow_route(exit,max_steps-1);
  }
  evaluate cost of this route;
}
```

Figure 2 A sample exit from a volume.　　**Figure 3** The motion generator algorithm.

ensure we consider as many volumes as possible whose exits actually *touch* the destination. As we are only examining a finite number of exits on each sub-volume, we must ensure that one of these points reaches the destination, which can be achieved by rotating sub-volumes so that one of the exits lies at the destination.

In order to consider plausible animations we must evaluate a wide variety of paths. This is achieved using the recursive algorithm outlined in Figure 3 where, at each point in time, we consider exiting a range of volumes, of increasing size, centred on the current point. Each chosen exit is then considered as the next step on the route. For each full route evaluated in the recursive tree, i.e., a route which has taken the maximum number of steps, we determine the total cost by adding the costs of each of the smaller movements which contribute to that path. The final approximate optimal path is then found by choosing the cheapest of all these contenders. Note that the variable max_steps allows us to control the resolution of the synthesised path, and so the quantity of work which must be performed.

To illustrate this process, Figure 4 shows two routes which have been evaluated as routes between A & B. A large cost-area of positive cost discourages routes which traverse it, and two paths are shown, with their component sub-volumes passing above and below. Each sub-volume is rotated so that one of its considered exits is oriented towards the destination. Note that every sub-volume is assumed to be traversed in constant time. This means that the lower route in Figure 4 takes longer to reach the destination than its counterpart.

3.4 Multi-Body Animation

An algorithm for generating a spacetime path, for a single actor, has now been

Sub-volumes generated
on the route

B

Obstacle

A

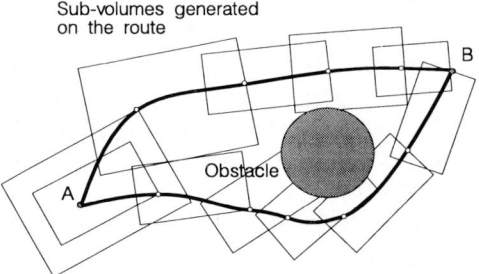

Figure 4 Two paths which are being considered,

described. However, most production animation involves the control of more complicated networks of bodies. Conventional spacetime approaches tackle this by treating the relationship between component bodies as additional dimensions in statespace, which, unfortunately, increases the synthesis times.

However we can treat each body independently, and consequently in parallel, to produce a series of statespace paths which describe the motion each component body wishes to traverse. The finished animation can then be constructed by post-processing each path to ensure connectivity is maintained. The algorithm is described in more detail elsewhere [10], and is based on previous constraint maintenance approaches [6].

Note that this approach causes the addition of a serial component to the application which cannot easily be implemented in parallel. However, this step requires little computation and, as we will see in section 7.3, will not unduly affect the scalability of the algorithm.

3.5 Algorithm Fundamentals

This motion synthesis technique has been described in abbreviated form, a more comprehensive discussion being available elsewhere [10]. In particular we have disregarded the details of finding the forces required to cause a particular motion, the production of high quality motion from the approximation (which is achieved by using these forces as impulses in a forward dynamic simulation), as well as the algorithms ability to handle collisions & control mechanisms which operate at a higher level than the placement of cost-areas.

However, none of these abilities change the fundamental algorithm, described in Figure 3, which influences the *expense* of using such a technique as a motion generation tool.

4 Parallel Properties of the Algorithm

In order to implement this synthesis technique in parallel we must determine a way of splitting the computation caused by evaluation of the algorithm (Figure 3), into a number of work units, which may be processed independently. Following an outline of the reasoning behind the chosen approach, we discuss the techniques employed to ensure the algorithm performs well using a variety of problems, in section 4.2.

4.1 Basic Parallel Design

As `follow_route` is evaluated an implicit tree is constructed, which maps out the search space that the algorithm processes. When the algorithm detects that it has taken the maximum number of steps (which have not *necessarily* brought it to the desired destination), it compares the suitability of the route taken to determine whether this is a candidate for the optimal path. When all the possible routes have been examined the cheapest is chosen as the trajectory.

At each node in the search space we are examining a particular volume around the 'current' point, and choosing the cheapest exit from it. As the size of this volume is dependent on the `cur_step` it is possible to characterise a node in this space by that value, and the depth of the node in the tree. A portion of the search space is shown in Figure 5, where the first figure in each node denotes the depth, and the second the magnitude of the relevant volume.

Each of these nodes corresponds to a single cycle through the loop described in Figure 3. The principal cost of this, once we disregard the cost of administration, is that of

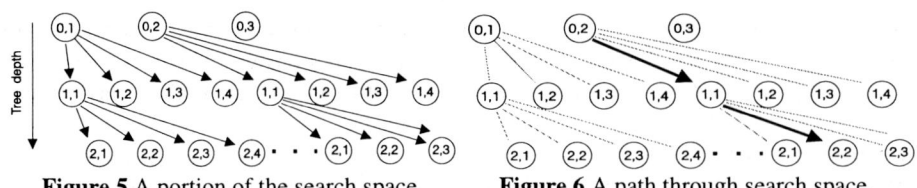

Figure 5 A portion of the search space.   **Figure 6** A path through search space.

finding the cheapest exit from a particular volume. However, as we achieve this by examining a finite number of exits, this expense is not great, and so this portion of the algorithm is not worth parallelising.

The expense of using this algorithm, however, is in the large number of sub-volumes which must be considered, which we can think of as the size of the search space. A productive method of parallelism, then, requires splitting this search space into smaller work units, and distributing these across the available processors.

It is tempting to choose a single node in the search space as our basic work unit, but there are problems with this. As we have seen each node corresponds to an iteration around the loop in Figure 3, which is intended to solve the problem "at a particular point in state-space, what is the best place to move to on the bounds of a particular volume?".

It is important, then, to note that this is meaningless without knowing the *current* position, or the place that the preceding route has brought the actor to, and so the volume which will be considered. This preceding route (Figure 6) is determined implicitly in a serial implementation as a result of the recursive nature of the algorithm, and so means that it is impossible to treat any single node in isolation. It is for this reason that the search space is not amenable to dynamic programming techniques [2].

The expense of determining the previous path to each node, for *every* node in the search space, would be prohibitive. However, this expense can be ameliorated by considering a number of nodes, which would be treated sequentially by the serial implementation, as our work unit. In this way the preceding route only needs to be evaluated once, and so causes less of a problem. The time taken to evaluate a work unit consisting of k nodes can be expressed simply as:

$$t_{unit} = t_{setup} + (k \times t_i) \tag{3}$$

where t_i is the time taken to evaluate a single node, and t_{setup} the time required to evaluate any preceding path.

The adoption of k nodes as our unit of parallelism permits an improvement of performance over that of using a single node, though it still requires substantially more work than a serial implementation. Fortunately we can reduce this still further by recognising that for much of the time we will be processing work units which occur consecutively in the search space. If this occurs it is not necessary to evaluate the preceding path, as it will have been examined already for the previous units.

This leaves us with a simple parallelisation strategy. The search space is split into j work units, each of which consists of k nodes to be evaluated. We store the position in this space for the *start* of each work unit. These positions can then be passed to processors to enable them to efficiently reach the start of their allotted work, and evaluate the relevant portion of search space.

To allow processes to quickly reach portions of the search space the algorithm shown in Figure 3 is complicated slightly to include flags which enable a processor searching for its start position to bypass any unrequired calculation. We can achieve this because the route to the start point includes the volumes chosen at each level in the tree.

4.2 Implementation Issues

We must decide how many work units to discretise space into (j). It is tempting to choose n, where n corresponds to the number of processors available. We will never achieve linear scalability with this approach though, as the parallel implementation must perform additional work to evaluate the preceding route, but it is not likely to have a pronounced effect. This simple splitting approach, however, suffers from a more serious problem.

The cost of evaluating a particular node is governed by the expense of evaluating (2). Unfortunately the time required to evaluate this is not uniform, as the positioning of cost-areas, and portions of the scenery, alter the expense of evaluating $CP(S_2) + CR(D)$. This means that certain nodes in the search space take longer to process than others. To demonstrate this a naïve implementation was produced, and the processing times of individual nodes was accumulated. Figure 7 shows these timings, arranged sequentially to indicate that certain areas of the search space are more expensive than others.

This implementation used 10 processors, and the timings clearly show 9 peaks where the cost of evaluating the preceding route impacted on performance (the first process, of course, requires no setup). However, as expected, there are the other peaks which indicate the presence of aspects of the statespace which take longer to process. By varying the animation problem the positioning of these peaks moves, but only vanishes with the most trivial of situations.

Such a simple implementation exhibits poor scalability because the work load is not being evenly balanced across the machine, in this case the processors evaluating the 'first' portion of the search space took longer to complete their work than others. In order to improve the performance of this approach it is necessary to perform better *load balancing*. As we cannot predict where the increased areas of work are likely to lie, it is necessary to adopt a *dynamic* load balancing strategy. That is, the algorithm must be capable of determining, during processing, which processors have been allotted too much work, and so must have their load reduced.

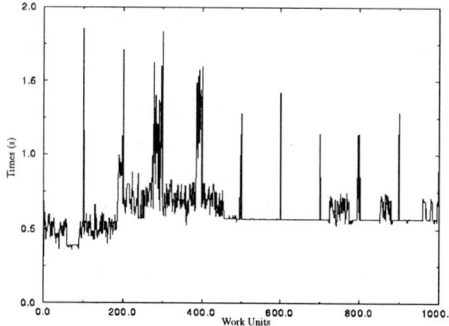

Figure 7 Timings for the different nodes.

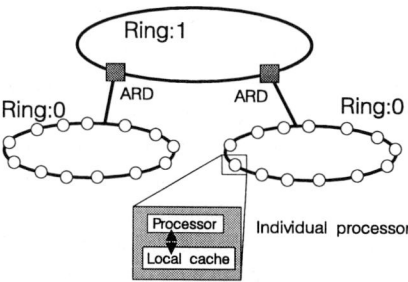

Figure 8 The KSR architecture.

5 The KSR-1 Basic Implementation

To evaluate load balancing approaches this synthesis tool was implemented on a parallel machine (the Kendall Square Research (KSR) 1) which exhibited properties which made it suitable as a test bed for algorithms which perform well on an optimal platform, but could be translated for use on more commonly available machines. Before discussing how these issues are addressed, we first outline the pertinent aspects of the architecture.

5.1 Machine Architecture

Heterogeneous parallel computers can be broadly categorised into 2 groups, those whose memory is shared between processors, and those where the memory is distributed. Unfortunately this has meant that when developing a parallel algorithm we must target one category, and be unable to employ this approach on the other group of machines.

However, recently a rival to this classification has been developed, virtual shared memory (VSM), which physically distributes the memory, but devotes considerable hardware effort into ensuring that the application running on any single processor has easy access to memory which is stored remotely. The first commercial implementation of this design is incorporated into the Kendall Square Research 1 supercomputer [4].

In the KSR-1, processors & memory units are distributed on a 2 level (0 & 1) hierarchy of rings (as shown in Figure 8). When an individual processor requires access to a portion of memory it initially looks in its own local memory/cache, but if it doesn't find it the KSR hardware (in the form of the ARD unit) fetches the memory for it. In practice, then, the memory across the entire machine is dynamic, and moves around to respond to the requirements of the applications currently executing.

From the our point of view the KSR-1 provides an ideal platform for the development of portable parallel codes, as it is capable of supporting VSM applications quickly, and so can highlight load problems, and once developed the VSM model can be emulated in more available workstation clusters.

5.2 Initial Implementation

It is common in dynamic load balanced parallel applications to employ a master/slave algorithm. Here a single process is responsible for ensuring a large number of slaves are kept occupied, which it does by doling out work from a *work list*, until the task is complete. Such a strategy is initially appealing, but for applications which are highly dynamic it has a serious flaw. If several processors finish their units of prescribed work, they must wait for the master to assign more. It takes the master some amount of time to assign a single work unit, and so several of these slaves may lie idle while waiting for jobs.

This bottleneck is caused by the physical location of the work list on a single processor, under the purview of a single process. In a distributed memory machine this is unavoidable, but in the VSM KSR-1 this is no longer the case. Given the ability to move the list around the machine, either wholly or in part, we can avoid the more serious bottlenecks.

The strategy for controlling the work performed by the motion generator operates as follows. Firstly the search space is split into some large number of work units, the number and size of which being dependent on the max_steps chosen by the anima-

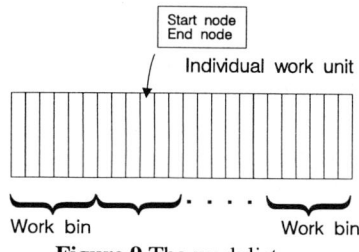

Figure 9 The work list.

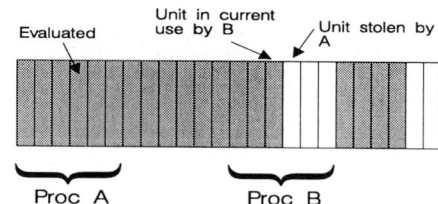

Figure 10 Stealing work units from victim processes.

tor. This list is made available to all processors as a global data structure.

The list is then split into *n* larger chunks of work (for *n* processors), which we call the *work bins* (as shown in Figure 9). A number, *n*, of worker processes are created, each of which evaluates portions of the search space, and is placed on its own processor. Each process refers to its work bin to find where in the search space it must begin work, and then starts processing, taking some time defined by (3). When they have each completed, they transfer back the optimal routes they have found, which the parent process chooses between by examining the costs.

6 Optimization of this Algorithm

As has been previously mentioned, a naïve implementation of such an algorithm, on any machine, is likely to perform poorly, principally due to load balancing problems. Having described the pertinent features of a KSR-1 implementation, it is now possible to address how we avoid these problems on both the target platform, and more commonly available networks of workstations.

6.1 Stealing Work

In a master/slave implementation, dynamic load balancing is performed as a result of the competitive market of slaves searching for work. A slave which is busy will concentrate on the work it has been assigned, while its colleagues will be assigned work which the busy slave would otherwise have processed. However, with a distributed work list, we cannot rely on a master distributing work fairly, and so must ensure that slaves perform the load balancing themselves, by searching the work list, and *stealing* unperformed work from other slaves' work bins (Figure 10).

This is achieved by maintaining, with the global work list, a flag which indicates whether the relevant work units are being/ have been processed yet. When a processor *begins* work on a unit it sets this flag, which prevents that unit being stolen.

Once a processor has completed the work bin it was initially allocated, it begins searching the work list. With a VSM implementation this is a cheap operation (as the machine will transfer the relevant portions of the list to local memory) but with workstation clusters this may cause expensive contention. To reduce the risk of such delays each processor traverses the list sequentially, beginning at the subsequent processors bin, and continuing in that direction, wrapping round when it reaches the end of the list. In this way we avoid the delays of several processors all beginning looking at the same place in the list.

Each worker process can be in one of two modes of operation

Victim: Here the process is working through the bin pre-allocated to it. While working, the unprocessed units within its bin are stealable, hence it is a potential victim.

192

Thief: Once a process can no longer find any work in its pre-allocated bin it begins looking elsewhere, using the algorithm previously described. When it finds a work unit which hasn't been used it 'marks' it as taken and begins evaluation.

Eventually all processes will enter thief mode. When each thief process can no longer find extra work it notifies its parent process, transfers the local optimal route found, and expires.

There are two principal problems with this, which we examine in the subsequent subsections, the cost of work faults, and the expense of traversing the list.

6.2 Work faults

The cost of evaluating a work unit is largely dependent on ensuring that we evaluate as many adjacent units as possible (due to the cost of evaluating the preceding route, as per (3)). However, once a thief process begins to steal work it will have to re-perform this setup, thereby causing a delay. Such a problem is analogous to the delay in an OS caused by a page fault, and is consequently termed a *work fault*.

We can avoid the worst effects of such a fault by also maintaining, along with each work bin, a *path cache* into which each processor keeps the data created during the traversal of the preceding sub-route to the current unit (i.e., the results of the work performed during each setup). Then, during each theft operation, the contents of this cache are copied along with the node information.

When the thief process begins operation it examines this cache, and reuses as much as possible, thereby reducing t_{setup} for this unit. We must allow thief processes to update the path cache, as it is possible for a considerable portion of certain bins to be evaluated by thieves, and so we would otherwise hamper the load balancing. Consequently some locking must be performed to enable multiple processors to update it correctly.

6.3 Traversing the list

On the KSR-1, thanks to the hardware support, the cost of traversing the list is low. However, on other platforms, including clusters of workstations, this expense may hamper the ability of the algorithm to balance load adequately.

This cost can be reduced, in such an environment, by increasing the granularity of the stolen units. So, rather than stealing individual units, a thief process marks a sequence of consecutive units as taken, which it would then process itself. This prevents fragmentation of the work list under extreme conditions, and enables even the slower environments to perform some load balancing.

Note that the granularity of such stolen work must be determined *experimentally* on different platforms by measuring the scalability of the implementation using animations which require extensive load-balancing. Once this size is determined it should apply to all animations, as well balanced problems will not require it, and we have tested it with the worst-case.

7 Case Studies

In order to evaluate the success of this algorithm we must examine its performance on the target platform. Whilst it is important that the algorithm produces results in acceptable time, it is equally necessary to validate that the approach is capable of using large numbers of processors, hopefully producing results faster that the minimum acceptable time.

Figure 11 A two bodied actor hopping.

The parallelised algorithm, as presented, allows the animator to control the efficiency of its operation by altering 2 parameters. In order to compare times meaningfully, then, we must choose example settings. These significant parameters are

• `max_steps`, which represents the number of steps the path will be discretised into, and,

• the number of work units which the search space is split into.

For the purposes of these tests `max_steps` is set to 7, as this produces paths which are sufficiently detailed to work with, and creates a search space large enough to evaluate the effects of the number of work units, or the size of j (section 4.1). The optimal choice for this second parameter is related to the number of processors we employ, the likelihood of any load imbalances and also the speed at which we can respond to these problems.

Consequently the choice of 'ideal' granularity is closely dependent on the problem, and so we cannot determine this value in advance. However, even a poor choice will only seriously effect performance with very large numbers of processors, and so it is possible to choose an acceptable setting without too much difficulty. During these tests a granularity of 2 nodes per work unit has been chosen, but in section 7.3 the results of a poor choice are presented to justify this.

7.1 Example Animations

In order to examine the algorithms performance on different animation problems, this paper presents timings for 2 motion examples. They are

• A 2 body actor, connected by a single joint. We wish the actor to perform the hopping motion beloved of spacetime motion researchers. This motion is caused by placing a floor and obstacle in the scene, each of which are costly to enter, which thereby encourage the actor to hop as it traverses the scene. To demonstrate how spacetime techniques may be used for production animation we generate motion for a skeleton, over which a NURBS body is skinned to create an interesting character. The strobed representation of the approximated resulting coffee cups' hopping motion is shown in Figure 11.

• A 5 body representation of a mannequin, which we wish to perform a walk cycle. This requires a large number of cost-areas (15) to cause the network to appear to walk, and is one of the more complicated examples we might use this technique with. The animation produced is shown in Figure 12.

Having described the problems we now discuss the speed at which the motion may be synthesised, and the ability of the algorithm to adequately exploit large numbers of processors.

7.2 The Hopping Cup

The measured timings for the KSR-1 implementation are shown in Table 1. We can see that the time of execution quickly drops to acceptable levels (~20 seconds). Of course, if the animator finds this delay excessive he or she can reduce the `max_steps` variable to allow the route to be more quickly evaluated. We also wish to measure the ability of the algorithm to fully exploit extra processors (the speedup), so for each sample taken on n processors, taking t_n seconds, we plot the number of virtual processors we are fully utilising.

$$vprocs = \frac{t_1}{n} t_n \tag{4}$$

where t_1 is the time taken on 1 processor. This graph is shown in Figure 13.

We can see that the performance of this algorithm continues to increase, though veers gradually from the ideal linear speedup (marked as the solid line). Recall that as we increase the number of processors we are actually increasing the amount of work which must be performed (due to the number of preceding routes we must process). The gentle slope away from the ideal increase indicates that this factor is having a progressively larger, but not especially critical, effect.

The kink exhibited by the graph at 50 processes is caused by the implementations' use of KSR processors which are also responsible for servicing I/O devices. It is interesting, therefore, to note that as we increase the number of processors beyond this value the load balancing strategy copes with this problem.

7.3 The Walker

The timings exhibited for this problem, and speedups measured, are shown in Table 2 and Figure 14. This problem seems to produce slightly poorer speedups, and we can

Figure 12 A walking mannequin.

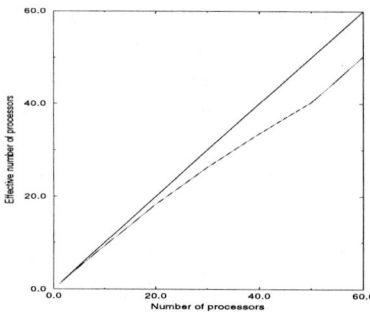

Figure 13 Speedup for the hopping cup.

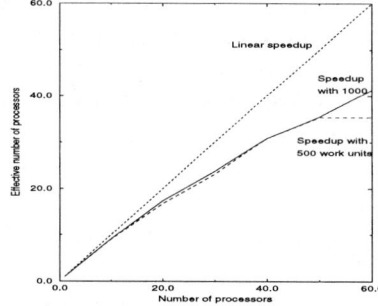

Figure 14 Speedup for the walker.

Table 1 Timings for hopping cup.					
# procs	Elapsed time (s)	Efficiency(%)	# procs	Time (500/1000)	Efficiency(%)
1	604	100	1	2290 / 2770	100 / 100
10	65	93	10	255 / 304	90 / 91
20	33	91.5	20	136 / 159	84 / 87
30	23	87.5	30	100 / 117	77 / 79
40	18	83.9	40	75 / 90	77 / 77
50	15	80.5	50	65 / 78	70.8 / 71.0
60	12	83.9	60	65 / 67	59 / 68.9

Table 1 Timings for hopping cup. **Table 2** Walker Times(500 & 1000 units).

ascribe this to the increased serial processing which takes place.

Recall (section 3.4) that in order to synthesise motion for networks of actors we perform serial constraint maintenance. Whilst this requires little work in the first example, the 5 body network sometimes requires extra processing. However the effect only really becomes serious on large numbers of processors, and as we can see from Table 2, the algorithm still improves in speed rapidly, the slowdown only being noticeable once we wish to plot speedup graphs.

As an indication of the effects of a poor choice for work granularity we plot, in Figure 14, the speedup measured for both 500 and 1000 work units in our search space. Both graphs remain similar for low numbers of processors, but for large processor sets the large granularity damages the load balancing algorithms ability to work effectively, and so does not scale well beyond 50 processors. However, the difference between them, when measured in absolute time, is of the order of seconds, and so is not critical.

8 Conclusions

Recent advances in motion synthesis techniques have improved the ease by which complicated, and realistic, animation may be produced. However, the computational expense of such approaches has largely restricted their use to the academic community.

This paper has advocated the application of parallel processing to these implementations, as a way of reducing the perceived expense of high level motion control techniques. To demonstrate how this may be achieved it has described the efficient distributed implementation of such a motion generator, which uses spacetime abstractions to enable an animator to interactively create production quality motion.

From this it is possible to conclude that parallelism presents a promising solution to the difficulties of using intuitive control methodologies in animation production. Furthermore, as modern commercial animation houses often possess networks of either single or multi-processor workstations, it is likely that such an approach could attract widespread use. The development of high level motion control techniques which can exploit parallelism, then, provides a large area for future work.

Appendix

To demonstrate the speed at which motion may be synthesised in parallel, Tables 1 & 2 present the measured times for the 2 motion examples. In any practical parallel machine the timings on identical runs will fluctuate slightly, due to events out of our control, and so these timings are each averages of 5 runs. Table 2 contains timings for the two different granularities shown in Figure 14.

It is difficult to compare these times meaningfully with previous parallel motion synthesis techniques. Ngo & Marks' [9] technique employs a machine (containing huge numbers of simple single bit processors) which is especially suited to their application, and they do not provide indications of the algorithms ability to execute on varying numbers of processors, as they set out to describe a tool which it is simply convenient to run in parallel.

Friedmann & Pentland [5] do try to achieve scalability on conventional networks of workstations, but only publish results for up to 5 processors (for which they achieve only 50% efficiency), and employ a very low bandwidth network, so a straight comparison is not strictly fair.

Acknowledgments

Thanks to the students and staff of Manchesters' Computer Science department and MC's Computer Graphics Unit for their support. Some of this work was undertaken while the author was an EPSRC sponsored student, so thanks also to my supervisors Prof. F. Sumner and W.T. Hewitt.

References

[1] William W. Armstrong, Mark Green and Robert Lake. Near Real-Time Control of Human Figure Models. *IEEE Computer Graphics & Applications*, 7:39-51, June 1987.

[2] R. Bellman. *Dynamic Programming*. Princeton University Press, 1957.

[3] Michael F. Cohen. Interactive Spacetime Control for Animation. *Computer Graphics*, 26(2):293-302, July 1992.

[4] Steven Frank, Henry Burkhardt III and James Rothnie. The KSR-1 : Bridging the Gap Between Shared Memory and MPPs. In *Proceedings of Compcon '93*, February 1993.

[5] Martin Friedmann and Alex Pentland. Distributed Physical Animation. In *3rd Eurographics Workshop on Animation & Simulation*, 1992.

[6] Jean-Dominique Gascuel and Marie-Paule Gascuel. Displacement Constraints: A New Method for Interactive Dynamic Animation of Articulated Solids. In *3rd Eurographics Workshop on Animation & Simulation*, 1992.

[7] Mark Green and W.W. Armstrong. Interactive Animation Responding to the Real World. In *4th Eurographics Workshop on Animation & Simulation*, 1993.

[8] Zicheng Liu, Steven J. Gortler and Michael F. Cohen. Hierarchical Spacetime Control. In *Proceedings of SIGGRAPH '94*, pages 35-42, 1994. In *Computer Graphics* proceedings, Annual Conference Series.

[9] J. Thomas Ngo and Joe Marks. Spacetime Constraints Revisited. In *Proceedings of SIGGRAPH '93*, pages 343-350, 1993. In *Computer Graphics* proceedings, Annual Conference Series.

[10] Martin Preston. Parallel Motion Synthesis with Space-Time Control. Ph.D. Thesis, University of Manchester, 1995.

[11] Martin Preston. Parallel Motion Synthesis. In *International Workshop on HPC for Computer Graphics and Visualisation*, Swansea, 1995, To appear.

[12] F. Van Reeth and E. Flerackers. Utilizing Parallel Processing in Computer Animation. In *Computer Animation '91*, Springer-Verlag, 1991.

[13] Karl Sims. Particle Animation and Rendering Using Data Parallel Computation. *Computer Graphics*, 24(4):405-413, August 1990.

[14] Nadia Magnenat-Thalmann and Daniel Thalmann. *Computer Animation: Theory and Practice*. Springer-Verlag, Second Edition. 1990.

[15] Michiel van de Panne, Eugene Fiume and Zvonko Vranesic. Reusable Motion Synthesis using State-Space Controllers. *Computer Graphics*, 24(4):225-234, August 1990.

[16] Andrew Witkin and Michael Kass. Spacetime Constraints. *Computer Graphics*, 22(4):159-168, August 1988.

General Animation and Simulation Platform

Stéphane Donikian and Rémi Cozot

IRISA

Campus de Beaulieu

35042 Rennes Cedex, FRANCE

donikian@irisa.fr, cozot@irisa.fr

Abstract. We present in this paper a platform which integrates the different animation models: descriptive, generative and behavioural models. The integration of these models in the same platform permits to offer to each dynamic entity a more realistic and a richer environment, and thereby to increase possible interactions between an actor and its environment. Therefore we describe the unification and the temporal extension of all animation models, within the animation and simulation platform. Theoretical and practical aspects of the platform implementation and experimental results on a driving simulation example are presented.

Key Words: Animation Platform, Motion Control Models, Real-Time

1 Introduction

Context. The objective of animation is the calculation of an image sequence corresponding to discrete time states of an evolving system. Animation consists at first in expressing relationships linking successive states (specification phase) and then making an evaluation of them (execution phase). Motion control models are the heart of any animation/simulation system that determines the friendliness of the user interface, the class of motions and deformations produced, and the application fields. Motion control models can be classified into three general families : descriptive, generative and behavioural models [14]. Descriptive models are used to reproduce an effect without any knowledge about its cause. This kind of models include key frame animation techniques and procedural methods. Unlike preceding models, generative models offer a causal description of objects movement (describe the cause which produces the effects), for instance, their mechanics. In this case, the user control consists in applying torques and forces on the physical model. Thus, it is not easy to determine causes which can impose some effects onto the mechanical structure to produce a desired motion. Two kinds of tools have been designed for the motion control problem: loosely and tightly coupled control. The loosely coupled control method consists in automatically computing the mechanical system inputs from the last value of the state vector and from the user specification of the desired behaviour, while in the other method, the motion control is achieved by determining constraint equations and by inserting directly these equations into the motion equations of the mechanical system. Motion control tools provide the user with a set of elementary actions, but it is difficult to control simulta-neously a large number of dynamic entities. The solution consists in adding a higher level which controls the set of elementary actions. This requires to make a deliberative choice of the object behaviour, and is done by the third model named *behavioural*. The goal of the behavioural model is to simulate autonomous entities like organisms and living beings. A behavioural entity possesses the following capabilities: perception of its environment, decision, action and communication. Nevertheless, in a simulation, all simulated entities do not require the same level of realism. The advantage of descriptive model is its low cost, while disadvantages of generative model are its high frequency and its important calculation cost. Then, it is interesting to mix these different models in a same system to benefit from advantages of each motion control model [30].

Organisation of the paper. The following section presents more precisely the three different motion control models. A set of characteristics needed to simulate these models in a single simulation platform are listed. Section 3 gives a structural view of this platform. Next, section 4 discusses about an architecture of this platform, and its implementation. A driving simulation example illustrates our purpose in the section 5. The paper concludes with an outline of forthcoming development on the platform.

2 Requirements to integrate the motion control models

As described in the introduction, three kinds of motion control models are commonly used in animation. We present here, in more details, these models and point out what each of them require to be integrated in a simulation platform.

2.1 Animation Models

The animation objective is the calculation of an image sequence corresponding to discrete time states of an evolving system. This system is represented by a suite $E(t_0)..E(t_n)$ giving the state of the system at different moments t_i, $i \in \{0, .., n\}$ which represent a regular time sampling ($t_i = t_{i-1} + \Delta t$). Animation consists, using a motion control model, at first to express relationships linking successive states (specification phase) and then to make an evaluation of them (execution phase). Motion control models can be classified into three general families : descriptive, generative and behavioural models [14].

The Descriptive Model. Descriptive models are used to reproduce an effect without any knowledge about its cause. Each object is described by a set of parameters $P \in R^n$. This model describes explicitly how these parameters varies over time ($P = f(t)$). This kind of models includes key frame animation techniques and procedural methods like inverse kinematics [6] or AFFD [8]. In key frame techniques, a subset of instantaneous states $\{P(t_0), \ldots, P(t_k)\}$ are expressed either absolutely or relatively over time, and by interpolation a spatio-temporal trajectory is obtained in the system description space. In this case, the state of the system at each instant $E(t)$ is equal to $P(t)$ which is expressed by a function of the following form $g(P(t_0), \ldots, P(t_k), t)$. In procedural methods, the set of parameters is decomposed in two parts: known X and unknown Q. Then we have to calculate the value of each $q_i \in Q$ by solving a system of nonlinear equations $\forall i \in 0, \ldots, n$, $f_i(X, Q) = 0$. Some particular solutions can be selected from the set of possible ones, by using some criteria. $E(t_i)$ is expressed by a function h of the following form $h(X(t_i), X(t_{i-1}))$.

The Generative Model. Unlike preceding models, generative models offer a causal description of object's movement (describe the cause which produces the effects), for instance, their mechanics. Using physical model to represent and simulate the object permits to take into account natural phenomena. Mechanic simulation enables to animate articulated rigid objects [19], deformable objects [5, 18] and particles models [17]. From a high level description of the rigid and deformable interconnected multibody systems, a simulation blackbox is generated whose inputs are torques and outputs are position and orientation parameters [9]. Motion equations of a mechanical system give a non-linear differential system of order 2: $\forall i \in 0, \ldots, n$, $f_i(q, \dot{q}, \ddot{q}, t, U(t)) = 0$, where q are parameters of the system, and U is the set of forces or torques applied to the object. The state of the system at time t_i is $E(t_i) = F(q(t_{i-1}), \dot{q}(t_{i-1}), t_i, U(t_i))$.

The Behavioural Model. The goal of behavioural models is to simulate the behaviour of different kinds of living things from plants [10, 22] to living beings like animals and persons [3, 4]. Behavioural models define the internal and external behaviour of an entity and its actions and reactions. The behavioural model is composed of the following characteristics: perception of the environment, decision, action and communication. In this case, the temporal dependency relation of the state of an entity $E(t_i)$ at the time t_i is globally expressed by a function $f(E(t_{i-l}), \ldots, E(t_{i-1}), P(t'_{j-k}, \ldots, t'_j), C(t_i), t_i)$, where $C(t_i)$ is the set of messages received by the entity at time t_i and P represents the environment perception function during the temporal interval $[t'_{j-k}, \ldots, t'_j]$, with $t'_j \leq t_i$.

Different approaches have been studied for the decision part: Sensor-Effector [28, 29], Behaviour Rule [15, 23, 26, 27], Predefined Environment [24] and State Machine [1, 11]. Most of these systems have been designed for some particular examples, in which modularity and concurrency are not necessary. This is due to the fact that entities possess only one activity line and because possible interactions between an object and its environment are very simple: sensors and actuators are reduced to minimal capabilities which, most of the time, permit only to avoid obstacles in a 2D or 3D world. Another point which is generally not treated is the notion of time. Paradigms needed for programming a *realistic* behavioural model are reactivity, data-flow, modularity, concurrency and hierarchical preemption [12].

2.2 Time

In a system mixing different objects described by different kinds of models (descriptive, generative and behavioural), it is necessary to take into account the explicit management of time, either during the specification phase (memorization, prediction, action duration, etc.) or during the execution phase (synchronization of objects with different internal times). Three different temporal notions are important for a simulation:

200

Absolute time.   It is the temporal reference of the external world. Interactions between the system and the external world, for a real-time simulation, imposes a strong constraint on the execution of the different tasks. The different tasks are scheduled depending on the absolute time, and this must be done by a global controller. The computer frequency is used to generate this physical time.

Internal time.   Each agent described by an adequate model is cadenced at its own internal frequency. For example, a generative model's internal frequency depends on the stiffness of the mechanical model. The state of the model must be evaluated depending on this internal time.

Execution time.   The execution time is the maximal value of the time necessary to calculate one simulation step. This time is dependent on the target architecture.

2.3   Communications

During the animation or the simulation, models have to exchange informations about their own state. These communication between agents can be both continuous or sporadic. The continuous communication between two agents can be managed by a synchronous data-flow communication. As each agent is cadenced at its own internal frequency, the data-flow communication channel must include all the mechanisms to adapt to the local frequency of the sender and receiver (over-sampling, sub-sampling, interpolation, extrapolation, etc...). Sporadic communications concern both event sending and distant information access.

2.4   Distribute the Simulation

Simulating different modules on a distributed architecture allows:

- interaction of more than one user with a virtual environment, during one simulation.

- to increase the complexity of scenes which can be simulated in real-time.

3   Logical Architecture of the Platform

As mentioned above, different models have to be integrated in a same system and moreover the calculation of the system has to be distributed for efficiency and multi-user interaction. Thus, a simulation platform has to synchronize and manage communications between a set of modules. We need three kinds of communication between modules:

Data-flow.   This is for continuous and predetermined data communication between two modules: a sender and a receiver. For example, a virtual driver has always to give the value of torques that he imposes on the mechanical model of the vehicle (cf figure 1).

Event. This is for symbolic information exchange between modules and a global controller. For example, the scenario can impose on the driver to realize a particular tasks, while the physical model can inform the global controller that it can not assume the real-time constraint, because its internal time is lower than its execution one.

Client-Server. As the platform is composed by a set of distributed modules, each module does not possess locally all the information about the environment. Behavioural modules needs some information about their perceptible environment, but by the fact that objects are in movement in the scene, the set of required data evolves during the simulation. It is not realistic to maintain a global knowledge of the environment in each behavioural module. A better way consists, in our opinion, by maintaining a unique global data-base, from which information can be accessed by a client-server mechanism. The data updating is performed by a data-flow communication between the data owner (producer) and the data-base. Because, sensors require a large amount of data, we have decided to implement them in the data-base module.

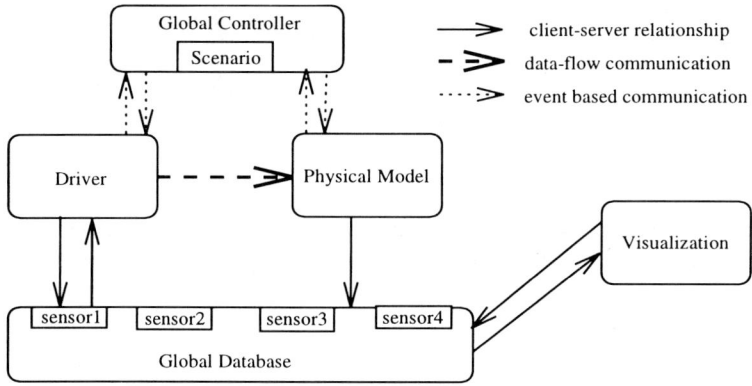

Figure 1: Communications between modules

To ensure the portability of the platform on different hardware architectures, a real-time kernel has been defined (cf figure 2) and is structured in different layers. The first layer is composed of a Communication Server and a Temporal Manager of Processes (scheduler), and is architecture dependent (we describe a particular implementation in the next section). The second layer consists in the implementation of a Global Controller, an Event Manager, a Dataflow Manager and a Client-Server Manager. The third layer is composed of Local Controllers, each of them is associated to an Animation Module. The set of the Animation Modules constitutes the fourth layer. The association between a local controller and an animation module is called an agent.

At each component is associated a specific task:

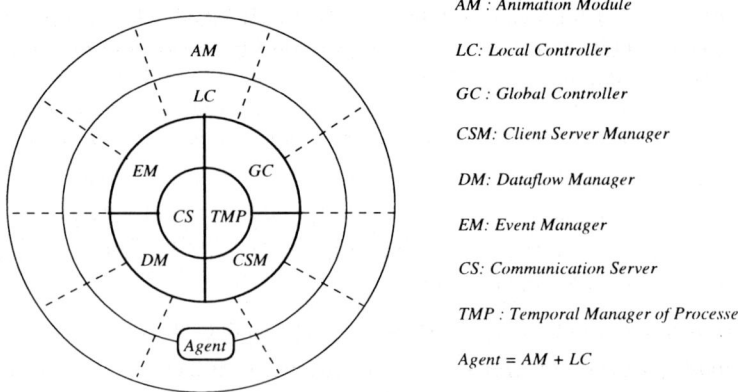

AM : Animation Module

LC: Local Controller

GC : Global Controller

CSM: Client Server Manager

DM: Dataflow Manager

EM: Event Manager

CS: Communication Server

TMP : Temporal Manager of Processes

Agent = AM + LC

Figure 2: layers of the logical architecture of the platform

Global controller: it is the centralised controller of an animation/simulation. It performs the scheduling of the agents execution in order to respect the real time constraint. It is responsible of the initialization and dynamic configuration of the set of agents through communications with the agent using events. The dynamic configuration depends of events generated by the agents or of the analysis of an external script describing the animation/simulation.

Local controller: this controller has to manage the communications by events to the global controller and by data-flow to the other agents. The temporal control of the animation module is also performed by this controller according to the global controller directives.

Animation module: this module is the effective computation module performing the animation task as user interaction, physically based models calculation, trajectories application, image synthesis and so on. Each animation module has a local frequency according to its functionality.

Dataflow Manager: this module has in charge the management of the dataflow communication and propose in fact a set of primitives which permits to open, close or modify a communication channel. A communication channel connects two agents with potentially different local frequencies. The structure of data which will be transported by the channel is initialized at the opening of the channel and can not be modified during the simulation. The data-flow communication is adapted according to these known frequencies. Let F_s be the frequency of the sender and F_r the frequency of the receiver. To limitate the communication flow, we have distinguished three case

1. $F_s = F_r$: this is the most simple case, at each one of the simulation step of the sender module, the datastructure is sent to the receiver.

2. $F_s < F_r$: the sender module transmit, at each one of its simulation step, the datastructure. Then, the receiver module can perform some interpolations to generate data according to its own frequency.

3. $F_s > F_r$: as the sender module has the knowledge of the receiver own frequency, it performs the interpolation of the data according to the frequency of the receiver.

For the interpolation mechanism, messages are temporally stamped. Possible actions are:

- *int create_channel(sender name, sender frequency, receiver name, receiver frequency, interpolation type, data type)*: this function creates a new channel and returns the number of the channel,

- *destroy_channel(channel number)*: this procedure destroy the channel,

- *modify_channel(channel number, sender frequency, receiver frequency, interpolation type)*: this procedure modifies the functionning mode of the channel (new frequency, new interpolation mode).

- *send_df(channel number, data type, data structure)*:

- *receive_df(receipt flag, channel number, data type, data structure)*:

The receipt flag permits to specify if we want a blocking or non-blocking procedure. This mechanism permits to synchronize modules by data-dependency.

Event Manager: this module has in charge the sporadic exchange of informations between agents. The content of the message is composed of the event type, the sender or receiver name and an attached data-structure.

Client-Server Manager: this module permits to access to distant data through a global database server. We use a producer/consumer system. The owner of the data send at its own frequency, the new value of the data to the global database module (*data_update(data name, data_structure)*). A process, who need the value of the data make a request to the global data-base (*request_data(client name, data_name)*) which send the in reply the data (*send_data(client name, data_name, data_structure), receive_data(data_name, data_structure)*).

4 Implementation of the Platform

Different experimentations have been realized:

- A mono-user modular version in which synchronization and control are specified in the synchronous reactive language SIGNAL[7].

- Two multi-processes version by using PVM (Parallel Virtual Machine) [13] and Chorus (micro-kernel technology) [25].

An object oriented distributed version of the simulation platform is currently in developpment. PVM is used to define the real-time kernel which is in charge of communication and synchronization between different processes, while SIGNAL is used to assume internal management of each process. PVM is a software package which permits to developp parallel programs executable on networked Unix computers. It allows a heterogeneous collection of workstations and supercomputers to function as a single high-performance parallel machine. It is portable ans runs on a wide variety of modern platforms. In PVM, we describe an application as a collection of cooperating tasks. Tasks access PVM resources through a library of standard interface routines. These routines allow the initiation and termination of tasks across the network as well as communication and synchronization between tasks. The PVM message-passing primitives involve a strongly typed constructs for buffering and transmission. Communication constructs include those for sending and receiving data structures.

SIGNAL is a synchronous real-time language, data flow oriented (i.e., declarative) and built around a minimal kernel of operators. It manipulates signals, which are unbounded series of typed values (`integer`, `logical`, ...). They have an associated clock determining the instants where values are present. For instance, a signal X denotes the sequence $(\mathbf{x}_t)_{t \in \mathbb{N}}$ of data indexed by time-index t. Signals of a special kind called `event` are characterized only by their clock i.e., their presence (they are given the boolean value `true` at each occurrence). The compiler performs the analysis of the consistency of the system of equations (absence of causal cycles), and determines whether the synchronization constraints between the signals are verified or not. If the relational program is constrained enough to be a function computing a deterministic solution, the compiler transforms the specification into an optimized executable code (in C, FORTRAN or ADA) computing and outputting the solutions to this system of equations at each reaction.

5 Application to the Praxitele Projet

Aims and goals of the Praxitele Project. The Praxitele project combines the efforts of two large government research institutes, one in transportation technologies (INRETS), the other in computer science and automation (INRIA), in cooperation with large industrial companies (RENAULT, EDF, CGEA). This project designs a novel transportation system based on fleet of small electric public cars under supervision from a central computer [21]. These public cars are driven by their users but their operation can be automated in specific instances. The system proposed here should bring a solution to the congestion and pollution in most cities through the entire world.

The concept of a public transport system based on a fleet of small electric vehicles has already been the subject of experiments several times but with poor results. The failure of these experiments can be traced to one main factor : poor avaibility of the vehicles when a customer needs one. To solve this main problem, Praxitele project develops and implements automated cooperative driving of a platoon of vehicles, only the first car is driven by a human operator [20]. This function is essential to move easily the empty vehicles from one location to another.

The realization of such a project requires experiments of the behaviour of autonomous vehicles in an urban environment. Because of the danger of this kind of experiments in a real site, it is necessary to design a virtual urban environment in which simulations can be done. Our platform permits to simulate a platoon of vehicules evolving in a virtual urban environment and so to test control algorithms of the automated cars.

Virtual urban environment simulation. An urban environment is composed of many dynamic entities evolving in a static scene. These dynamic entities have to be both autonomous and controllable and also realistic in term of behaviour. It is necessary to combine the three motion control models to describe dynamic entities of the environment. For example, to describe traffic lights it is not necessary to use a generative model when a descriptive model (finite state automata) is sufficient. On the other hand, for a realistic car driving, we need both generative and behavioural models (the first one to simulate the dynamic of the vehicle and the second one to simulate the driver).

To illustrate our purpose, we developp now an example composed of the three kinds of motion control models, integrated in a same simulation platform. This example is composed of seven dynamic vehicles, with three kinds of motion control (driven by a user, autonomous praxi-vehicles, virtual driver) and a bicycle with a descriptive motion control. A vehicle is an articulated rigid object structure if we do not consider the deformations of the tires and the component flexibility [2]. The vehicle is defined by a generative model which is parametrized by a state vector and three torques (brake, motor and guidance).

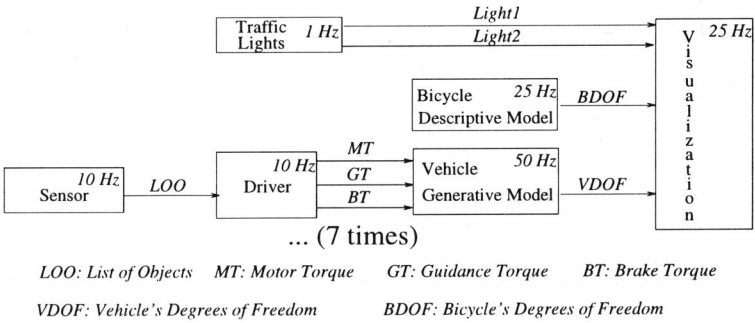

Figure 3: Data-flow aspect of the example

In the case of an automatic control of the vehicle, we have to describe the behaviour of a virtual driver depending on how is its perception of its environment. A feedback state control algorithm [16] determines what torques are applied to the vehicle from actions decided by the virtual driver. The virtual driver is described by a behavioural model in which the decision part is defined by a hierarchical parallel transition system [12]. The Bicycle model is described by six parameters (cf figure 4):

- (x, y, z, ϕ_1) for the position and orientation of the frame.

- ϕ_2 for the orientation of the fork relating to the frame orientation.

- ψ_1 for the rotation of the two wheels and the crank gear.

The descriptive motion control model determines the value of (x, y) so that the bicycle follow a predefined trajectory, which is the middle of a lane. z is constant (height of the gravity center of the frame). The two angles ϕ_1 and ϕ_2 are calculated so that the frame and the front wheel stay tangent to the trajectory. The value of ψ_1 depends on the speed of the bicycle.

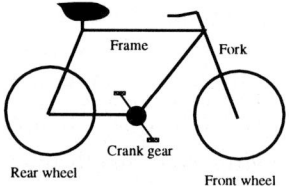

Figure 4: Bicycle model

The figure 5 shows the initial state of a simulation example. The eight images reproduced in the appendix are extracted from the same simulation sequence. This example illustrates possible interactions between objects controlled by different motion control models. At the beginning, three Praxicars (blue cars) are parked and are waiting for the head of the platoon which is coming slowly: the viewpoint of the figure 3 corresponds to the point of view of the virtual driver of this vehicle. Another car is stopped at the crossroads while other vehicles are in a free driving state and the bicycle follows slowly its traffic lane. During this simulation, we can observ an interaction between the bicycle and the platoon, because the driver of the first vehicle has decided to overtake the bicycle. On the other hand, the bicycle passes through the car which stopped at the crossroads, because of its motion control model. Another possible interaction is between a dynamic object and the static scene (for example knowledge of the qualitative aspect of the road and colour of traffic lights for the driver), thanks to the management of a knowledge basis which contains geometrical informations but also topological and semantic knowledges.

Figure 5: One view of the initial state of the simulation example.

6 Conclusion

In this paper, we have pointed out different requirements to integrate in a unique platform the three kinds of motion control models. Such a platform offers to each dynamic entity a more realistic and a richer environment, and thereby increases possible interactions between an agent and its environment. We have then described the logical architecture of the platform, and one implementation. This work is directly applied as part of the PRAXITELE project. Our work will permit to first simulate the line of vehicles evolving in a virtual urban environment with the intention of giving experimenters the ability to test their control algorithms whose inputs are informations from virtual sensors.

References

1. O. Ahmad, J. Cremer, S. Hansen, J. Kearney, and P. Willemsen. – Hierarchical, concurrent state machines for behavior modeling and scenario control. – In *Conference on AI, Planning, and Simulation in High Autonomy Systems*, Gainesville, Florida, USA, 1994.

2. B. Arnaldi and G. Dumont. – Vehicle simulation versus vehicle animation. – In *Third Eurographics Workshop on Animation and Simulation*, Cambridge, September 1992.

3. N. I. Badler, C. B. Phillips, and B. L. Webber. – *Simulating Humans : Computer Graphics Animation and Control.* – Oxford University Press, 1993.

4. Norman I. Badler, Bonnie L. Webber, Jugal Kalita, and Jeffrey Esakov, editors. – *Making them move: mechanics, control, and animation of articulated figures.* – Morgan Kaufmann, 1991.

5. D. Baraff and A. Witkin. – Dynamic simulation of non-penetrating flexible bodies. – *Computer Graphics*, 26(2):303–308, July 1992. – In Proceedings of SIGGRAPH'92.

6. R. Boulic. – Combined direct and inverse kinematic control for articulated figure motion editing. – *Computer Graphics Forum*, 11(4):189–202, 1992.

7. Patricia Bournai, Bruno Chéron, Thierry Gautier, Bernard Houssais, and Paul Le Guernic. – Signal manual. – Technical Report 745, IRISA, July 1993.

8. Sabine Coquillard and Pierre Jancène. – Animated free-form deformation: An interactive animation technique. – *Computer Graphics*, 25(4):225–234, jul 1991. – In proceedings of SIGGRAPH'91.

9. R. Cozot, B. Arnaldi, and G. Dumont. – A unified model for physically based animation and simulation. – In *Applied Modelling, Simulation and Optimization*, Cancun, Mexico, June 1995. IASTED.

10. Phillippe de Reffye, Claude Edelin, Jean Francon, Marc Jaeger, and Claude Puech. – Plant models faithful to botanical structure and development. – In John Dill, editor, *Computer Graphics (SIGGRAPH '88 Proceedings)*, volume 22, pages 151–158, August 1988.

11. S. Donikian and B. Arnaldi. – Complexity and concurrency for behavioral animation and simulation. – In G. Hégron and O. Fahlander, editors, *Fifth Eurographics Workshop on Animation and Simulation*, Oslo, Norvège, September 1994.

12. Stéphane Donikian and Eric Rutten. – Reactivity, concurrency, data-flow and hierarchical preemption for behavioural animation. – In *Fifth Eurographics Workshop on Programming Paradigms in Graphics*, Maastricht, The Netherlands, September 1995.

13. Al Geist, Adam Beguelin, Jack Dongarra, Weicheng Jiang, Robert Manchek, and Vaidy Sunderam. – *PVM: Parallel Virtual Machine.* – The MIT Press, 1994.

14. G. Hégron and B. Arnaldi. – *Computer Animation : Motion and Deformation Control.* – Eurographics'92 Tutorial Notes, Eurographics Technical Report Series, Cambridge (Grande-Bretagne), September 1992.

15. D. Kalra and A.H. Barr. – Modeling with time and events in computer animation. – In A. Kilgour and L. Kjelldahl, editors, *Eurographics*, pages 45–58, Cambridge, United Kingdom, September 1992. Blackwell.

16. Ch. Lecerf, B. Arnaldi, and G. Hégron. – Mechanical systems motion control for computer animation. – In Bulent Ozguc and Varol Akman, editors, *First Bilkent Computer Graphics Conference on Advanced Techniques in Animation, Rendering and Visualization, ATARV-93, July 12-14, 1993*, pages 207–222. Bilkent University, Ankara, Turkey, jul 1993.

17. A. Luciani, S. Jimenez, O. Raoult, C. Cadoz, and J.L. Florens. – An unified view of multitude behavior, flexibility, plasticity and fractures balls, bubbles and agglomerates. – In Springer-Verlag, editor, *Modeling in Computer Graphics*, pages 55–74. IFIP Working conference 91 (TC 5/WG5. 10), apr 1991.

18. D. Metaxas and D. Terzopoulos. – Dynamic deformation of solid primitives with constraints. – *Computer Graphics*, 26(2):309–312, July 1992. – In Proceedings of SIGGRAPH'92.

19. C. W. A. M. Van Overveld. – A simple approximation to rigid body dynamics for computer animation. – *The Journal of Vizualisation and Computer Animation*, 5:17–36, 1994.

20. M. Parent and P. Daviet. – Automatic driving for small public urban vehicles. – In *Intelligent Vehicle Symposium*, Tokyo, Japon, July 1993.

21. M. Parent and P.Y. Texier. – A public transport system based on light electric cars. – In *Fourth International Conference on Automated People Movers*, Irving, Texas, U.S.A., March 1993.

22. Przemyslaw Prusinkiewicz, Mark S. Hammel, and Eric Mjolsness. – Animation of plant development. – In James T. Kajiya, editor, *Computer Graphics (SIGGRAPH '93 Proceedings)*, volume 27, pages 351–360, August 1993.

23. Craig W. Reynolds. – Flocks, herds, and schools: A distributed behavioral model. – In Maureen C. Stone, editor, *Computer Graphics (SIGGRAPH '87 Proceedings)*, volume 21, pages 25–34, July 1987.

24. Gary Ridsdale and Tom Calvert. – Animating microworlds from scripts and relational constraints. – In N. Magnenat-Thalmann and D. Thalmann, editors,

Computer Animation '90 (Second workshop on Computer Animation), pages 107–118. Springer-Verlag, April 1990.

25. M. Rozier, V. Abrassimov, F. Armand, M. Boule, M. Gien, M. Guillemont, F. Herrman, C. Kaiser, S. Langlois, P. Leonard, and W. Neuhauser. – Overview of the chorus distributed operating system. – In *Usenix Symposium on micro-kernels and other kernels architectures*, pages 39–69, Seattle, April 1992.

26. Hanqiu Sun and Mark Green. – The use of relations for motion control in an environment with multiple moving objects. – In *Graphics Interface*, pages 209–218, Toronto, Ontario, May 1993.

27. Xiaoyuan Tu and Demetri Terzopoulos. – Artificial fishes: Physics, locomotion, perception, behavior. – In *Computer Graphics (SIGGRAPH'94 Proceedings)*, pages 43–50, Orlando, Florida, July 1994.

28. Michiel van de Panne and Eugene Fiume. – Sensor-actuator networks. – In James T. Kajiya, editor, *Computer Graphics (SIGGRAPH '93 Proceedings)*, volume 27, pages 335–342, August 1993.

29. Jane Wilhelms and Robert Skinner. – A "notion" for interactive behavioral animation control. – *IEEE Computer Graphics and Applications*, 10(3):14–22, May 1990.

30. David Zeltzer. – Task-level graphical simulation: abstraction, representation, and control. – In Norman I. Badler, Brian A. Barsky, and David Zeltzer, editors, *Making them move: mechanics, control, and animation of articulated figures*, pages 3–33. Morgan Kaufmann, 1991.

Editors' Note: see Appendix, p. 235 for coloured figure of this paper

An Efficient Symbolic Interface to Constraint Based Animation Systems

Zicheng Liu

Department of Computer Science

Princeton University

Princeton, NJ 08544

zl@cs.princeton.edu

Michael F. Cohen

Microsoft Research

Redmond, WA 98052

mcohen@microsoft.com

Abstract. Symbolic methods have been used to provide a general user interface in optimization based animation systems. However, previous methods suffer from the exponential growth in the length of the symbolic expressions of the objectives, constraints and their derivatives. In this paper, we present a symbolic language which is general enough to represent common kinematic and dynamic quantities. The evaluation of these symbolic expressions and their gradients are as fast as numerical methods. In particular, the computational complexity is only a low degree polynomial compared to exponential growth of previous methods, and the optimum performance is achieved for computing the gradients of the generalized forces by extending Hollerbach's technique of compuing inverse dynamics. Furthermore, in this new language the expressions are usually very small so that they can be easily typed in, therefore this method provides a general and efficient interface to optimization based linked figure animation systems.

1 Introduction

Symbolic methods have been used to represent constraints and objectives in many optimization based animation systems ([6, 1, 5]). The major advantage of symbolic methods is that they are general enough to represent various kinds of constraints and objectives. In addition, the gradients and Hessians can be obtained automatically by symbolic differentiation at runtime. However, one major disadvantage of previous approaches is that the length of the resulting symbolic expressions are exponential in the depth of the tree of degrees of freedom (DOFs). This problem has been noticed and subexpression elimination techniques have been used to reduce the sizes of the evaluation trees [3, 5]. However, this does not fully solve the problem since the size of the evaluation trees after subexpression elimination are still exponential in general. To see why, let's consider an n-link chain. Each link is attached to a local coordinate system, and let W_i be the orientation matrix of link i in the world coordinate system.

Let R_i be the orientation matrix of link i in the local coordinate system of link $i - 1$. Then

$$W_n = R_0 R_1 ... R_{n-1} \tag{1}$$

Each R_i is a function of the rotation angles (say X-Y-Z angles) between link $i - 1$ and link i. Denote $W_n = (a_{uv})_{1 \leq u,v \leq 3}$, and $R_i = (a_{uv}^i)_{1 \leq u,v \leq 3}$, then

$$a_{uv} = \sum_{1 \leq i_1, i_2, ..., i_{n-1} \leq 3} a_{ui_1}^0 a_{i_1 i_2}^1 ... a_{i_{n-2} i_{n-1}}^{n-2} a_{i_{n-1} v}^{n-1}. \tag{2}$$

So a_{uv} contains 3^{n-1} summation terms. Notice that the common subexpression elimination applied to a_{uv} would not necessarily reduce the number of summation terms since no two terms are guaranteed to be the same. However, if we don't expand W_n but instead evaluate $R_0, ..., R_{n-1}$ first and then do matrix multiplication numerically we can compute W_n in linear time.

This suggests that expanding the matrices as explicit functions of DOFs is not a good idea. So we propose to use position vectors and orientation matrices as first class symbolic variables in the symbolic expressions, (i.e., we don't expand them). Together with a few special operators which will be defined later in the paper, we will show that with this paradigm common kinematic and dynamic expressions can be represented as a small number of operations on the joint positions and link orientations. These expressions are usually small enough to be simply typed in. More importantly there are very efficient ways to evaluate these expressions.

We do not want to claim this as a completely new idea, as the same insight has been used in developing fast dynamics algorithms [2]. This paper extends these ideas to the constrained optimization area and discusses a simple language and implementation.

2 The Language

This section will not discuss the full syntax of the simple symbolic language described here, but will rather focus on the interesting extensions that provide the efficiencies discussed above.

In this paper, we assume the figure structure is a tree of links. Each link can rotate around its parent about a joint. Each joint can have 1 to 3 degrees of freedom and we use Euler angles (rotated around X, Y and Z successively) to represent the rotation angles at each joint. We assume the links are labeled L_1, ..., L_n, and the joint angles are labeled θ_0, ..., θ_{m-1}. Each link is attached to a local coordinate system which rotates with the link.

2.1 Variables

Normal scalar variables representing DOF functions and their time derivatives are represented by **dof_name[derivative, t]**) where *name* is the variable name, and t is time. In addition, three new types of variables are introduced: position variables, orientation variables, and torque variables. A position variable has the form: **pos_**name[der-info, t , x, y, z] where name is the label of the link at which this position is located, t is either a real number representing a specific time or simply the symbol **T** indicating "at all times", (x,y,z) is the coordinate of this position in the local coordinate system, and finally der-info is a sequence of integers of the form $(i_1, i_2, ..., i_p, j)$ which store the derivative information representing the operator $\frac{\partial^p}{\partial\theta_{i_1}\partial\theta_{i_2}...\partial\theta_{i_p}}\frac{d^j}{dt^j}$. When (x, y, z) represents the center of gravity, it can be omitted. That is, we can simply write **pos_**name[der-info, t].

For example, suppose we have three links labeled $L1$, $L2$, and $L3$. If we use $E(t)$ to denote the world coordinates of the end effector at time t. Then $E(t)$, $\dot{E}(t)$, and $\ddot{E}(t)$ can be represented as **pos_**$L3[0, T, ex, ey, ez]$, **pos_**$L3[1, T, ex, ey, ez]$, and **pos_**$L3[2, T, ex, ey, ez]$, respectively, where (ex, ey, ez) is the coordinates of the end effector relative to the local coordinate system of $L3$. The partial derivative $\frac{\partial\dot{E}(t)}{\partial\theta_2}$ can be represented as **pos_**$L3[(2, 1), t, ex, ey, ez]$, $\frac{\partial^2\dot{E}(t)}{\theta_2(t)\theta_3(t)}$ can be represented as **pos_**$L3[(2, 3, 1), t, ex, ey, ez]$. How do we represent the partial derivatives with respect to the time derivatives of angles such as $\frac{\partial\dot{E}(t)}{\partial\dot{\theta}_2(t)}$? Actually $\frac{\partial\dot{E}(t)}{\partial\dot{\theta}_2(t)} = \frac{\partial E(t)}{\partial\theta_2(t)}$. In general, any partial derivatives with respect to time derivatives of angles can always be reduced to partial derivatives with respect to angles (without time derivatives). In most cases where only up to second order derivatives are under consideration, the following formulas are sufficient for the reductions:

$$\frac{\partial E(t)}{\partial\dot{\theta}(t)} = 0, \tag{3}$$

$$\frac{\partial E(t)}{\partial\ddot{\theta}(t)} = 0, \tag{4}$$

$$\frac{\partial\dot{E}(t)}{\partial\dot{\theta}(t)} = \frac{\partial E(t)}{\partial\theta}, \tag{5}$$

$$\frac{\partial\dot{E}(t)}{\partial\ddot{\theta}(t)} = 0, \tag{6}$$

$$\frac{\partial\ddot{E}(t)}{\partial\dot{\theta}(t)} = 2 * \frac{\partial\dot{E}(t)}{\partial\theta(t)}, \tag{7}$$

$$\frac{\partial\ddot{E}(t)}{\partial\ddot{\theta}(t)} = \frac{\partial E(t)}{\partial\theta(t)}. \tag{8}$$

Similarly, an orientation variable has the form **ori_**name[der-info, t] which denotes the orientation matrix of the link name or its derivatives including mixed partial and time derivatives.

Notice that an orientation variable is a 3×3 matrix[1], while a position variable is a 3D vector. For example, if the orientation matrix of link $L1$ in the world

---

[1] Alternatively, the orientation can berepresented as a quaternion. In this case, the derivations which follow would require the corresponding quaternion algebra.

coordinate system is $M_1(t)$, then

$$\frac{dM_1(t)}{dt} = \mathbf{ori\_}L1[1, t]. \tag{9}$$

A torque variable has the form $\mathbf{tor\_}id[t]$, which represents the generalized force with respect to the rotational angle named id at time t. Notice that torque variables are not essential to this symbolic system since torques(generalized forces) can be represented as functions of positions and orientations in a short form (see the appendix or [2]). The reason to introduce the torque variables is to gain the optimum efficiency for computing torques and their gradients since torques are the most expensive quantities . We will show how to extend Hollerbach's technique[2] of computing Lagragian inverse dynamics to evaluate the gradients of all the torques in $O(m^2)$ time, which is the optimum since we have to evaluate $O(m^2)$ entries. Without such special treatment, it would take $O(m^3)$ time.

2.2 Operations

Many operations on scalar variables are defined with the expected syntax and differentiation rules. Similarly, common matrix and vector operations are defined. In addition to normal matrix operations, we need two special operations to represent quantities like kinetic energy and angular momentum of a rigid link. Given two 3×3 matrices M_1 and M_2, and a link L, we define operators $\mathbf{Vdot}$ and $\mathbf{Vcross}$ as the following:

$$\mathbf{Vdot}(L, M_1, M_2) = \int (M_1 X) \cdot (M_2 X) \tau(X) dX \tag{10}$$

and

$$\mathbf{Vcross}(L, M_1, M_2) = \int (M_1 X) \times (M_2 X) \tau(X) dX \tag{11}$$

where X ranges over the coordinates of all the points on the link L in its local coordinate system, and $\tau(X)$ is the mass density at X.

Given a link L with a centroidal local coordinate system and assuming its orientation matrix is M, then the rotational energy of L is

$$0.5 \int (\dot{M} X) \cdot (\dot{M} X) \tau(X) dX = 0.5 \mathbf{Vdot}(L, \dot{M}, \dot{M}), \tag{12}$$

and its angular momentum about its center of mass is

$$\int (M X) \times (\dot{M} X) \tau(X) dX = \mathbf{Vcross}(L, M, \dot{M}). \tag{13}$$

Notice that the computation of both integrals can be reduced to the computation of the nine elements of $\int X X^T \tau(X) dX$ (they are constants) which is the inertia tensor of the link with respect to its local coordinate system.

3 An Example

We give an example to show all the expressions in a spacetime constraint formulation by using this new language. The example is extracted from [5]. Suppose we want to animate a planar three link arm which starts holding a ball in its rest position at time $t0$, throws the ball at time $t1$, and comes back to its rest position at time $t2$. The requirement is that the ball has to go into basket.

Assume the basket position is at (Bx, By, Bz), the local coordinate of the end of the hand is (Hx, Hy, Hz). And let $g = 9.8$ be the gravity constant. Assume T is the time period during which the ball flies from leaving the hand to getting into the basket.

The objective function is the integral of the sum of squares of the three torques. There are three types of constraints:

1. The ball should go into the basket.

2. At time $t0$ and tf, the arm is still at its rest position.

3. Each joint angle has a limited range.

The third constraint is a built-in constraint, i.e., each rotational angle has an upper and lower bound which are stored in the figure data structure. So the user doesn't have to input joint limit constraints.

Using our language, the objective function can be written as

$$\mathbf{itg}[t0, tf](\mathbf{sqr}(\mathbf{tor\_0}[\mathbf{T}]) + \mathbf{sqr}(\mathbf{tor\_1}[\mathbf{T}]) + \mathbf{sqr}(\mathbf{tor\_2}[\mathbf{T}])), \tag{14}$$

the constraint (1) is derived from simple physics equated the position and velocity of the ball at the time of release with the position of the ball T time later,

$$\begin{aligned} &\mathbf{pos\_hand}[(0), t1, Hx, Hy, Hz] + \mathbf{pos\_hand}[(1), t1, Hx, Hy, Hz] * T + \\ &0.5 * \mathbf{colv}(0, -g, 0) * T * T = \mathbf{colv}(Bx, By, Bz), \end{aligned} \tag{15}$$

and the constraint (2) consists of twelve simple constraints,

$$\mathbf{dof\_0}[0, t0] = 0, \mathbf{dof\_1}[0, t0] = 0, \mathbf{dof\_2}[0, t0] = 0, \tag{16}$$

$$\mathbf{dof\_0}[1, t0] = 0, \mathbf{dof\_1}[1, t0] = 0, \mathbf{dof\_2}[1, t0] = 0, \tag{17}$$

$$\mathbf{dof\_0}[0, tf] = 0, \mathbf{dof\_1}[0, tf] = 0, \mathbf{dof\_2}[0, tf] = 0, \tag{18}$$

$$\mathbf{dof\_0}[1, tf] = 0, \mathbf{dof\_1}[1, tf] = 0, \mathbf{dof\_2}[1, tf] = 0, \tag{19}$$

where $\mathbf{itg}[t0, tf]$ denotes the definite integral from $t0$ to tf, $\mathbf{sqr}$ is the square function, $\mathbf{colv}(\text{x,y,z})$ is the column vector $(x, y, z)^T$.

If we instead use the change of energy as the objective function (for example, see [4]), we can represent the objective function as

$$\begin{aligned} \mathbf{itg}[t0, tf](&\mathbf{sqr}(m_1 * \mathbf{trans}(\mathbf{pos\_}L1[1, \mathbf{T}]) * \mathbf{pos\_}L1[2, \mathbf{T}] \\ + \quad &\mathbf{Vdot}(L1, \mathbf{ori\_}L1[1, \mathbf{T}], \mathbf{ori\_}L1[2, \mathbf{T}])) \\ + \quad &\mathbf{sqr}(m_2 * \mathbf{trans}(\mathbf{pos\_}L2[1, \mathbf{T}]) * \mathbf{pos\_}L2[2, \mathbf{T}] \\ + \quad &\mathbf{Vdot}(L2, \mathbf{ori\_}L2[1, \mathbf{T}], \mathbf{ori\_}L2[2, \mathbf{T}])) \\ + \quad &\mathbf{sqr}(m_2 * \mathbf{trans}(\mathbf{pos\_}L3[1, \mathbf{T}]) * \mathbf{pos\_}L3[2, \mathbf{T}] \\ + \quad &\mathbf{Vdot}(L3, \mathbf{ori\_}L3[1, \mathbf{T}], \mathbf{ori\_}L3[2, \mathbf{T}]))) \end{aligned} \tag{20}$$

where **trans** is the matrix transpose function.

4 Symbolic Differentiation

The ability to automate the gradient computation using symbolic differentiation is one of the major advantages of a symbolic language. The symbolic differentiation can be carried out essentially the same way as the previous method [5] except at the leaves representing either a position or a matrix variable, der-info should be updated correpondingly by using the reductions (3)-(8) if necessary (Basically the task is to store the differentiation information). The details are omitted. For the torque variables, the partial derivative information is stored in the node, and we will show how to compute the torques and their partial derivatives efficiently at evaluation time in the next section.

One should also notice that there are two special operators: **Vdot** and **Vcross**. The differentiation formulae of these two operators are simply

$$\frac{\partial \mathbf{Vdot}(L, M_1, M_2)}{\partial \theta} = \mathbf{Vdot}(L, \frac{\partial M_1}{\partial \theta}, M_2) + \mathbf{Vdot}(L, M_1, \frac{\partial M_2}{\partial \theta}), \quad (21)$$

and

$$\frac{\partial \mathbf{Vcross}(L, M_1, M_2)}{\partial \theta} = \mathbf{Vcross}(L, \frac{\partial M_1}{\partial \theta}, M_2) + \mathbf{Vcross}(L, M_1, \frac{\partial M_2}{\partial \theta}). \quad (22)$$

5 Torque Variables

In this section, we show how to extend Hollerbach's technique[2] to compute the gradients of torques with optimum efficiency. We only give the formulas here. The detailed derivations are given in the appendix.

Let W_i represent the 4×4 transformation matrix of link i. Let r_i be its center of gravity. Let $G = (0, g, 0)$ be the gravity vector. Denote u_j to be the index of the link where θ_j is located (i.e., θ_j is one of the degrees of freedom allowing this link to rotate around its parent). Let $K(l)$ be the set of indices of the kids of link l. Let $D(l)$ be the set of indices of all the decendents of link l. Let $\bar{D}(l) = D(l) \cup \{l\}$. We use $u_k \preceq u_j$ to denote the relationship that u_k is either an ancestor of u_j or $u_k = u_j$. Given a matrix M, let $tr(M)$ be the trace of M. Then the generalized force with respect to θ_j is

$$f_{\theta_j} = \sum_{i \in \bar{D}(u_j)} (tr\{\frac{\partial W_i}{\partial \theta_j} J_i(\ddot{W}_i)^T\} + m_i G \frac{\partial W_i}{\partial \theta_j} r_i) \quad (23)$$

Let

$$A_l = \sum_{i \in \bar{D}(l)} W_i^l J_i \ddot{W}_i^T, \quad (24)$$

$$b_l = \sum_{i \in \bar{D}(l)} m_i W_i^l r_i, \quad (25)$$

$$B_{l,k} = \sum_{i \in \bar{D}(l)} W_i^l J_i \frac{\partial \ddot{W}_i^T}{\partial \theta_k}, \tag{26}$$

$$C_{l,k} = \sum_{i \in \bar{D}(l)} 2 W_i^l J_i \frac{\partial \dot{W}_i^T}{\partial \theta_k}, \tag{27}$$

and

$$D_{l,k} = \sum_{i \in \bar{D}(l)} W_i^l J_i \frac{\partial W_i^T}{\partial \theta_k}. \tag{28}$$

Then

$$f_{\theta_j} = tr(\frac{\partial W_{u_j}}{\partial \theta_j} A_{u_j}) + G \frac{\partial W_{u_j}}{\partial \theta_j} b_{u_j} \tag{29}$$

The formula for computing partial derivatives with respect to a DOF variable and its 1st and second order derivatives are

$$\frac{\partial f_{\theta_j}}{\partial \theta_k} = \begin{cases} tr\{\frac{\partial^2 W_{u_j}}{\partial \theta_j \partial \theta_k} A_{u_j} + \frac{\partial W_{u_j}}{\partial \theta_j} B_{u_j,k}\} + G \frac{\partial^2 W_{u_j}}{\partial \theta_j \partial \theta_k} b_{u_j}, & u_k \preceq u_j \\ tr\{\frac{\partial^2 W_{u_k}}{\partial \theta_j \partial \theta_k} A_{u_k} + \frac{\partial W_{u_k}}{\partial \theta_j} B_{u_k,k}\} + G \frac{\partial^2 W_{u_k}}{\partial \theta_j \partial \theta_k} b_{u_k}, & \text{otherwise} \end{cases} \tag{30}$$

$$\frac{\partial f_{\theta_j}}{\partial \dot{\theta}_k} = tr\{\frac{\partial W_{u_j}}{\partial \theta_j} C_{u_j,k}\}, \tag{31}$$

and

$$\frac{\partial f_{\theta_j}}{\partial \ddot{\theta}_k} = tr\{\frac{\partial W_{u_j}}{\partial \theta_j} D_{u_j,k}\}. \tag{32}$$

The recursive formulas for computing A_l, b_l, $B_{l,k}$, $C_{l,k}$ and $D_{l,k}$ are

$$A_l = J_l \ddot{W}_l^T + \sum_{u \in K(l)} R_u A_u, \tag{33}$$

$$b_l = m_l r_l + \sum_{u \in K(l)} R_u b_u, \tag{34}$$

$$B_{l,k} = J_l \frac{\partial \ddot{W}_l^T}{\partial \theta_k} + \sum_{u \in K(l)} R_u B_{u,k}, \tag{35}$$

$$C_{l,k} = 2 * J_l \frac{\partial \dot{W}_l^T}{\partial \theta_k} + \sum_{u \in K(l)} R_u C_{u,k}, \tag{36}$$

$$D_{l,k} = J_l \frac{\partial W_l^T}{\partial \theta_k} + \sum_{u \in K(l)} R_u D_{u,k}, \tag{37}$$

In order to compute the gradients, for each k, we traverse the figure tree to compute A_l, b_l, $B_{l,k}$, $C_{l,k}$, and $D_{l,k}$ for all l by using (33)-(37). Then (29)-(32)

are applied to compute the torques and all of their partial derivatives. So in total, the gradient computation takes $O(m^2)$ time. Notice that we have m^2 components to evalute (the gradient of each torque contains m components), so in average each component takes constant time. Clearly this is the optimum.

6 Evaluation

The evaluation of the expressions boils down to the the evaluation of the variables at the leaves. The DOF variables are evaluated by using DOF representations (e.g., B-splines, B-spline wavelets, piecewise Hermite splines, etc.). From the last section we can see that the evaluation of torque variables reduces to the evaluation of orientation matrices. In addition, it is easy to see that the evaluation of positions and their time or partial derivatives can be computed recursively from the orientation matrices too. We thus need to recursively compute all the orientation matrices, their 1st and second order time derivatives, and their partial derivatives. Formally we need to evaluate W_i, $\dot{W}_i$, $\ddot{W}_i$, $\frac{\partial W_i}{\partial \theta_k}$ $\frac{\partial \dot{W}_i}{\partial \theta_k}$ $\frac{\partial \ddot{W}_i}{\partial \theta_k}$ for all i and k.

These evaluations can be done recursively by using the formulas below where we assume L_{i-1} is the parent of the link L_i.

$$W_i = W_{i-1} R_i \tag{38}$$

$$\dot{W}_i = \dot{W}_{i-1} R_i + W_{i-1} \dot{R}_i \tag{39}$$

$$\ddot{W}_i = \ddot{W}_{i-1} R_i + 2\dot{W}_{i-1} \dot{R}_i + W_{i-1} \ddot{R}_i. \tag{40}$$

$$\frac{\partial \dot{W}_i}{\partial \theta_j} = \frac{\partial \dot{W}_{i-1}}{\partial \theta_j} R_i + \dot{W}_i \frac{\partial R_i}{\partial \theta_j} + \frac{\partial W_{i-1}}{\partial \theta_j} \dot{R}_i + W_{i-1} \frac{\partial \dot{R}_i}{\partial \theta_j} \tag{41}$$

$$\frac{\partial \ddot{W}_i}{\partial \theta_j} = \frac{\partial \ddot{W}_{i-1}}{\partial \theta_j} R_i + \ddot{W}_{i-1} \frac{\partial R_i}{\partial \theta_j} + 2\frac{\partial \dot{W}_{i-1}}{\partial \theta_j} \dot{R}_i + 2\dot{W}_{i-1} \frac{\partial \dot{R}_i}{\partial \theta_j} + \frac{W_{i-1}}{\partial \theta_j} \ddot{R}_i + W_{i-1} \frac{\partial \ddot{R}_i}{\partial \theta_j} \tag{42}$$

In general, an optimization formulation may contain multiple expressions, and some expressions may need to be evaluated at multiple sampling time points(such as integral expression). In order to avoid redundant recursive matrix evaluations, for each time sampling point one can do a recursive matrix evaluation once and evaluate all the expressions at this time.

7 Experiments

We did some tests to compare the computation time of the previous method and this new method. The test cases are linear chains with the number of links ranging from 9 to 16. Each joint has one degree of freedom. The expression is

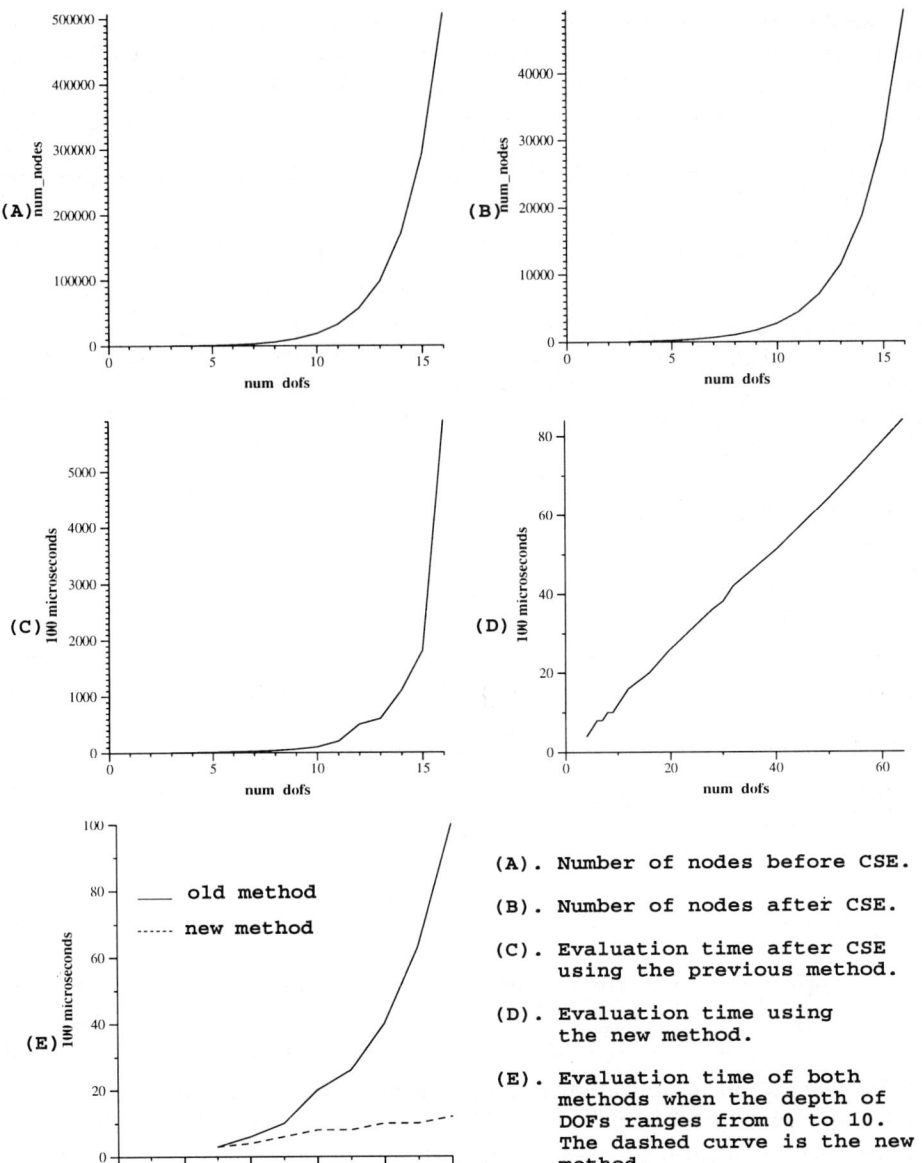

Figure 1: Comparisons of previous CSE method and the new symbolic method

the position of the end effector. The results are shown in Figure 1. The upper-left graph shows the number of nodes of the evaluation trees vs. the number of links using previous symbolic method before common subexpression elimination. The upper-right graph shows the number of nodes of the evaluation trees vs. the number of links after common subexpression elimination as described in [5]. The lower-left graph shows the evaluation time vs. the number of links using previous symbolic method with common subexpression elimination. Finally, the lower-right graph shows the evaluation time vs. the number of links using our new symbolic method.

We can see that in previous method, even after subexpression elimination, both the number of nodes and the evaluation time grow exponentially as the number of links increases. In contrast, the new symbolic method exhibits linear growth in the evalutation time. This provides the means to consider much more complex examples.

8   Conclusion

In this extended abstract, we have described a symbolic method and showed that this method is general enough to represent the kinematic and dynamic quantities that arise in the spacetime constraint method for animating linked figures. The evaluation of the resulting symbolic expressions and their gradients are in complexity, the same as the equivalent numerical methods. Furthermore, the expressions are usually very small, so this method makes a general, easy to use, and efficient interface to optimization based linked figure animation systems. Clearly, work needs to be done to provide more graphically based and/or intuitive means to generate, modify and inspect specifications in the language described here.

Appendix

In this appendix, we give the derivations of the formulas for computing torques and their gradients as listed in section 5. The formulas for computing the torques were derived by Hollerbach[2]. But for self containment, we give the derivations here also.

For each link i, its kinetic energy is

$$E_i = 0.5 \int X^T \dot{W}_i^T \dot{W}_i X \tau_i dx dy dz \tag{43}$$

where $X = (x, y, z, 1)^T$. So

$$
\begin{aligned}
E_i &= 0.5 \int tr(\dot{W}_i X X^T \dot{W}_i^T) \tau_i dx dy dz \\
&= 0.5 tr(\dot{W}_i \int X X^T \tau_i dx dy dz \dot{W}_i^T) \\
&= 0.5 tr(\dot{W}_i J_i \dot{W}_i^T),
\end{aligned}
\tag{44}
$$

where $J_i = \int X X^T \tau_i dx dy dz$ is the inertial tensor of the ith link with respect to its local coordinate system.

We have

$$\frac{\partial E_i}{\partial \theta_j} = 0.5tr(\frac{\partial \dot{W}_i}{\partial \theta_j} J_i \dot{W}_i^T + \dot{W}_i J_i \frac{\partial \dot{W}_i^T}{\partial \theta_j}) \tag{45}$$

$$\frac{\partial E_i}{\partial \dot{\theta}_j} = 0.5tr(\frac{\partial \dot{W}_i}{\partial \dot{\theta}_j} J_i \dot{W}_i^T + \dot{W}_i J_i \frac{\partial \dot{W}_i^T}{\partial \dot{\theta}_j}) = 0.5tr(\frac{\partial W_i}{\partial \theta_j} J_i \dot{W}_i^T + \dot{W}_i J_i \frac{\partial W_i^T}{\partial \theta_j}) \tag{46}$$

$$\frac{d}{dt}\frac{\partial E_i}{\partial \dot{\theta}_j} = 0.5tr(\frac{\partial \dot{W}_i}{\partial \theta_j} J_i \dot{W}_i^T + \frac{\partial W_i}{\partial \theta_j} J_i \ddot{W}_i^T + \ddot{W}_i J_i \frac{\partial W_i^T}{\partial \theta_j} + \dot{W}_i J_i \frac{\partial \dot{W}_i^T}{\partial \theta_j}) \tag{47}$$

So

$$\frac{d}{dt}\frac{\partial E_i}{\partial \dot{\theta}_j} - \frac{\partial E_i}{\partial \theta_j} = 0.5tr(\frac{\partial W_i}{\partial \theta_j} J_i \ddot{W}_i^T + \ddot{W}_i J_i \frac{\partial W_i^T}{\partial \theta_j}) = tr(\frac{\partial W_i}{\partial \theta_j} J_i \ddot{W}_i^T) \tag{48}$$

The potential energy due to gravity is $P_i = m_i G W_i r_i$.
So

$$\frac{d}{dt}\frac{\partial P_i}{\partial \dot{\theta}_j} - \frac{\partial P_i}{\partial \theta_j} = -m_i G \frac{\partial W_i}{\partial \theta_j} r_i \tag{49}$$

Therefore the generalized force with respect to θ_j is

$$f_{\theta_j} = \sum_{i=1}^{n}[tr(\frac{\partial W_i}{\partial \theta_j} J_i \ddot{W}_i^T) + m_i G \frac{\partial W_i}{\partial \theta_j} r_i] \tag{50}$$

Let's assume the index of the link where θ_j is located is u_j. And let $K(l)$ be the set of indices of the kids of link l. Let $D(l)$ be the set of indices of all the decendents of link l. Let $\bar{D}(l) = D(l) \cup \{l\}$. Let W_v^u be the orientation matrix of link v in the coordinate system of link u, i.e. $W_v = W_u * W_v^u$. Then we have

$$f_{\theta_j} = \sum_{i \in \bar{D}(u_j)} (tr\{\frac{\partial W_i}{\partial \theta_j} J_i \ddot{W}_i^T\} + m_i G \frac{\partial W_i}{\partial \theta_j} r_i) \tag{51}$$

$$= \sum_{i \in \bar{D}(u_j)} (tr\{\frac{\partial (W_{u_j} W_i^{u_j})}{\partial \theta_j} J_i (\ddot{W}_i)^T\} + m_i G \frac{\partial (W_{u_j} W_i^{u_j})}{\partial \theta_j} r_i) \tag{52}$$

$$= tr\{(\frac{\partial W_{u_j}}{\partial \theta_j}) \sum_{i \in \bar{D}(u_j)} (W_i^{u_j} J_i \ddot{W}_i^T)\} + G \frac{\partial W_{u_j}}{\partial \theta_j} \sum_{i \in \bar{D}(u_j)} (m_i W_i^{u_j} r_i) \tag{53}$$

$$= tr(\frac{\partial W_{u_j}}{\partial \theta_j} A_{u_j}) + G \frac{\partial W_{u_j}}{\partial \theta_j} b_{u_j}, \tag{54}$$

which is (29). To derive (30), when $u_k \preceq u_j$ we have

$$\frac{\partial f_{\theta_j}}{\partial \theta_k} = \sum_{i \in \bar{D}(u_j) \cap \bar{D}(u_k)} (tr\{\frac{\partial^2 W_i}{\partial \theta_j \partial \theta_k} J_i (\ddot{W}_i)^T + \frac{\partial W_i}{\partial \theta_j} J_i \frac{\partial \ddot{W}_i^T}{\partial \theta_k}\}$$

$$+m_i G \frac{\partial^2 W_i}{\partial \theta_j \partial \theta_k} r_i) \tag{55}$$

$$= \sum_{i \in \bar{D}(u_j)} (tr\{ \frac{\partial^2 W_{u_j}}{\partial \theta_j \partial \theta_k} W_i^{u_j} J_i (\ddot{W}_i)^T + \frac{\partial W_{u_j}}{\partial \theta_j} W_i^{u_j} J_i \frac{\partial \ddot{W}_i^T}{\partial \theta_k} \}$$

$$+ m_i G \frac{\partial^2 W_{u_j}}{\partial \theta_j \partial \theta_k} W_i^{u_j} r_i) \tag{56}$$

$$= tr\{ \frac{\partial^2 W_{u_j}}{\partial \theta_j \partial \theta_k} \sum_{i \in \bar{D}(u_j)} W_i^{u_j} J_i (\ddot{W}_i)^T + \frac{\partial W_{u_j}}{\partial \theta_j} \sum_{i \in \bar{D}(u_j)} W_i^{u_j} J_i \frac{\partial \ddot{W}_i^T}{\partial \theta_k} \}$$

$$+ G \frac{\partial^2 W_{u_j}}{\partial \theta_j \partial \theta_k} \sum_{i \in \bar{D}(u_j)} m_i W_i^{u_j} r_i \tag{57}$$

$$= tr\{ \frac{\partial^2 W_{u_j}}{\partial \theta_j \partial \theta_k} A_{u_j} + \frac{\partial W_{u_j}}{\partial \theta_j} B_{u_j,k} \} + G \frac{\partial^2 W_{u_j}}{\partial \theta_j \partial \theta_k} b_{u_j} . \tag{58}$$

The case when u_k is u_j's decendent is similar. What follows are the derivations of (31) and (32). From (51), we have

$$\frac{\partial f_{\theta_j}}{\partial \dot{\theta}_k} = \sum_{i \in \bar{D}(u_j)} tr\{ \frac{\partial W_i}{\partial \theta_j} J_i \frac{\partial \ddot{W}_i^T}{\partial \dot{\theta}_k} \} \tag{59}$$

$$= tr\{ \sum_{i \in \bar{D}(u_j)} 2 \frac{\partial W_{u_j}}{\partial \theta_j} W_i^{u_j} J_i \frac{\partial \dot{W}_i^T}{\partial \theta_k} \} \tag{60}$$

$$= tr\{ \frac{\partial W_{u_j}}{\partial \theta_j} \sum_{i \in \bar{D}(u_j)} 2 W_i^{u_j} J_i \frac{\partial \dot{W}_i^T}{\partial \theta_k} \} \tag{61}$$

$$= tr\{ \frac{\partial W_{u_j}}{\partial \theta_j} C_{u_j,k} \}, \tag{62}$$

$$\frac{\partial f_{\theta_j}}{\partial \ddot{\theta}_k} = \sum_{i \in \bar{D}(u_j)} tr\{ \frac{\partial W_i}{\partial \theta_j} J_i \frac{\partial \ddot{W}_i^T}{\partial \ddot{\theta}_k} \} \tag{63}$$

$$= tr\{ \sum_{i \in \bar{D}(u_j)} \frac{\partial W_{u_j}}{\partial \theta_j} W_i^{u_j} J_i \frac{\partial W_i^T}{\partial \theta_k} \} \tag{64}$$

$$= tr\{ \frac{\partial W_{u_j}}{\partial \theta_j} \sum_{i \in \bar{D}(u_j)} W_i^{u_j} J_i \frac{\partial W_i^T}{\partial \theta_k} \} \tag{65}$$

$$= tr\{ \frac{\partial W_{u_j}}{\partial \theta_j} D_{u_j,k} \}. \tag{66}$$

The derivations of (33)-(37) are similar to each other. So we only give the one

222

for (33).

$$A_l = J_l \ddot{W}_l^T + \sum_{i \in D(l)} (W_i^l J_i \ddot{W}_i^T) \tag{67}$$

$$= J_l \ddot{W}_l^T + \sum_{k \in K(l)} \sum_{i \in \bar{D}(k)} (W_i^l J_i \ddot{W}_i^T) \tag{68}$$

$$= J_l \ddot{W}_l^T + \sum_{k \in K(l)} \sum_{i \in \bar{D}(k)} (W_k^l W_i^k J_i \ddot{W}_i^T) \tag{69}$$

$$= J_l \ddot{W}_l^T + \sum_{k \in K(l)} R_k \sum_{i \in \bar{D}(k)} (W_i^k J_i \ddot{W}_i^T) \tag{70}$$

$$= J_l \ddot{W}_l^T + \sum_{k \in K(l)} R_k A_k \tag{71}$$

References

1. Michael F. Cohen. Interactive spacetime control for animation. *Computer Graphics*, 26(2):293–302, July 1992.
2. John M. Hollerbach. A recursive lagrangian formulation of manipulator dynamics and a comparative study of dynamics formulation complexity. *IEEE Transactions on Systems, Man, and Cybernetics*, 10(11):730–736, November 1980.
3. Michael Kass. Condor: Constraint-based dataflow. In *Proceedings of SIG-GRAPH'92 (Chicago, July 26–31, 1992)*, pages 321–330. ACM, July 1992.
4. Zicheng Liu and Michael F. Cohen. Keyframe motion opimization by relaxing speed and timing. In *Proceedings of 6th EuroGraphics Workshop on Animation and Simulation*, (Maastricht, The Netherlands, September2-3 1995).
5. Zicheng Liu, Steven Gortler, and Michael F. Cohen. Hierarchical spacetime control. *Computer Graphics*, pages 35–42, July 1994.
6. Andrew Witkin and Michael Kass. Spacetime constraints. *Computer Graphics*, 22(4):159–168, August 1988.

Appendix:
Colour Illustrations

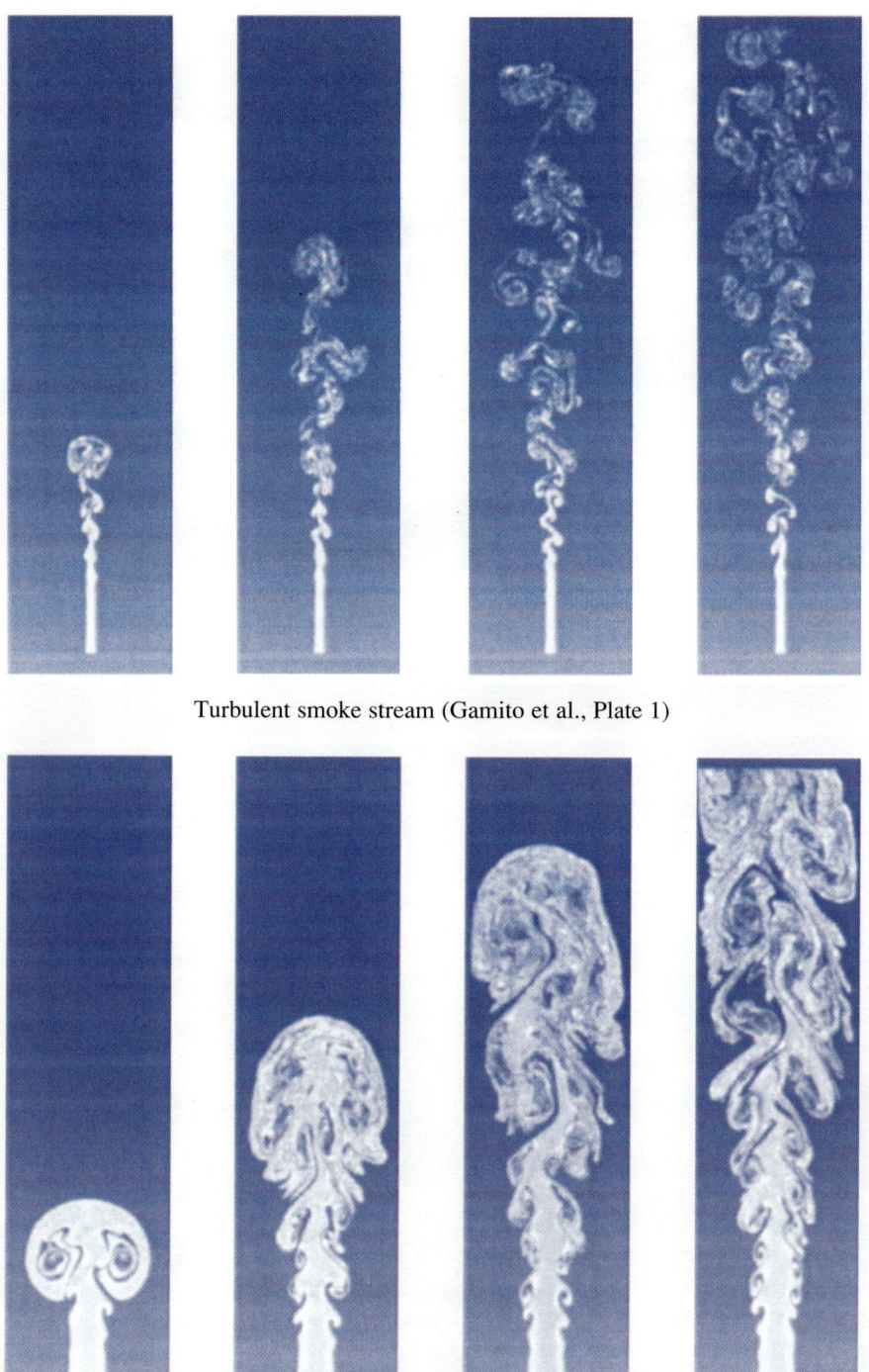

Turbulent smoke stream (Gamito et al., Plate 1)

Turbulent smoke stream with increased thickness (Gamito et al., Plate 2)

226

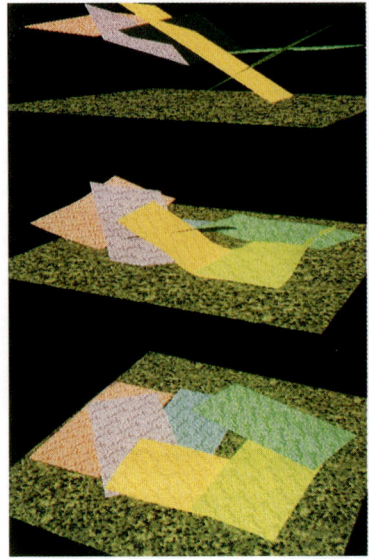

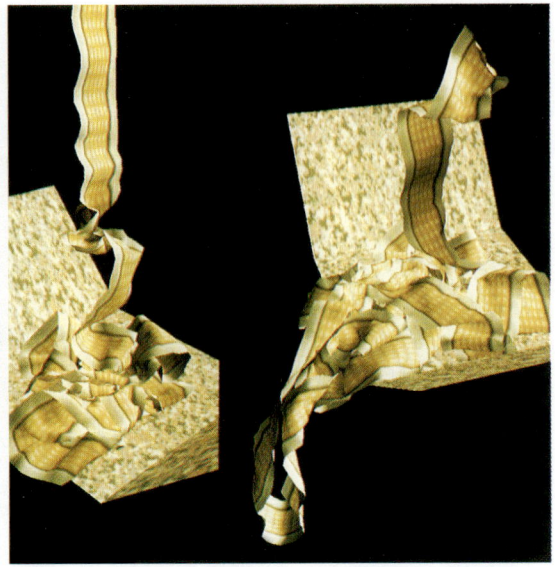

Collision consistency correction in a set of falling surfaces (Volino and Thalmann, Photo A)

Complex collisions: A crumpling ribbon (Volino and Thalmann, Photo B)

Complex collisions: Crumpling objects in a rotating cylinder (Volino and Thalmann, Photo C)

(van Overveld and Barenbrug)

A lawn in the wind (Neyret, Fig. 3)

Top: a scaffolding flag. Left: a single texel. Right: zoom on one corner
(Neyret, Fig. 4)

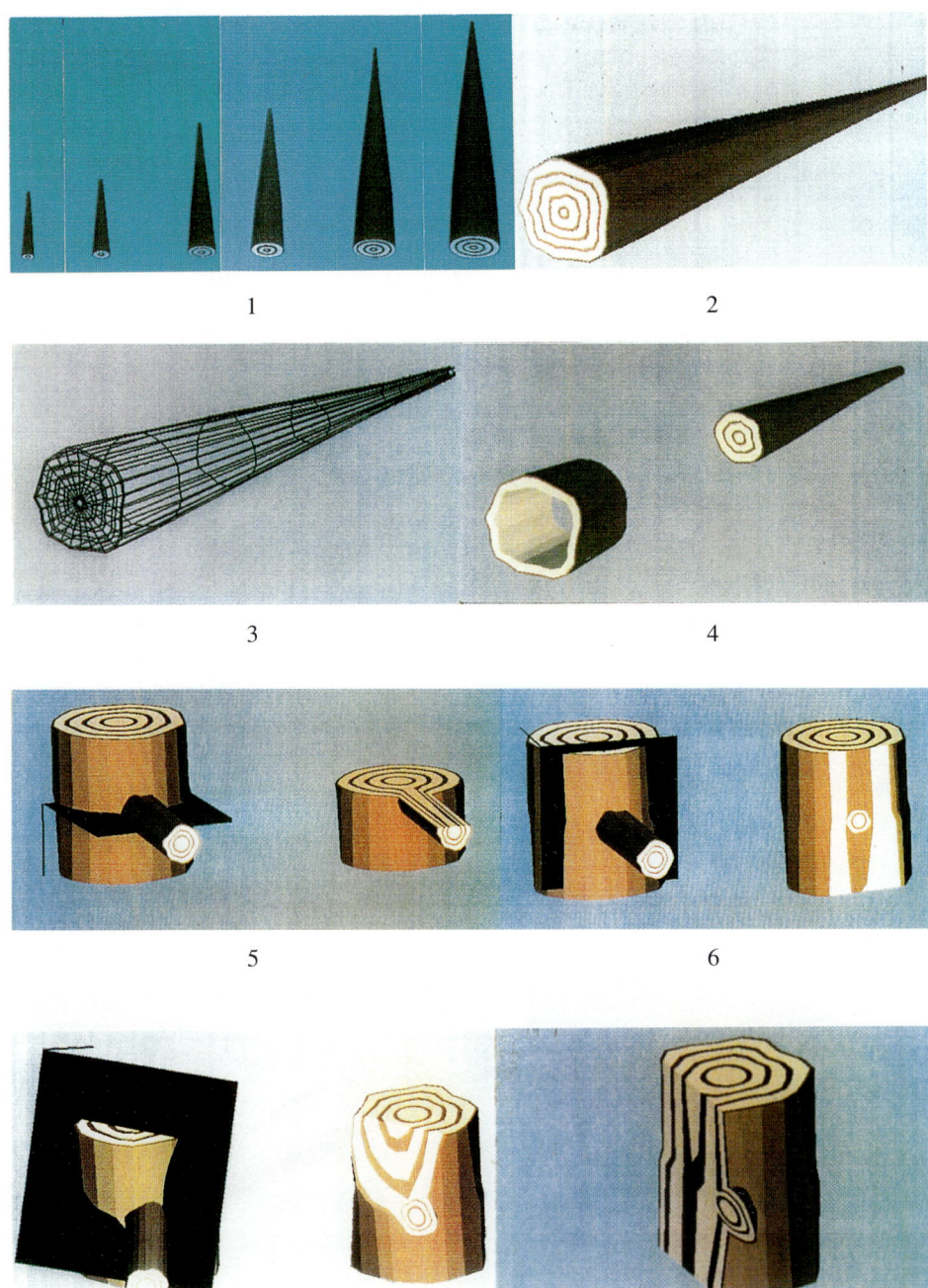

1

2

3

4

5

6

7

8

(Terraz and Lienhardt, Fig. A)

230

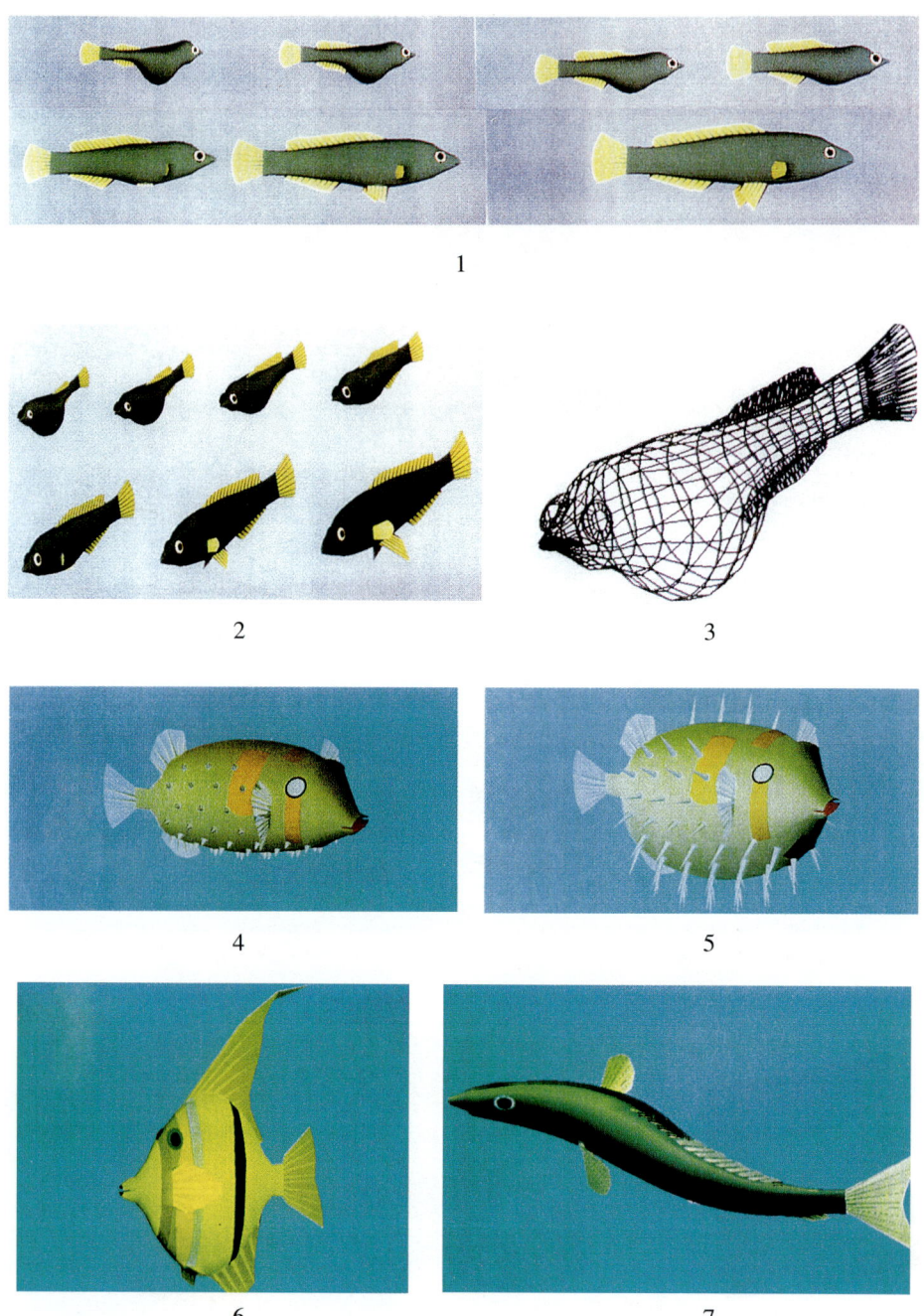

1

2

3

4

5

6

7

(Terraz and Lienhardt, Fig. B)

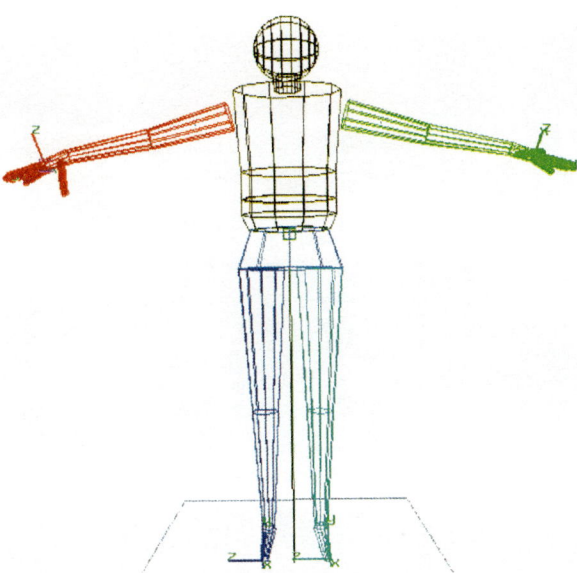

Propagating the support influence. **a** Equal support (0.25) for each site: right and left hands and feet (Boulic et al.)

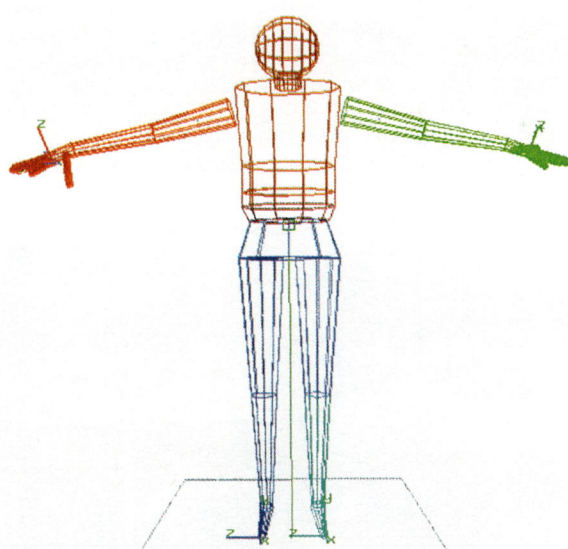

Propagating the support influence. **b** Higher support (0.4 each) for right hand and foot than left hand and foot (0.1 each) (Boulic et al.)

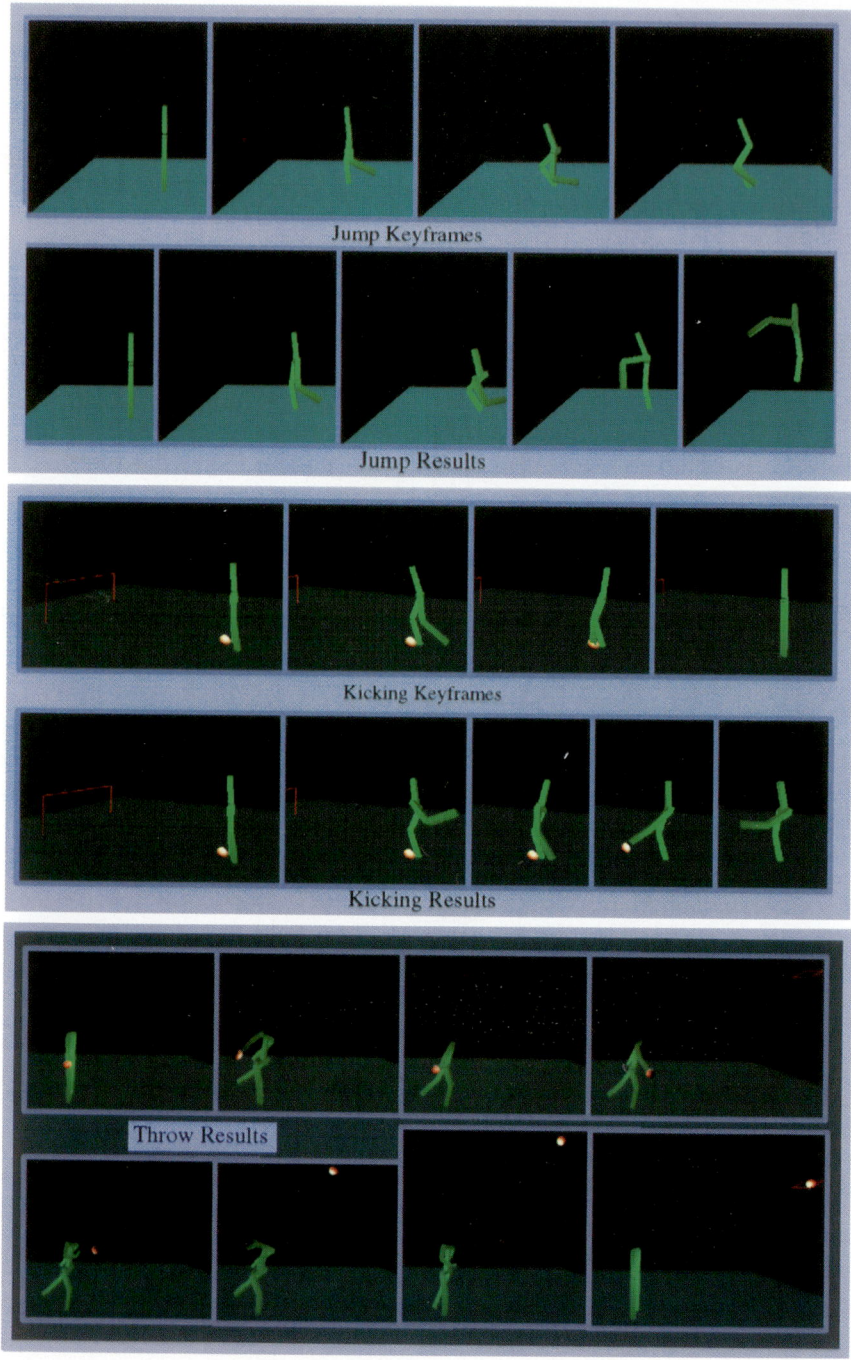

Jumping, kicking, throwing (Liu and Cohen)

Pulse modulated locomotion: the paddling pattern is regulated in real-time in order to steer the kayak's course for the desired direction, at the desired speed (Nougaret and Arnaldi, Fig. 1)

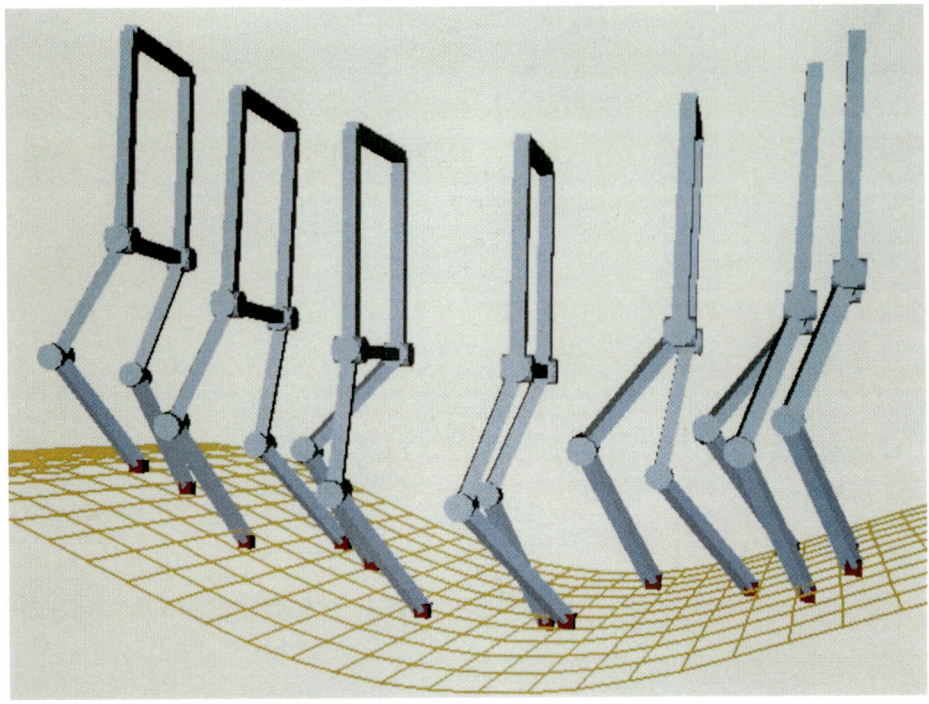

Simpleton (van de Panne and Lamouret, Plate A)

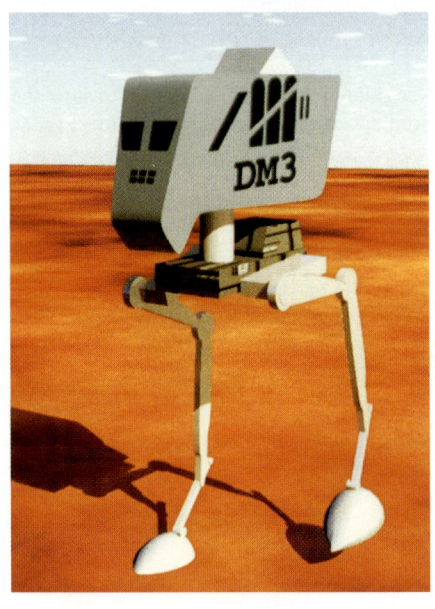

Robo-bird (van de Panne and Lamouret, Plate B)

A human model (van de Panne and Lamouret, Plate C)

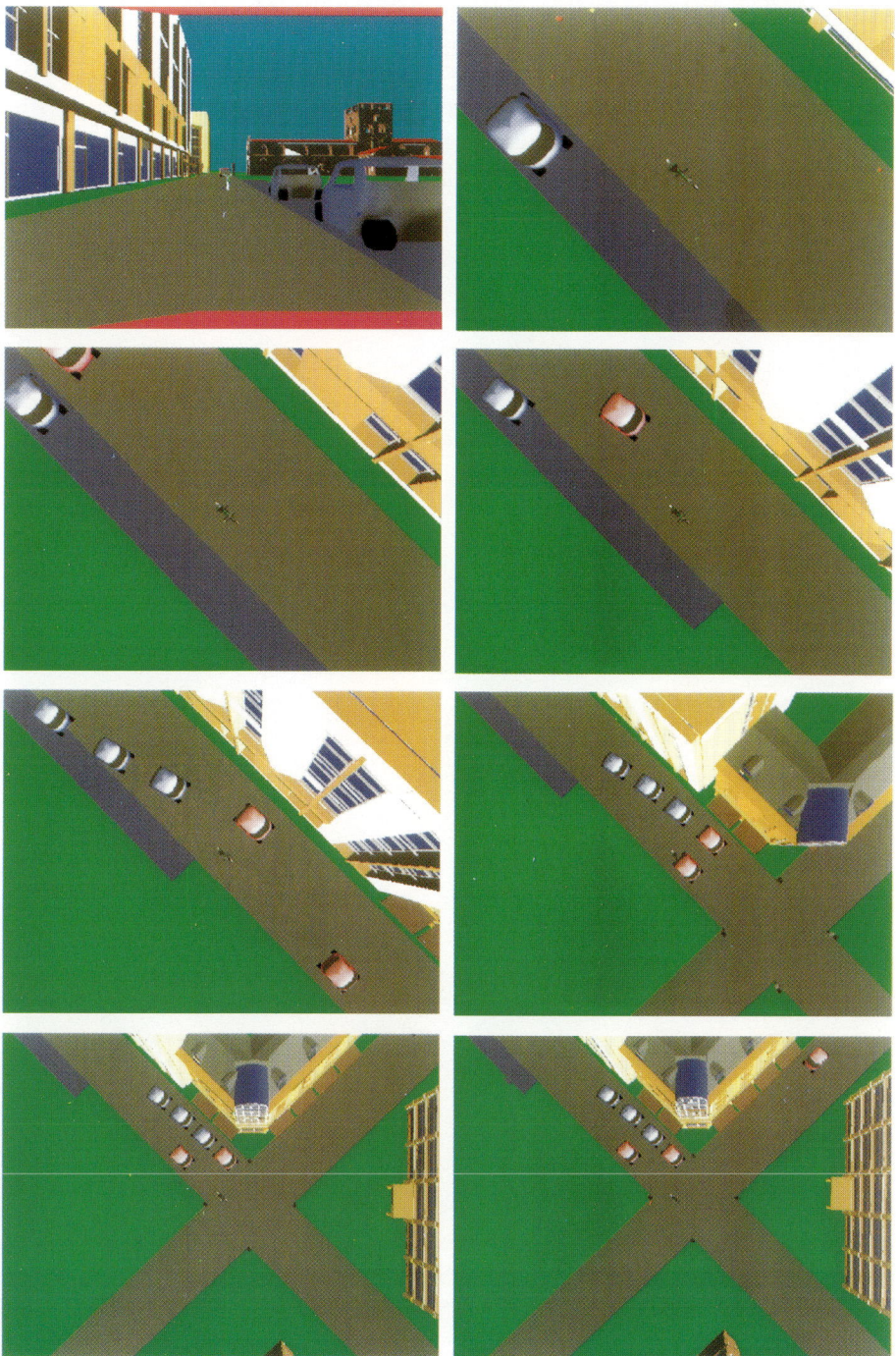

Illustration of a simulation sequence (Donikian and Cozot, Fig. 1)

Riccardo Scateni, Jarke J. van Wijk, Pietro Zanarini (eds.)

Visualization in Scientific Computing '95

**Proceedings of the Eurographics Workshop
in Chia, Italy, May 3–5, 1995**

1995. 110 figures. VII, 161 pages. ISBN 3-211-82729-3
Soft cover DM 85,–, öS 595,–. (Eurographics)

13 contributions cover a wide range of topics, ranging from detailed algorithmic studies to searches for new metaphors. The reader will find state-of-the-art results and techniques in this discipline, which he can use to find solutions for his visualization problems.

Patrick M. Hanrahan, Werner Purgathofer (eds.)

Rendering Techniques '95

**Proceedings of the Eurographics Workshop
in Dublin, Ireland, June 12–14, 1995**

1995. 198 figures. XI, 372 pages. ISBN 3-211-82733-1
Soft cover DM 118,–, öS 826,–. (Eurographics)

31 contributions give an overview on hierarchical radiosity, Monte Carlo radiosity, wavelet radiosity, nondiffuse radiosity, radiosity performance improvements, ray tracing, reconstruction techniques, volume rendering, illumination, use interface aspects, and importance sampling. Also included are two invited papers by James Arvo and Alain Fournier.

Prices are subject to change without notice

Springer-Verlag Wien New York

Sachsenplatz 4–6, P.O.Box 89, A-1201 Wien · 175 Fifth Avenue, New York, NY 10010, USA
Heidelberger Platz 3, D-14197 Berlin · 3-13, Hongo 3-chome, Bunkyo-ku, Tokyo 113, Japan

Martin Göbel, Heinrich Müller, Bodo Urban (eds.)

Visualization in Scientific Computing

1995. 150 figures. VIII, 238 pages. ISBN 3-211-82633-5
Soft cover DM 118,–, öS 826,–. (Eurographics)

Visualization is the most important approach to understand the huge amount of data
produced in today's computational and experimental sciences. Selected contributions
treat topics of particular interest in current research, for example visualization of
multidimensional data and flows, time control, interaction, and volume visualization.
Readers may profit in getting insight in state-of-the-art techniques which might help
to solve their visualization problems.

Wolfgang Herzner, Frank Kappe (eds.)

Multimedia/Hypermedia
in Open Distributed Environments

Proceedings of the Eurographics Symposium
in Graz, Austria, June 6–9, 1994

1994. 105 figures. VIII, 330 pages. ISBN 3-211-82587-8
Soft cover DM 118,–, öS 826,–. (Eurographics)

This book represents the results from the Eurographics symposium on "Multi-
media/Hypermedia in Open Distributed Environments", June 6–9, 1994, Graz,
Austria. Its six sessions "Standards and Standards Exploitation", "Demonstrations",
"Tools", "Hypermedia and Authoring", "Architectures", and "CSCW and
Information Services" give a comprehensive overview about current research and
development, including the future mm/hm standards MHEG and PREMO. The
reader will profit in getting up-to-date information about the current trends in (the
development of) mm/hm services and applications in open, distributed environments.

Prices are subject to change without notice

Springer-Verlag Wien New York

Sachsenplatz 4–6, P.O.Box 89, A-1201 Wien · 175 Fifth Avenue, New York, NY 10010, USA
Heidelberger Platz 3, D-14197 Berlin · 3-13, Hongo 3-chome, Bunkyo-ku, Tokyo 113, Japan

Springer-Verlag
and the Environment

WE AT SPRINGER-VERLAG FIRMLY BELIEVE THAT AN international science publisher has a special obligation to the environment, and our corporate policies consistently reflect this conviction.

WE ALSO EXPECT OUR BUSINESS PARTNERS – PRINTERS, paper mills, packaging manufacturers, etc. – to commit themselves to using environmentally friendly materials and production processes.

THE PAPER IN THIS BOOK IS MADE FROM NO-CHLORINE pulp and is acid free, in conformance with international standards for paper permanency.